LITERARY BRITAIN

PHOTOGRAPHED BY
BILL BRANDT

WITH AN INTRODUCTION BY
JOHN HAYWARD

EDITED AND WITH AN AFTERWORD BY
MARK HAWORTH-BOOTH

AN APERTURE BOOK

The original edition of *Literary Britain* was published by Cassell & Company Ltd in 1951. Photographs reproduced by kind permission of Mrs. Noya Brandt.

Copyright © 1986 Aperture Foundation Inc.
Photographs: © the Estate of Bill Brandt, 1986
Essays: © the authors, 1986
Designed by Simon Rendall
Printed by Westerham Press

ISBN 0–89381–223–4 (cloth)
ISBN 0–905–209–66–4 (UK paper)
Library of Congress Catalogue Number: 85–052456

Aperture Foundation Inc. publishes a periodical, books, and portfolios of fine photography to communicate with serious photographers and creative people everywhere. A complete catalogue is available upon request. Address: 20 East 23 Street, New York, New York 10010.

Contents

Foreword by Sir Roy Strong

Introduction by John Hayward

The Plates

		PLATE NO
JANE AUSTEN	Chawton	1
ARNOLD BENNETT	Burslem Town Hall	2
WILLIAM BLAKE	Blake's Cottage at Felpham	3
GEORGE BORROW	Norwich, from Mousehold Heath	4
JAMES BOSWELL	Isle of Skye	5
THE BRONTËS	In Haworth Parsonage	6
	Haworth Churchyard	7
CHARLOTTE BRONTË	In the Ruins of Wycoller Hall	8
EMILY BRONTË	Wuthering Heights	9
	Withens	10
	Withens	11
	Yorkshire Moors	12
ELIZABETH BARRETT BROWNING	Coxhoe Hall	13
GEORGE GORDON, LORD BYRON	Newstead Abbey	14
	Lord Byron's Bedroom	15
JOHN CLARE	Clare's Birthplace	16
WILLIAM COBBETT	Church and Barn, Hurstbourne Tarrant	17
SAMUEL TAYLOR COLERIDGE	Greta Hall, Keswick	18
GEORGE CRABBE	Aldeburgh	19
	Aldeburgh Beach	20
	Aldeburgh	21
CHARLES DICKENS	Gad's Hill Place	22
	Cooling Graveyard	23
	The Chalet, Gad's Hill	24
	The Forge, Chalk	25

		PLATE NO
HENRY FIELDING	Prior Park, near Bath	26
THOMAS GRAY	The Churchyard, Stoke Poges	27
THOMAS HARDY	Abbotsbury	28
	Stonehenge	29
	Egdon Heath	30
	Tess's Cottage	31
	Stair Hole, Lulworth Cove	32
	Avebury	33
WILLIAM HENRY HUDSON	The Wiltshire Downs	34
HENRY JAMES	The Reform Club, London	35
RICHARD JEFFERIES	Barbary Castle, Marlborough Downs	36
DR SAMUEL JOHNSON	The House where Johnson was Born	37
	Lord Macdonald's Forest, Skye	38
	The Graveyard at Strath	39
	Isle of Skye	40
JOHN KEATS	Wentworth Place, Hampstead	41
RUDYARD KIPLING	The Roman Wall	42
WILLIAM LANGLAND	The Malvern Hills	43
DAVID HERBERT LAWRENCE	Lawrence's Birthplace	44
	The Garden of Garsington Manor	45
CHRISTOPHER MARLOWE	Berkeley Castle	46
GEORGE MEREDITH	Flint Cottage, Boxhill	47
JOHN MILTON	In the Gardens of Christ's College, Cambridge	48
THE PASTONS	Caister Castle, Norfolk	49
SAMUEL PEPYS	Buckden Cottage, Brampton	50
ALEXANDER POPE	In the Garden of Stourhead, Wiltshire	51
SAMUEL RICHARDSON	The Grange, North End Crescent, Fulham	52
SIR WALTER SCOTT	Melrose Abbey	53
WILLIAM SHAKESPEARE	From Glamis Castle	54
	Flint Castle	55
GEORGE BERNARD SHAW	Shaw's Corner, Ayot St Lawrence	56

PLATE NO

SIR PHILIP SIDNEY	Penshurst Place	57
ROBERT LOUIS STEVENSON	Rannoch Moor, Perth	58
ALFRED, LORD TENNYSON	The Old Rectory, Somersby	59
ANTHONY TROLLOPE	St Nicholas Hospital, Salisbury	60
	Salisbury Cathedral	61
HORACE WALPOLE	Strawberry Hill	62
OSCAR WILDE	Reading Gaol	63
WILLIAM WORDSWORTH	Wordsworth's Room in Dove Cottage	64
	Between Ullswater and Thirlmere in Early Spring	65

Additional Plates

Aldeburgh	66
Gordale Scar	67
Gordale Scar	68
Giant's Causeway	69
Giant's Causeway	70
Tom Moore's House, Dublin	71
Christmas Eve, Campden Hill	72
Fountains Abbey	73
Fountains Abbey	74
West Wycombe Park	75

POETRY: Bill Brandt — Photographer
and *A Retrospect* by Tom Hopkinson

Afterword by Mark Haworth-Booth

Acknowledgements & Notes

Foreword

The original exhibition on which this publication is based was planned as an 80th birthday tribute to the great photographer Bill Brandt. He became increasingly ill during 1983 and died on 20 December. Through the kind help of his widow, Noya Brandt, the project continued to be developed and stands as a tribute to Bill Brandt's achievement and in memory of his personal distinction.

Bill Brandt, for all the charm and humour he showed in private life, was an uncompromisingly serious photographer. In him, for very many people in all parts of the world, was enshrined an image of the eloquence of photography and a rare artistic integrity. He excelled in all its branches. I remember with pleasure Bill Brandt's enthusiastic collaboration with the Victoria and Albert Museum in devising and selecting the exhibition *The Land: 20th century landscape photographs* held there in 1975 and subsequently shown in national museums in Cardiff, Edinburgh and Belfast. He worked for a year and a half with Mark Haworth-Booth, the Assistant Keeper of Photographs, who has brought this project to fruition.

In 1981 they discussed the form the original exhibition should take. The first idea was to assemble a collection of 80 of Bill's 'vintage' photographic prints. The term 'vintage' as applied to photographs is somewhat rebarbative but a better one has not yet been found to describe prints made at or about the same time as the original negative. It would be naïve to assume that such prints are always more interesting or valuable than later prints from the same negative, but with Bill Brandt's photographs the matter has an especial significance. Darkroom work was always of the greatest importance to him and was an essential ingredient of his creativity. In the late 1950s he radically changed his style of printing. His photographs had always been simplified into clear tonal patterns but from the later 1950s he printed in dazzling chiaroscuro patterns on the hardest available grades of paper. At the same period he abandoned the Rolleiflex camera, with which he had worked so successfully from the early 1930s, in favour of the princely Superwide Hasselblad. The new camera provided him with high-energy, swooping perspectives much in keeping with his graphic printing

style and, as it happened, thoroughly consonant with the style of the 1960s. He disparaged the milder, fuller toned prints typical of his production in the 'Thirties and 'Forties. However, in recent years his admirers and critics found much to recommend the earlier prints. He kindly gave the Museum a set of some earlier prints in 1981. In 1982 a section of his splendid exhibition of portraits, held at the National Portrait Gallery, presented a group of the early prints. Marina Vaizey, art critic of *The Sunday Times*, spoke for many when she remarked that compared to the later prints 'the vintage prints of the 1940s are much smaller, exquisitely sharply detailed, toned in silvery, iridescent muted brown. It's heresy to say so, but the latter are much more aesthetically satisfying'.

Brandt came to regard with more tolerance the qualities of the early prints and agreed to our request to show them. There were to be 80 prints in the exhibition simply because it was to be held in honour of his 80th birthday, due to fall on 2 May 1984. During spring and summer 1983 the idea of such a celebration became a burden to him and so it was decided instead to devote the exhibition to the one large theme of his photography which had not been substantially shown or published in recent years. It is well known that his publishers have brought out a series of books covering his nudes, the portraits and his documentary series on *London in the Thirties* (Gordon Fraser, 1983). The photographs assembled into the collection *Literary Britain* remain among Bill Brandt's most impressive explorations, bringing together the best of such 'vintage' prints on this theme as Bill Brandt had retained. This publication includes the original introduction to *Literary Britain* written by John Hayward. Next follow the plates, which include photographs not originally published in the first edition but of strong interest to all students of Brandt's landscape photography. There follows the first serious appreciation of Bill Brandt as a photographer, written in 1942 by his friend and editor (Sir) Tom Hopkinson and published in *Lilliput*, the magazine in which most of the landscapes first appeared. Sir Tom has kindly added a retrospect which brings his exceptionally perceptive view of Bill Brandt up to date.

Mark Haworth-Booth contributes an afterword on *Literary Britain* and the publication is completed by a further group of plates – unknown to most of Bill Brandt's admirers – which show the range of the photographer's interest in the theme. All but a handful of the exhibits have been very kindly lent by the Estate of Bill Brandt and the Museum is most grateful, as on many previous occasions, to Noya Brandt.

SIR ROY STRONG *Director*
Victoria and Albert Museum

Introduction by John Hayward to Literary Britain (1951)

When we look at a collection of photographs, whether it is a family portrait album or a packet of amateur snapshots or a series taken to illustrate a particular theme, two faculties are brought into play. The first is that of recognition, the second that of association. Our immediate reaction is to discover what the picture represents. At first sight, that is to say, our eyes see exactly what the lens of the camera transmitted to the sensitized plate or film, and the appropriate cells in our brain inform us directly that we are looking, for instance, at the image of an old gentleman with side-whiskers, or at a group of children playing on the sands, or, as in this volume, at a building or a landscape. This relatively simple reflex act of recognition of the object is, of course, only a preliminary stage in the complicated process of understanding and appreciation. We may not feel inclined to proceed further than this; the old gentleman with side-whiskers, as far as we are concerned, is merely an old gentleman with side-whiskers, and we feel neither desire nor curiosity to know more about him, to give him, so to speak, a second thought. So we turn over the pages of the family album or run through the pack of glossy prints aimlessly, pausing only to admire some technical effect. But the moment our interest and curiosity are stimulated, the exquisitely delicate mechanism of association is engaged, and we begin to see, as it were, with the mind's eye. It is this faculty of association, mysteriously coupled with memory, that enables us to relate the present moment of experience with the past. We can never be sure what trains of thought it will set in motion, and we do not know why or how the impulse is given when it is. A particular phrase of music, the taste or smell or touch of some particular thing, or the faded sepia photograph of another old gentleman with side-whiskers, will inexplicably recompose, in the form of a mental picture, the scattered elements of some past experience. Thus a single photograph of no immediately apparent significance in our eyes may have the power in certain circumstances to conjure up for us, and re-present to the mind's eye, a whole range of sympathetic associations.

This book is a collection of such photographs and, though they are, in themselves, very fine examples of the taste and technique of a distinguished professional photographer, their purpose, so it seems to me, is to transcend mere representation of their subject and to arouse, through association and memory, a deeper response in those who are disposed to study and enjoy them in the mind's eye. In so far, however, as they are illustrations of a particular theme, and one that is no more than vaguely suggested by the title, *Literary Britain*, they necessarily require some explanation, or rather aid, to their identification. This is supplied by the letterpress facing each plate. These descriptive texts, whether in the form of allusive quotations in verse or prose, or of biographical memoranda, should, I suggest, be used simply as helpful clues to the fullest possible understanding of the pictures. They will be more or less useful according to the individual reader's knowledge of the facts or allusions they contain about books and authors; and to his capacity for responding, through the association of his personal experience of life and literature with the scenes recorded here, to the evocative element in each picture. These *aides-mémoire*, it is true, may not be indispensable, and some of them, in my opinion, are more effective than others; but they are certainly not otiose, for it would be difficult, not to say impossible, for any one person to be so well informed as to be able to recognize every one of the hundred scenes in this collection, without some assistance. It is nevertheless important to bear in mind that the text throughout is subordinate to the plates; because it would be a natural temptation, or at least an inclination, to regard the latter as illustrations of the printed commentary. The possibility of this misunderstanding is indeed raised by the first reproduction in this book – that of the beach at Dover in full moonlight. Such confusion of purpose would become so much the worse confounded if it were mistakenly supposed that text and illustrations together are intended to provide a comprehensive guide to the landmarks of English literature. They do nothing of the sort, even incidentally, and the omissions should be sufficiently obvious to make this clear to anyone with some general knowledge of literary history. At the same time it can fairly be claimed that the famous writers commemorated here – a trifle too formally, it may seem, in strict alphabetical order – do, on the whole, adequately represent and recall to mind the panorama of English literature from Chaucer to the present day.

This book is indeed in a more literal sense a panorama in so far as it is a pictorial representation or recollection of places scattered, some prominently, some obscurely, throughout the length and breadth of Great Britain, and each hallowed in one way or another, either by a writer or by one or all of his works. Many of these pictures convey much more than the obvious features they display and should be regarded rather as *points de repère* in an extensive literary landscape – each one a focus for innumerable associations. Our island is so small that there is scarcely any part of it where some literary association or other is not valid. 'Where'er we tread 'tis haunted, holy ground.' We are, perhaps, bound to forget this in our daily lives, particularly if we happen to live in a place where the old landmarks have gone, or the ground is hidden by new building or has been otherwise 'developed' beyond recognition. The camera, however, may still be able to remind us of what we cannot actually see for ourselves – even in London, whose prodigious growth has, within two generations, obliterated so much of the material evidence of her literary past, and where living conditions are now so different from what they were a single lifetime ago, that it is hardly possible to imagine, even in a still relatively unspoilt and quiet street like Cheyne Row, for example, that Thomas and Jane Carlyle lived and worked at number 24, and that the immediate neighbourhood was once familiar to Sir Thomas More and Donne, to Swift and Smollett, to Leigh Hunt and George Eliot, and to Rossetti, Morris, Swinburne and Henry James. But however cunningly the photographer may direct his viewfinder, so as to exclude the temporal from the scene and leave it open to the free play of associated ideas, there is a limit to what he can do with his subject. He cannot take photographs in mid-twentieth century London of the London of Dickens, or Dr Johnson, or Shakespeare. Thus it is that the majority of the photographs in this book are of places which have not changed in appearance since they were frequented by the writers or the fictional characters with whom they have come to be traditionally connected.

As one would expect, many of these literary landmarks are houses, such as Newstead Abbey, Dove Cottage, Kelmscott, which were once the homes of great writers; or houses, again, once peopled in the imagination of poets and novelists by such figures as Lady Macbeth, Joe Gargery, James Forsyte, and so on. But the best of them, to my mind, are those most numerous ones in which the personal element is merged in the impersonal, the temporal in the timeless, and the writer and his work, and all that we associate with both, seem to dissolve in their natural setting. I am thinking here not of those photographs, striking though they are, which were taken intentionally to arouse associations with a specific masterpiece – Marlowe's *Edward II* for example, or *Wuthering Heights*, or *The Pickwick Papers*, or Arnold's *Dover Beach* – but rather of those which suggest far more than a single novel or poem or play – the views which record (and this means literally to bring back to the heart) the Kentish Weald; the Pilgrims' Way; a Suffolk churchyard and the bleak salt marshes of the Thames estuary; Cranborne Chase, the Marlborough Downs, and the Malvern Hills; the Roman Wall and the hills overlooking Yarrow; the Border Country and Rannoch by Glencoe; and the farthest Hebrides, the subject of so many haunting allusions by the Romantic poets of Western Europe.

It is in the reproductions of such scenes as these that we are aware not only of the relationship of a particular writer with his environment, with the localities which nourished his thought and sensibility, and which in their turn have become for ever associated with his work, but of the general inter-relationship of literature and the external world. Here this communion is only hinted at (for a photograph and a few lines of description can offer only hints and intimations), and is moreover confined to the literature and landscape of a single country; but it sufficiently reveals how much each owes to the other; and how deeply involved they are in our understanding and enjoyment of each. To contribute to this understanding and enjoyment is the purpose of this book; and, in order that this purpose should be served as fully as possible, it is not enough to consider each picture on its own merits, to nail a text to it, and let specific associations play their part, however much this may conduce to 'our pastime and our happiness'.

We need, I think, to apprehend this larger relationship at every turn of the page until, at the end of the book, the time and the place of the individual genius become merged in a single timeless setting. To realize this is to realize how profoundly and permanently the poets and dramatists, the novelists and men of letters commemorated here, have impressed themselves and their achievements upon the face of Britain. We speak, as a matter of course, of the 'Border' Ballads, of the 'Shakespeare' Country, of the 'Lake' Poets, of Hardy's 'Wessex'; and the literary associations of the 'Five Towns', Stoke Poges, Kelmscott, Strawberry Hill, Jarrow, Wenlock Edge, to name at random only a few of the most familiar places recorded here, are common knowledge wherever English literature is read. We should have less cause and less desire to know about these places and to cherish them, if we had not first been drawn to them by those whom they inspired to write. But it is perhaps in the least familiar spots, so suggestively presented here in such views as those of Prior Park, of the 'Nymph of the Grot' at Stourhead, of Cooling graveyard, of the garden at Garsington, or of Barbary Castle on the Marlborough Downs, that we are liable to realize most completely the extent of this relationship. Therein, I believe, lies the fullest delight that this book is capable of giving. That it may also tempt some of those who turn its pages to visit the places and scenes they illustrate I have no doubt; as I do not doubt it will send some people back with renewed powers of appreciation, to the works of the writers associated with them. But just as it does not pretend to be a guide to literature, so it cannot claim to be a guide to 'places of literary interest'. It is designed essentially for the contemplative man's recreation, for those who care, with the mind's eye, to unite the word and the image, and by integrating the meaning of both, give to the whole an ulterior significance.

THE PLATES

JANE AUSTEN

Born: *Steventon, Basingstoke, 16 December, 1775*
Died: *Winchester, 18 July, 1817*

In 1809 Jane Austen and her family settled in the cottage at Chawton where she wrote *Mansfield Park, Emma, Persuasion* and some minor pieces.

'This house stood in the village of Chawton, about a mile from Alton, on the right-hand side, just where the road to Winchester branches off from that to Gosport. It was so close to the road that the front door opened upon it; while a very narrow enclosure, paled in on each side, protected the building from danger of collision with any runaway vehicle. I believe it had been originally built for an inn, for which purpose it was certainly well situated. Afterwards it had been occupied by Mr Knight's steward; but by some additions to the house, and some judicious planting and screening, it was made a pleasant and commodious abode. Mr Knight was experienced and adroit at such arrangements, and this was a labour of love to him. A good-sized entrance and two sitting-rooms made the length of the house, all intended originally to look upon the road, but the large drawing-room window was blocked up and turned into a book-case, and another opened at the side which gave to view only turf and trees, as a high wooden fence and hornbeam hedge shut out the Winchester road, which skirted the whole length of the little domain. Trees were planted each side to form a shrubbery walk, carried round the enclosure, which gave a sufficient space for ladies' exercise. There was a pleasant irregular mixture of hedgerow, and gravel walk, and orchard, and long grass for mowing, arising from two or three little enclosures having been thrown together.'

Memoir of Jane Austen, by her
nephew J. E. Austen-Leigh

1. CHAWTON

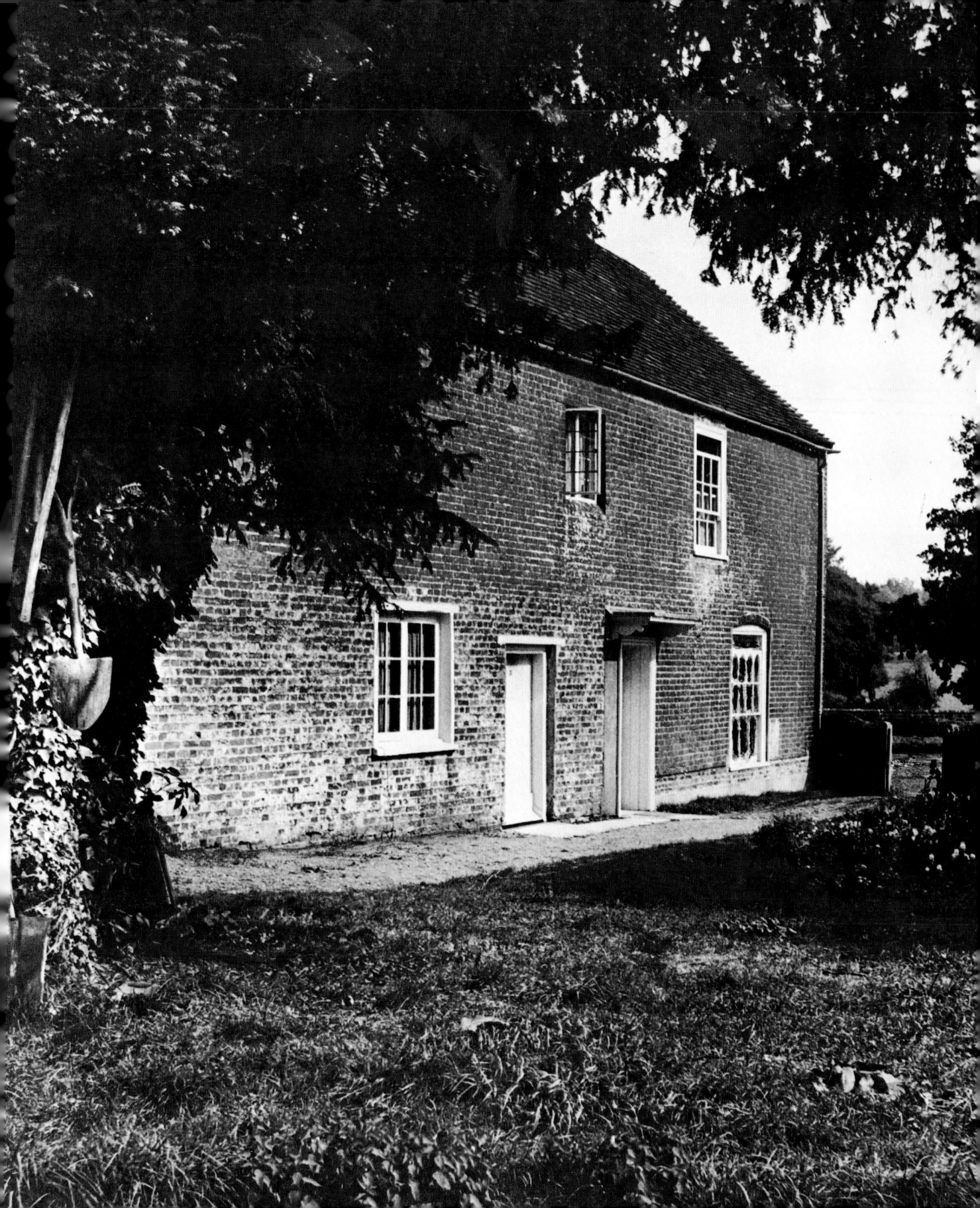

ARNOLD BENNETT

Born: *Hanley, Staffordshire, 27 May,* 1867
Died: *London, 27 March,* 1931

'Big James led him through the market-place, where a few vegetable, tripe and ginger-bread stalls – relics of the day's market – were still attracting cusomers in the twilight. These slatternly and picturesque groups, beneath their flickering yellow flares, were encamped at the gigantic foot of the Town Hall porch as at the foot of a precipice. The monstrous black walls of the Town Hall rose and were merged in gloom; and the spire of the Town Hall, on whose summit stood a gold angel holding a gold crown, rose right into the heavens and was there lost. It was marvellous that this town, by adding stone to stone, had upreared this monument which, in expressing the secret nobility of its ideals, dwarfed the town.'

Clayhanger

2. BURSLEM TOWN HALL

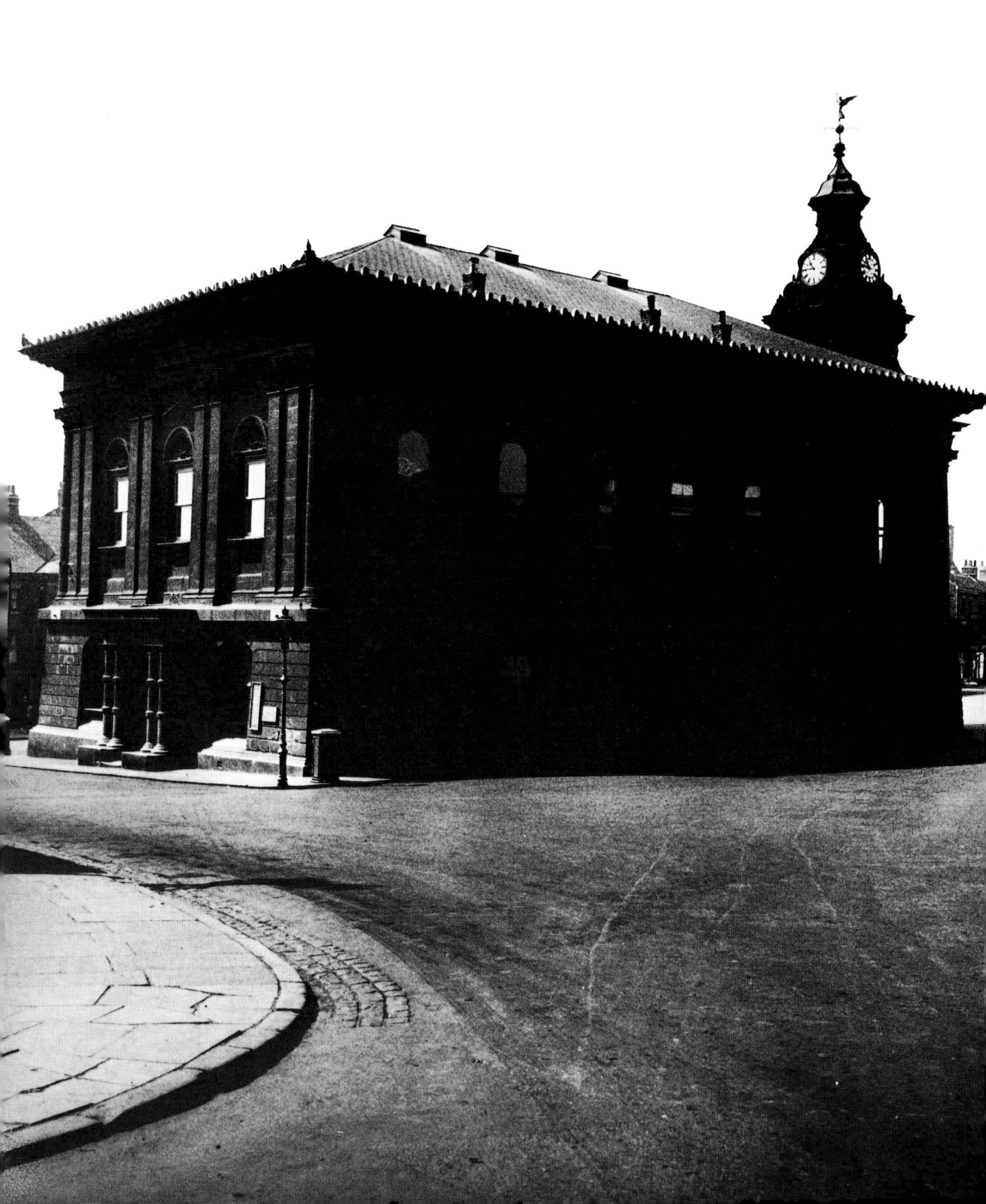

WILLIAM BLAKE

Born: *London, 28 November, 1757*
Died: *London, 12 August, 1827*

From 1800 to 1804 Blake lived in this cottage at Felpham, working on designs for the poet, William Hayley, who lived nearby. Of Felpham Blake wrote in September, 1800: 'The villagers of Felpham are not mere rustics; they are polite and modest. Meat is cheaper than in London; but the sweet air and the voices of winds, trees, and birds and the odours of the happy ground, make it a dwelling for immortals. Work will go on here with God-speed.'

3. BLAKE'S COTTAGE AT FELPHAM

GEORGE BORROW

Born: *East Dereham, 5 July,* 1803
Died: *Oulton, 26 July,* 1881

'A fine old city, truly, is that, view it from whatever side you will; but it shows best from the east, where the ground, bold and elevated, overlooks the fair and fertile valley in which it stands. Gazing from those heights, the eye beholds a scene which cannot fail to awaken, even in the least sensible bosom, feelings of pleasure and admiration. . . . Yes, there the city spreads from north to south, with its venerable houses, its numerous gardens, its thrice twelve churches . . . and yonder, rising three hundred feet above the soil, from among those noble forest trees, behold that old Norman master-work, that cloud-encircled cathedral spire, around which the garrulous army of rooks and choughs continually wheel their flight. Now, who can wonder that the children of that fine old city are proud of her, and offer up prayers for her prosperity?'

Lavengro

4. NORWICH, FROM MOUSEHOLD HEATH

JAMES BOSWELL

Born: *Auchinleck, 29 October,* 1740
Died: *London,* 19 *May,* 1795

'We passed through a wild moor, in many places so soft that we were obliged to walk, which was very fatiguing to Dr Johnson. Once he had advanced on horseback on a very bad step. There was a steep declivity on his left, to which he was so near, that there was not room for him to dismount in the usual way. He tried to alight on the other side, as if he had been a young buck indeed, but in the attempt he fell at his length upon the ground; from which, however, he got up immediately without being hurt. During this dreary ride, we were sometimes relieved by a view of branches of the sea, that universal medium of connection between mankind.'

Journal of a Tour to the Hebrides

5. ISLE OF SKYE

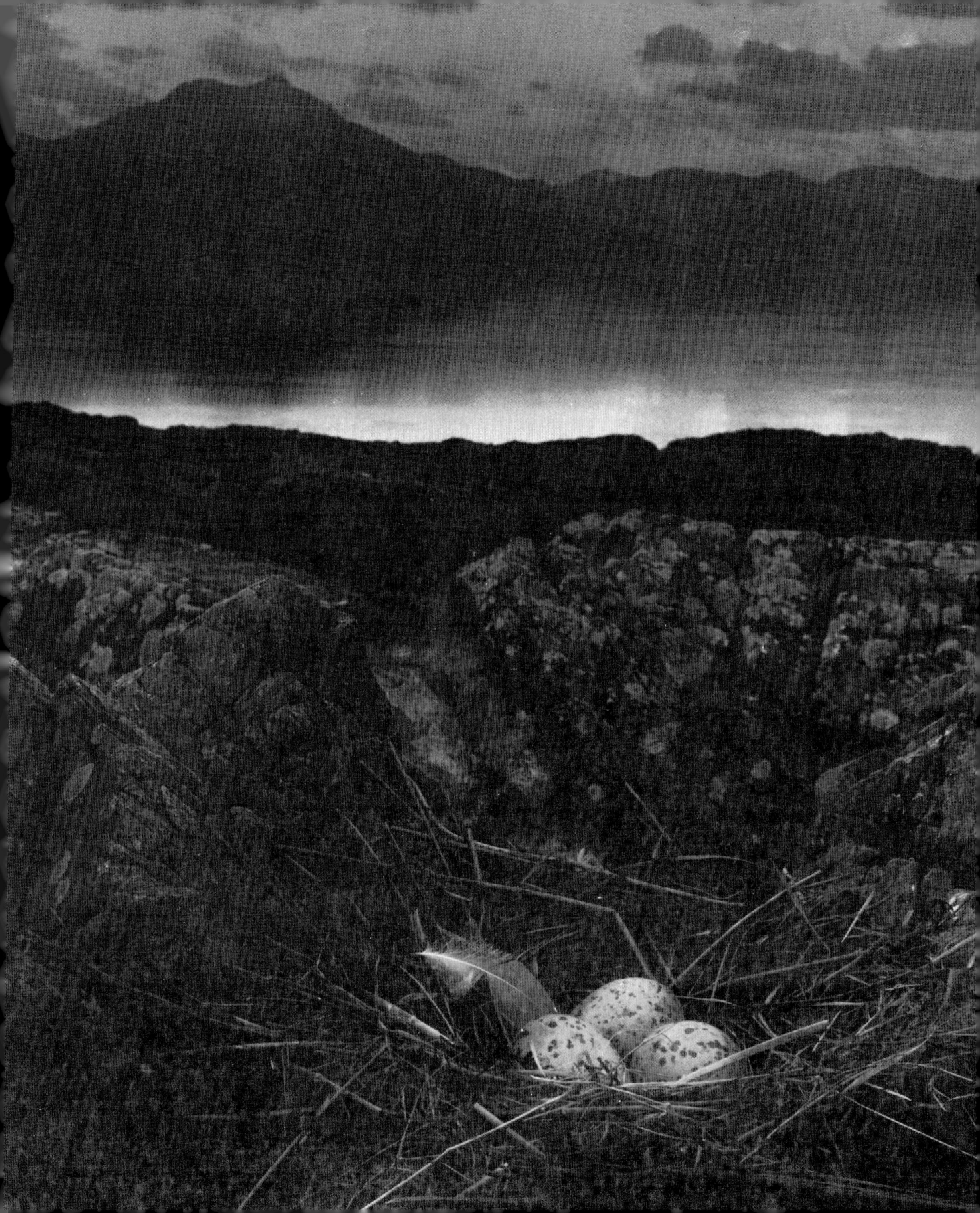

THE BRONTËS

CHARLOTTE

Born: *Haworth, 21 April, 1816*
Died: *Haworth, 31 March, 1855*

EMILY

Born: *Haworth, 20 August, 1818*
Died: *Haworth, 19 December, 1848*

ANNE

Born: *Haworth, 25 March, 1820*
Died: *Scarborough, 28 May, 1849*

In the background is the sofa on which Emily died. Above it is a painting of the girls' father. The trunk is the same one which Charlotte and Emily packed with such excitement before the trip to Brussels. Charlotte Brontë wrote to Ellen Nussey: 'I have had letters to write lately to Brussels, to Lille and to London – I have lots of chemises – night-gowns – pocket handkerchiefs and pockets to make – beside clothes to repair – and I have been every week since I came home expecting to see Branwell and he has never been able to get over yet – we fully expect him however next Saturday. Under these circumstances how can I go a-visiting?'

6. IN HAWORTH PARSONAGE

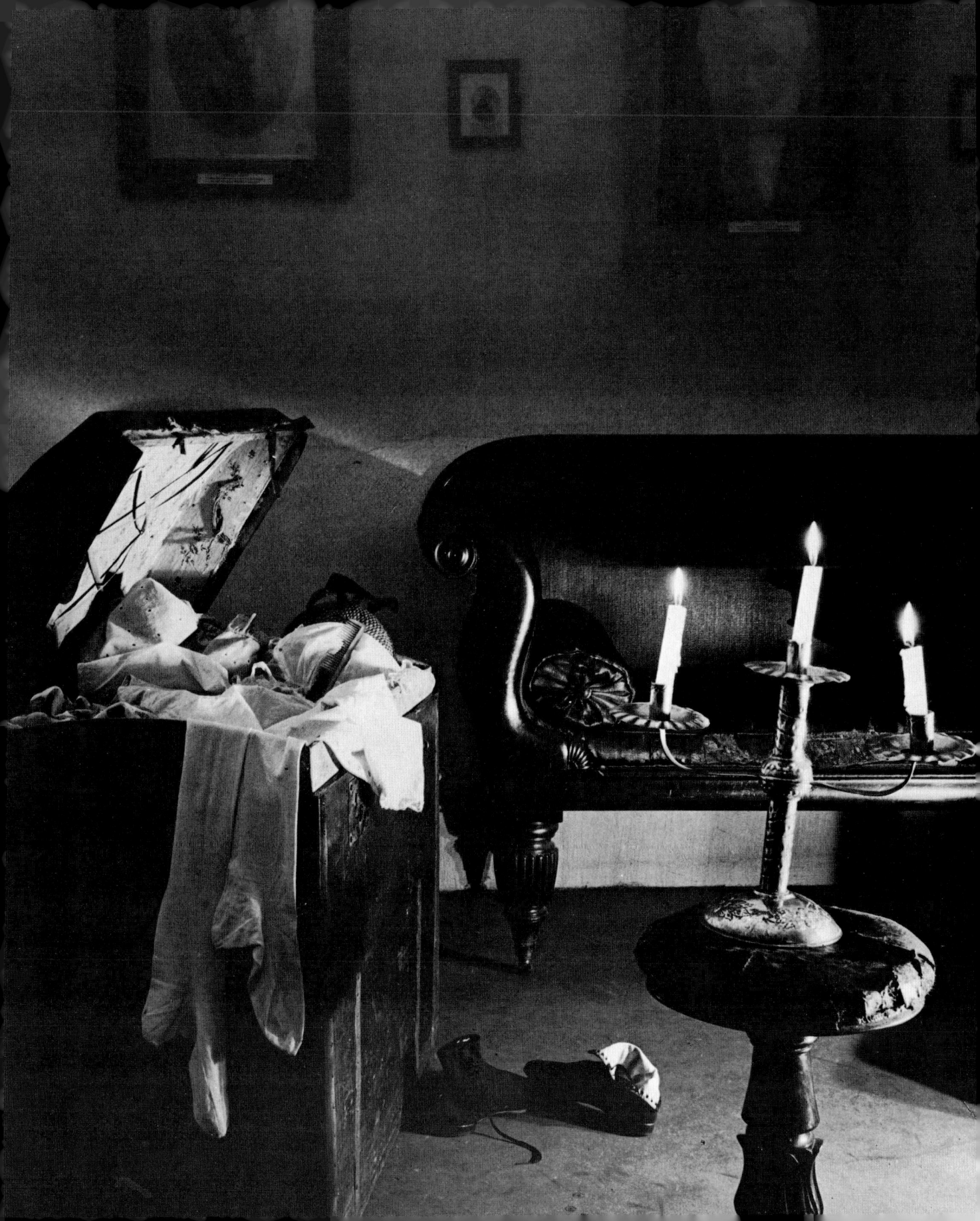

THE BRONTËS

In a letter to Ellen Nussey, Charlotte Brontë wrote: 'There have I sat on the low bedstead, my mind fixed on the window through which appeared no other landscape than a monotonous stretch of moorland, a grey church-tower rising from the centre of a church-yard so filled with graves that the rank weeds and coarse grass scarce had room to shoot up between the monuments.'

7. HAWORTH CHURCHYARD

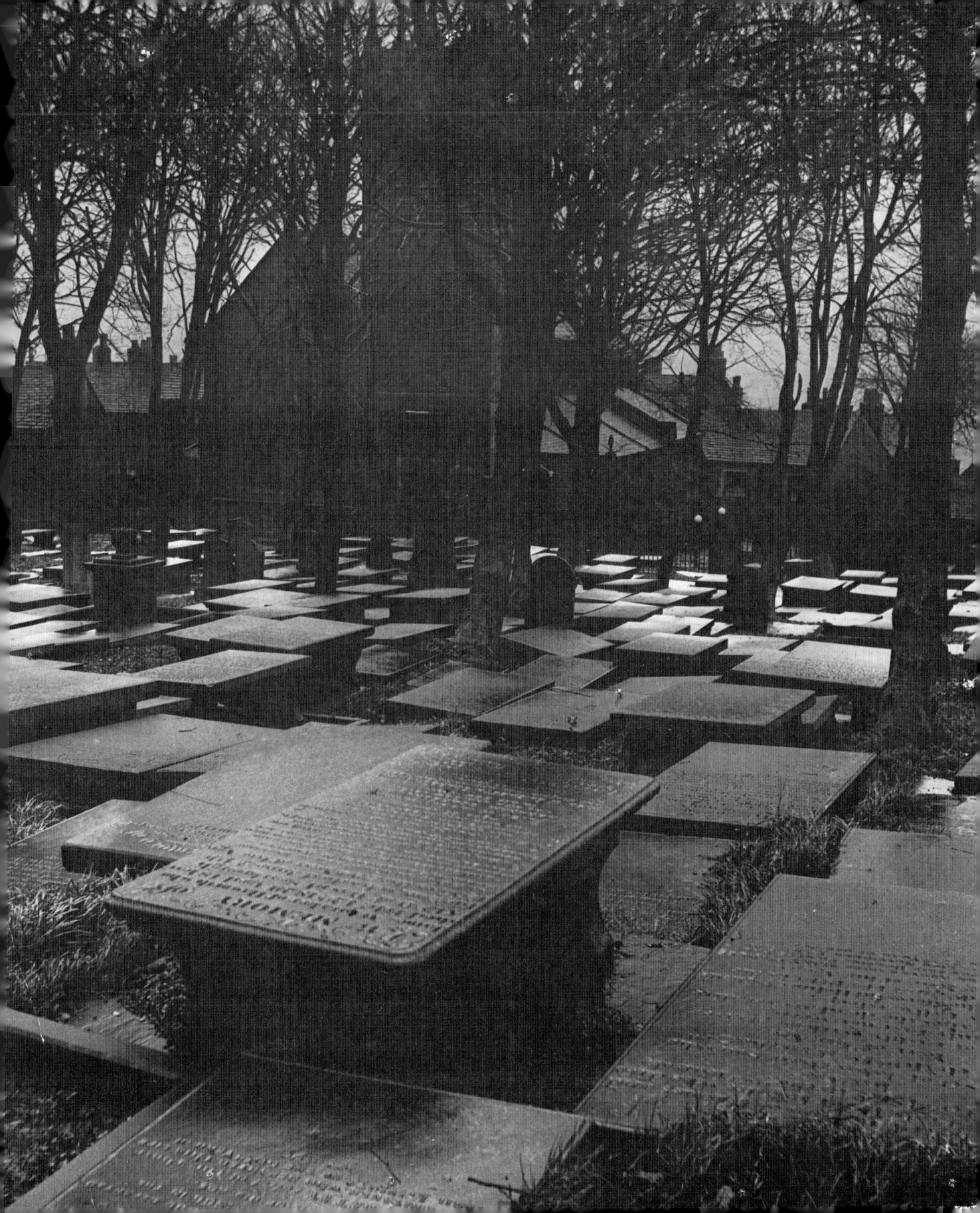

CHARLOTTE BRONTË

Charlotte Brontë took Wycoller Hall, six miles or so from Haworth, for the original of Ferndean Manor. The Hall is now in ruins, but the mantelpiece against which Mr Rochester leaned can still be seen.

'This parlour looked gloomy: a neglected handful of fire burnt low in the grate; and leaning over it, with his head supported against the high, old-fashioned mantlepiece, appeared the blind tenant of the room. His old dog, Pilot, lay on one side, removed out of the way, and coiled up as if afraid of being inadvertently trodden upon. Pilot pricked up his ears when I came in; then he jumped with a yelp and a whine and bounded towards me . . . Mr Rochester turned mechanically to see what the commotion was; but as he *saw* nothing he returned and sighed.'

Jane Eyre

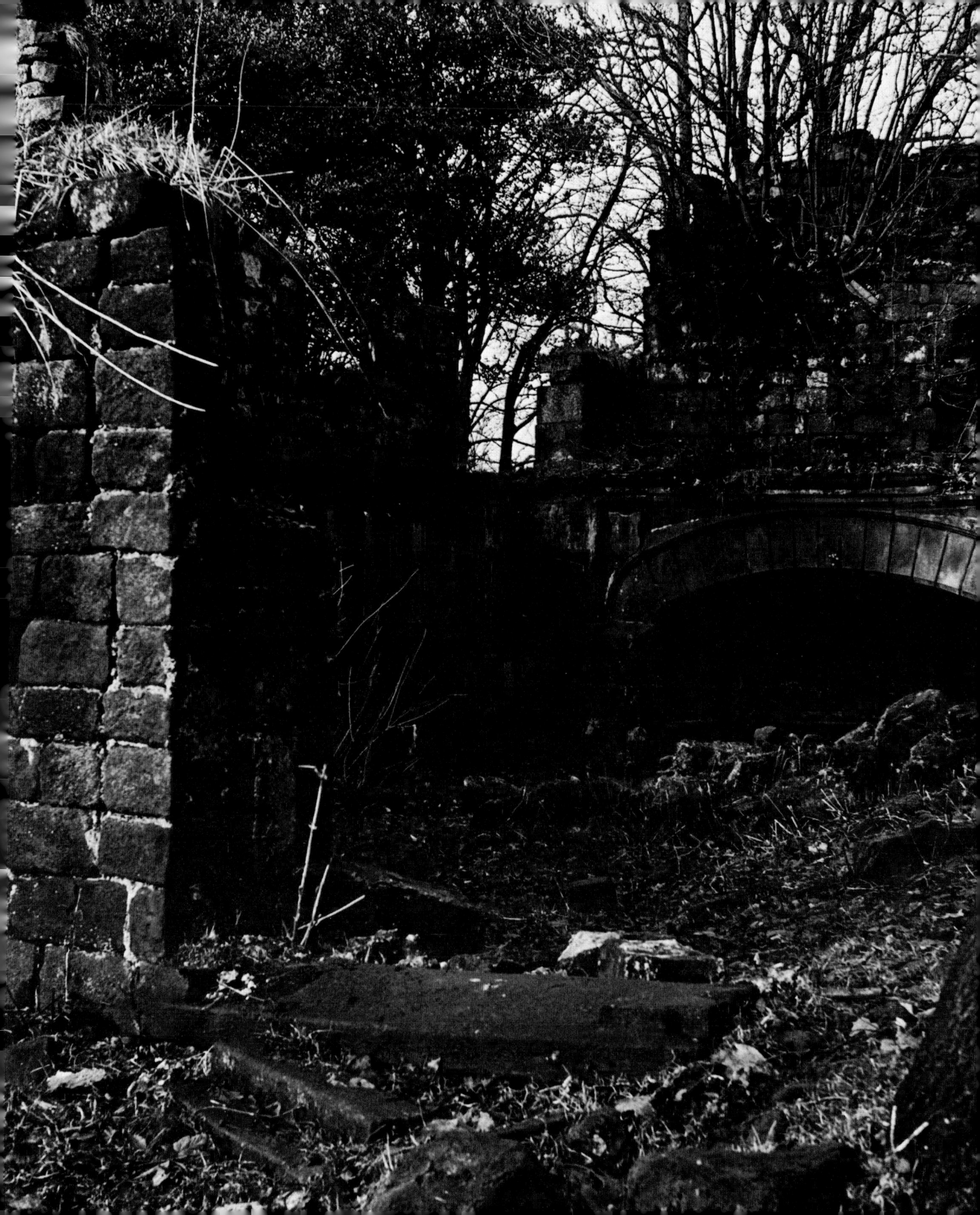

EMILY BRONTË

'Some West Riding folk call this empty shell of a building "Top Whithens", but it is generally known by the name which gave Emily the title for her novel. She was deeply attached to her home. When for brief periods she left Haworth to go to school or as a governess, she sickened and pined until her family were forced to bring her back to her beloved moors. "All round the horizon there is the same line of sinuous wave-like hills; the scoops into which they fall only revealing other hills beyond, of similar colour and shape, crowned with wild, bleak moors."'

Mrs Gaskell, *The Life of Charlotte Brontë*

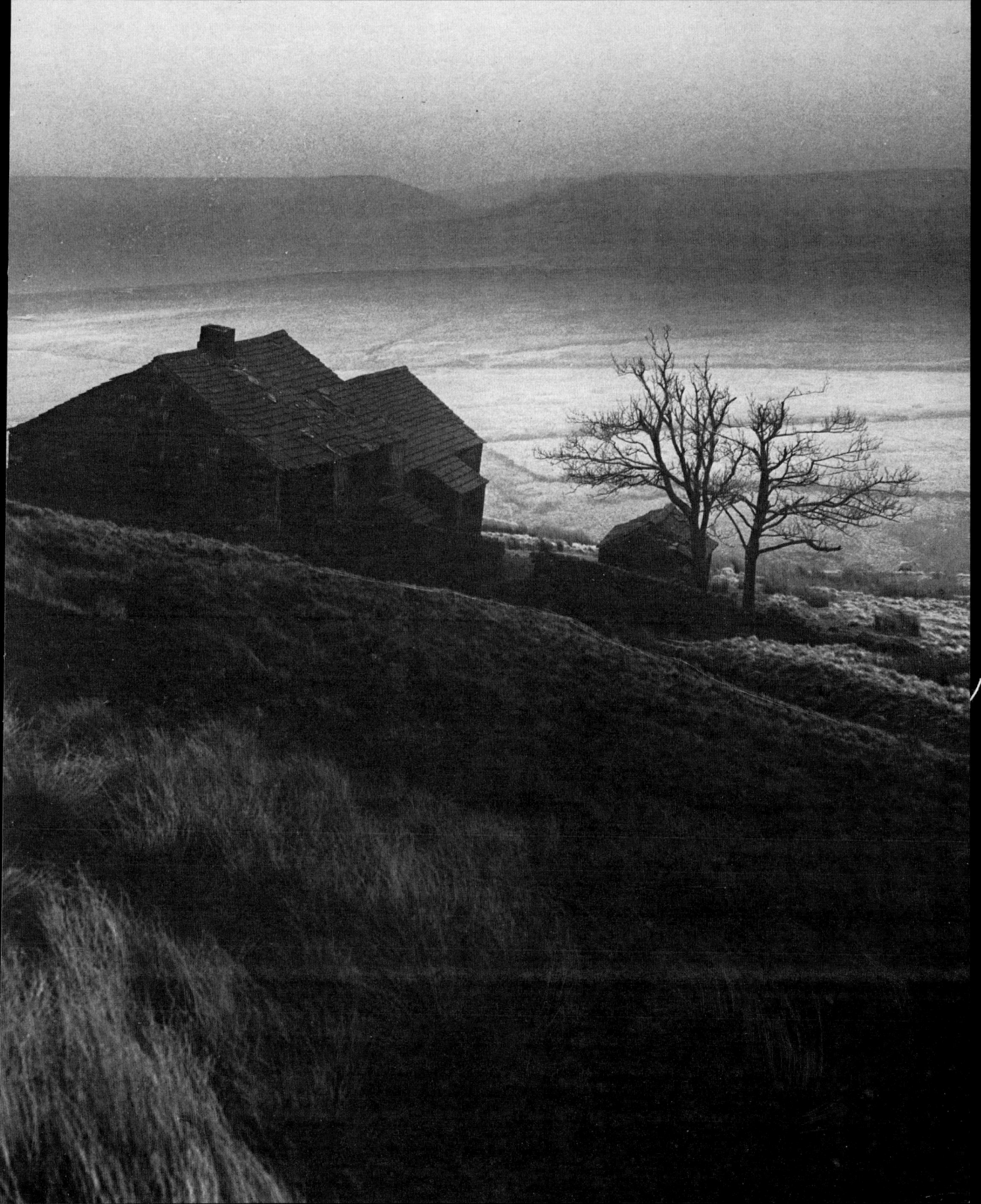

EMILY BRONTË

'Wuthering Heights is the name of Mr Heathcliff's dwelling, "Wuthering" being a significant provincial adjective, descriptive of the atmospheric tumult to which its station is exposed in stormy weather. Pure, bracing ventilation they must have up there at all times, indeed. One may guess the power of the north wind blowing over the edge by the excessive slant of a few stunted firs at the end of the house, and by a range of gaunt thorns all stretching their limbs one way, as if craving alms of the sun. Happily, the architect had foresight to build it strong; the narrow windows are deeply set in the wall, and the corners defended with large jutting stones.'

Wuthering Heights

10. WITHENS

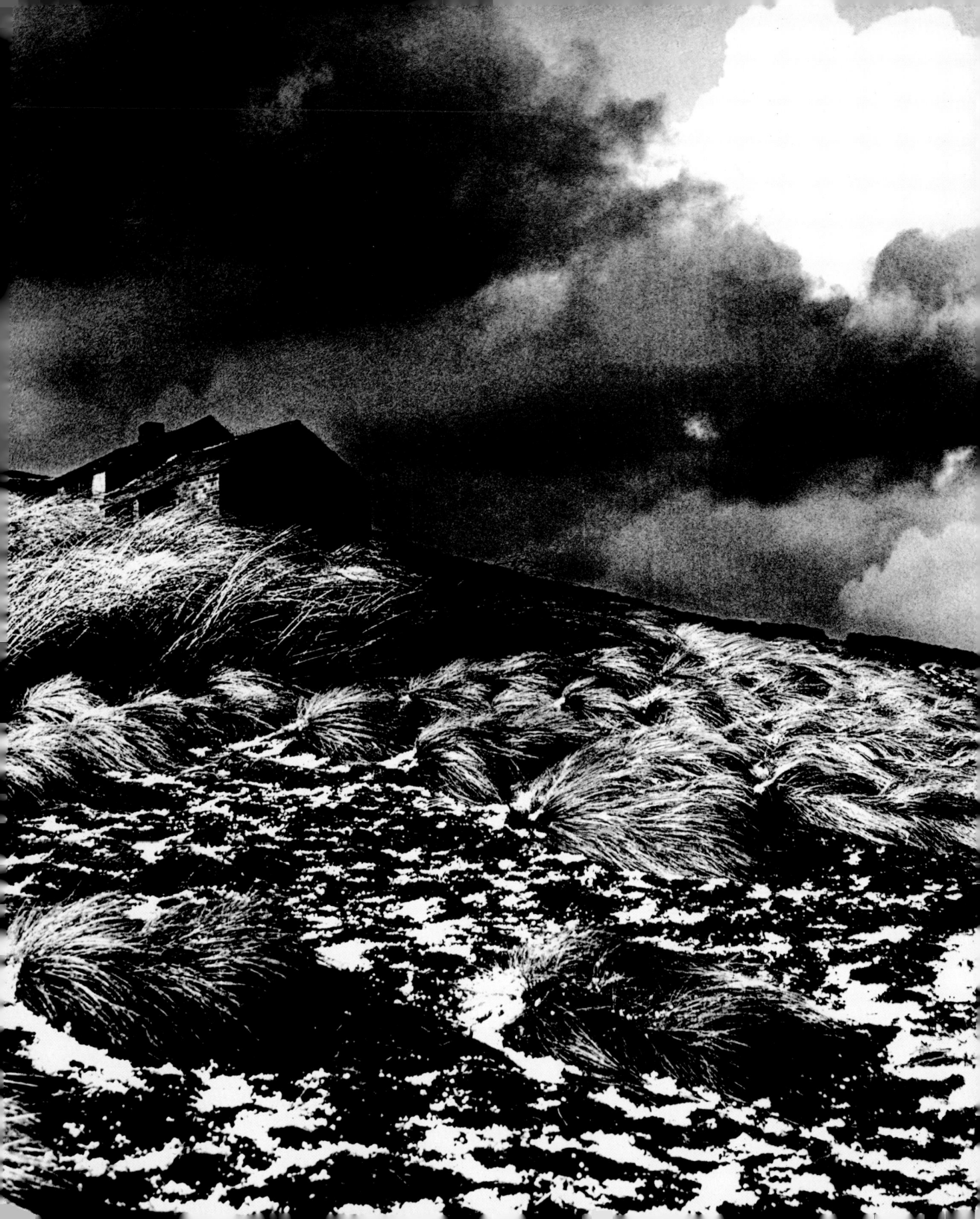

EMILY BRONTË

Wuthering Heights is a ruin now, a refuge for sheep on wild nights. Ninety years ago, an admirer of Emily Brontë bought and reconstructed it as he imagined it had been in Heathcliff's day. But in 1905, the Brontë Society pulled down the repairs and left the house to moulder away in peace.

'. . . beneath its walls I perceived decay had made progress: . . . many a window showed black gaps deprived of glass; and slates jutted off, here and there, beyond the right line of the roof, to be gradually worked off in coming autumn storms'.

Wuthering Heights

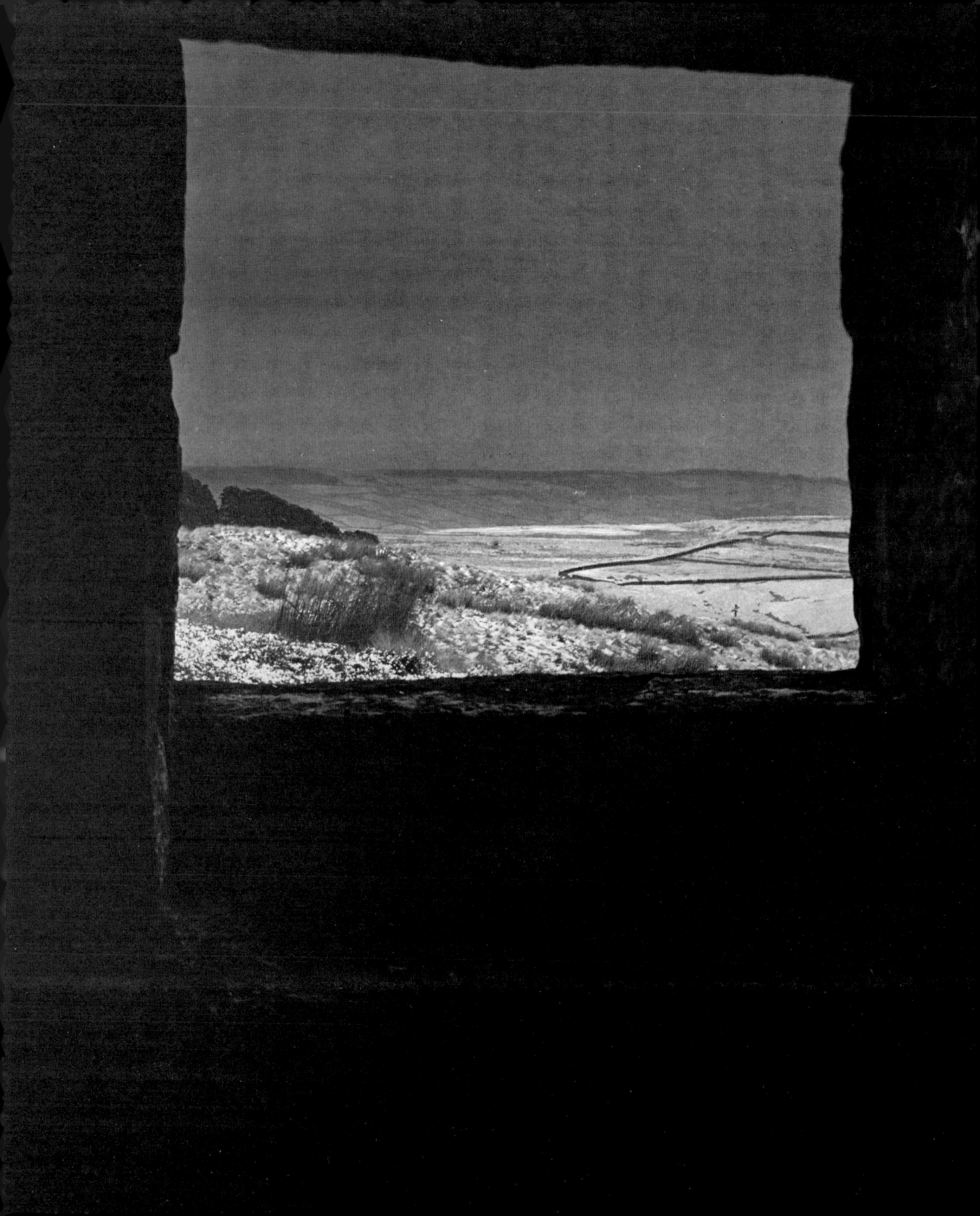

EMILY BRONTË

'My sister loved the moors. Flowers brighter than the rose bloomed in the blackest of the heath for her; out of a sullen hollow in a livid hill-side her mind could make an Eden. She found in the bleak solitude many and dear delights; and not the least and best-loved was – liberty'.

Charlotte Brontë writing about Emily Brontë

ELIZABETH BARRETT BROWNING

Born: *Coxhoe, 6 March,* 1806
Died: *Florence, 30 June,* 1861

At the time of her birth, Elizabeth Barrett's parents were living at Coxhoe Hall, some six miles to the south of Durham. While she was still an infant they moved to Herefordshire where her childhood was spent.

13. COXHOE HALL

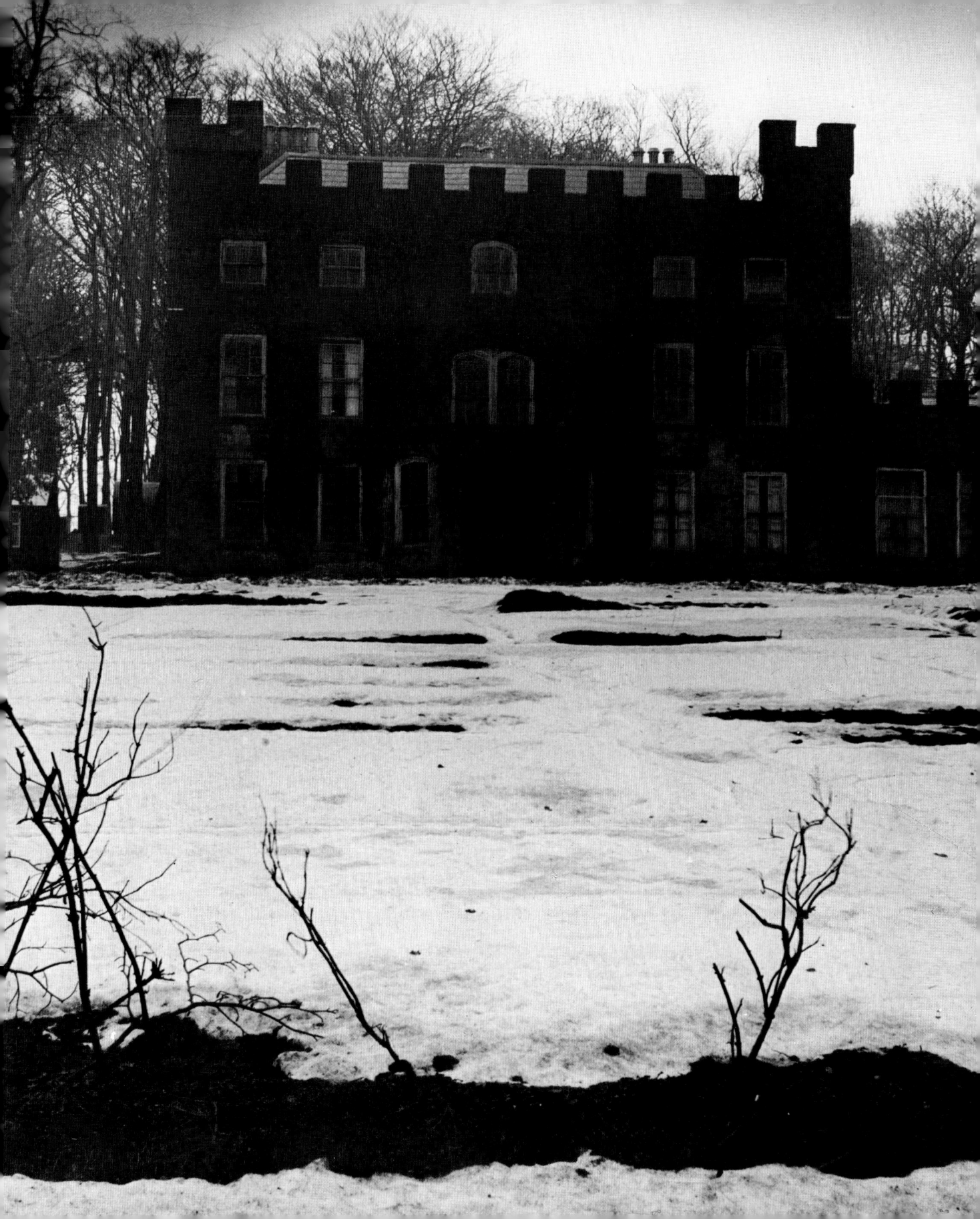

GEORGE GORDON BYRON

LORD BYRON

Born: *London*, 22 *January*, 1788
Died: *Missilonghi, Greece*, 19 *April*, 1824

Through thy battlements, Newstead, the hollow winds whistle;
Thou, the hall of my fathers, are gone to decay;
In thy once smiling garden, the hemlock and thistle
Have choked up the rose which late bloom'd in the way.

On Leaving Newstead Abbey

14. NEWSTEAD ABBEY

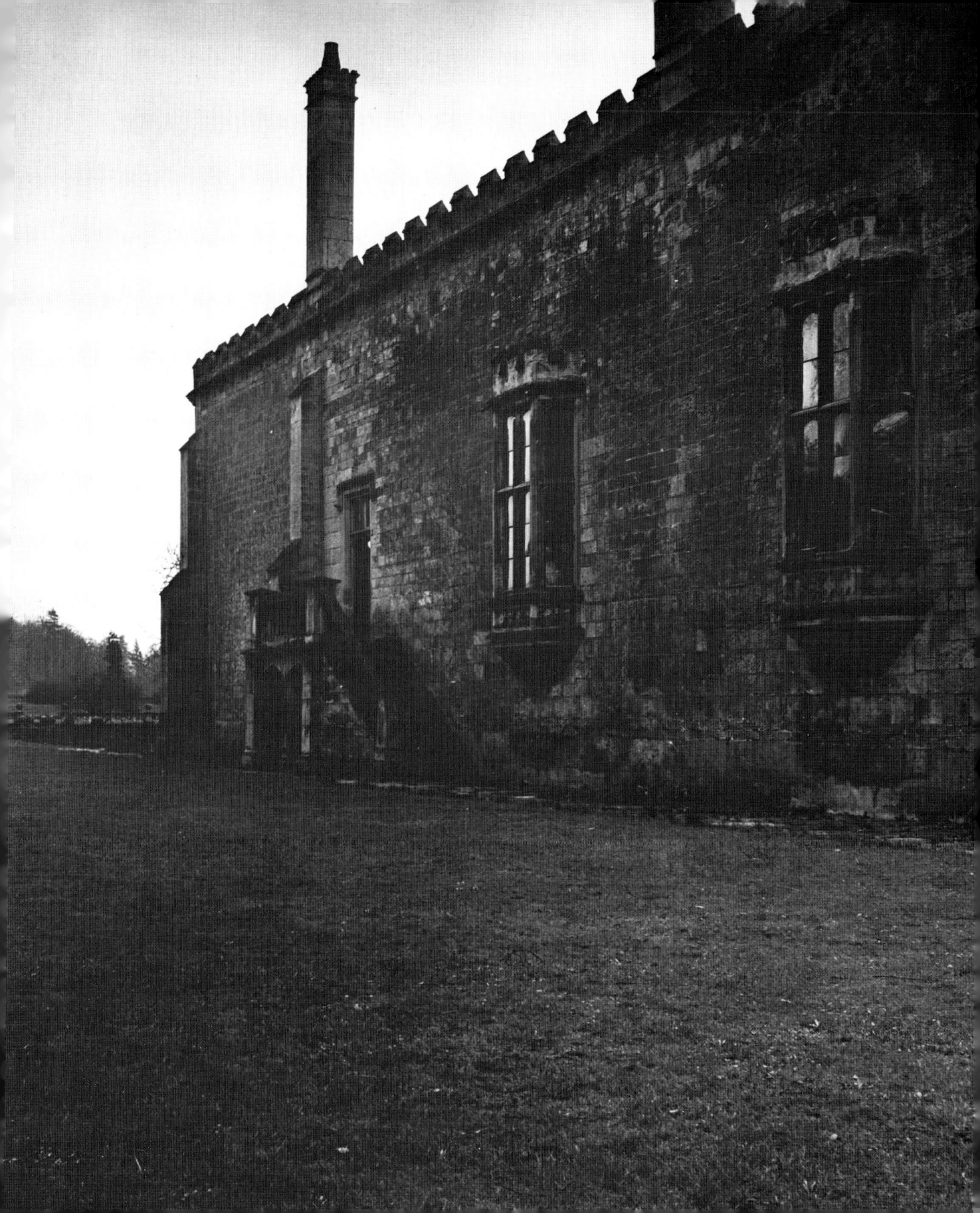

LORD BYRON

The poet's bedroom in Newstead Abbey remains much as he left it when he quitted England in 1816.

15. LORD BYRON'S BEDROOM

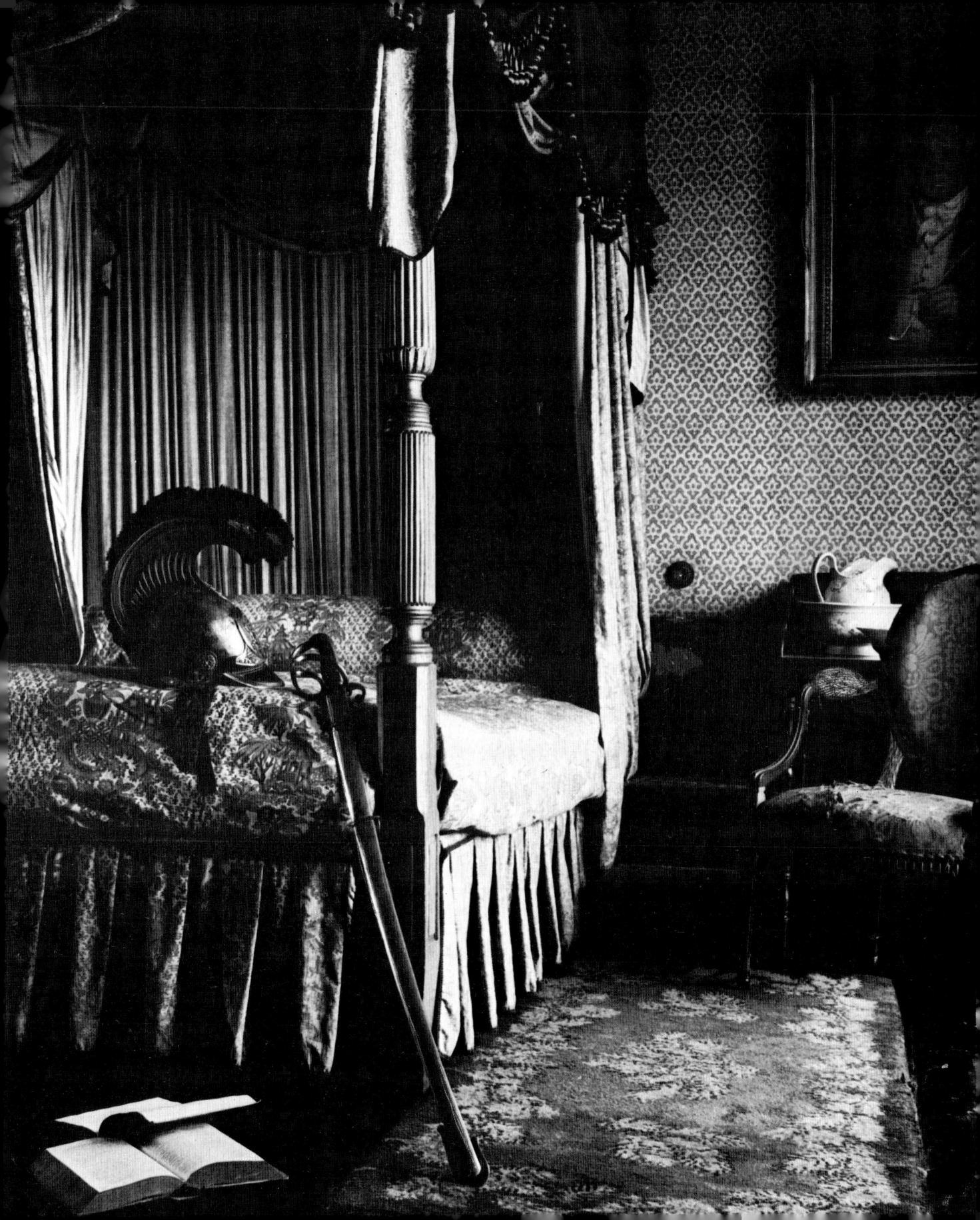

JOHN CLARE

Born: *Helpstone, Northamptonshire*, 13 *July*, 1793
Died: *Northampton*, 20 *May*, 1864

His native scenes! O sweet endearing sound;
Sure never beats a heart, howe'er forlorn,
But the warm'd breast has soft emotions found
To cherish the dear spot where he was born:
E'en the poor hedger in the early morn
Chopping the pattering bushes hung with dew,
Scarce lays his mitten on a branching thorn,
But painful memory's banish'd thoughts in view
Remind him, when 'twas young, what happy days he knew.

The Village Minstrel

16. CLARE'S BIRTHPLACE

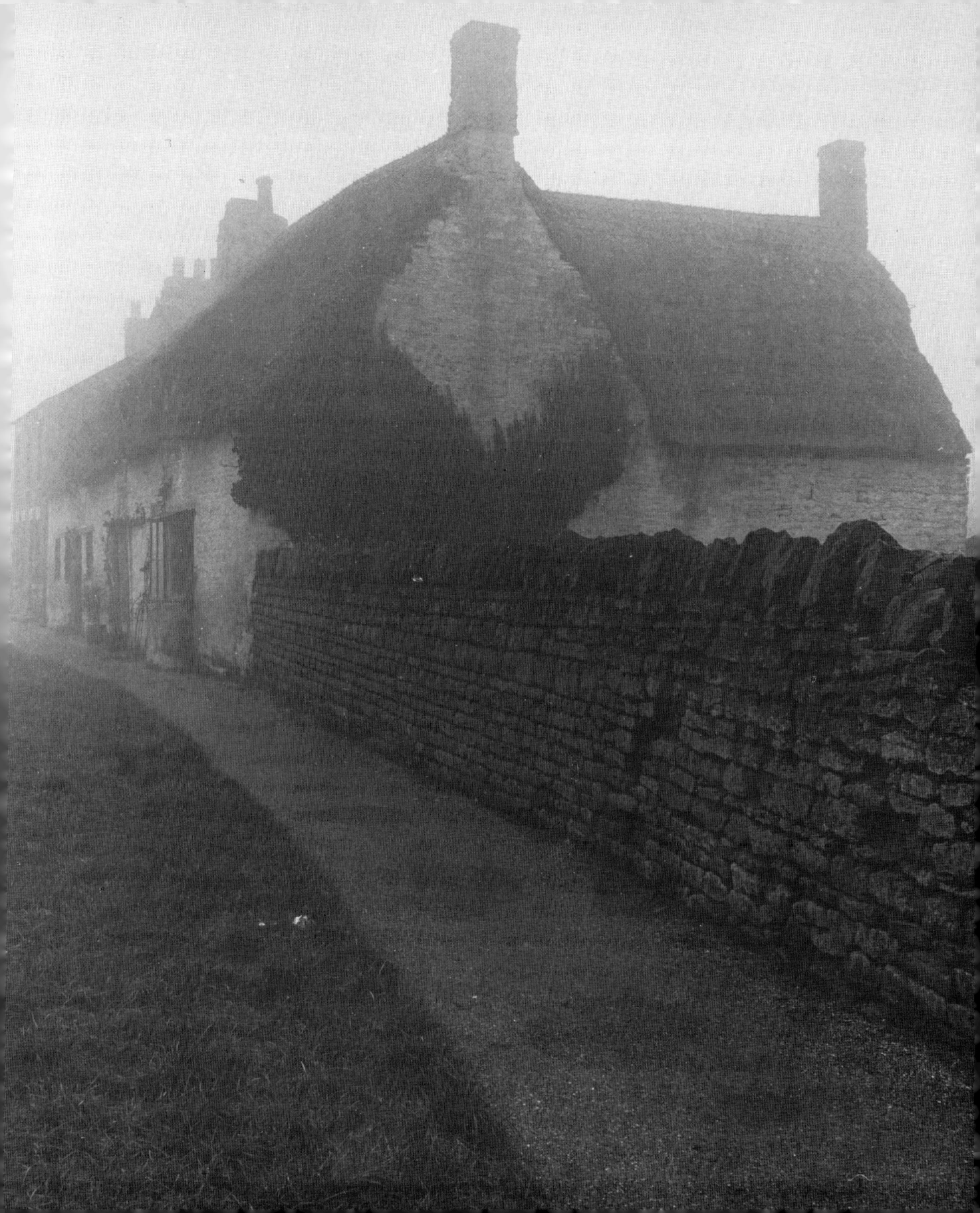

WILLIAM COBBETT

Born: *Farnham, 9 March,* 1762
Died: *Guildford,* 18 *June,* 1835

'In this North of Hampshire, as everywhere else, the churches and all other things exhibit indubitable marks of decay. There are along under the north side of that chain of hills, which divide Hampshire from Berkshire, in this part, taking into Hampshire about two or three miles wide of the low ground under the chain, eleven churches in a string, in about fifteen miles the chancels of which would contain a great many more than all the inhabitants, men, women, and children, sitting at their ease with plenty of room . . . In some instances the small farmhouses and homesteads are completely gone; in others, the buildings remain, but in a tumble-down state; in others, the house is gone, leaving the barn for use as a barn, or as a cattle-shed; in others the out-buildings are gone, and the house, with rotten thatch, broken windows, rotten door-sills, and all threatening to fall, remains as the dwelling of a half-starved, and ragged family of small farmers, that formerly lived happily in this very house.'

Rural Rides

17. CHURCH AND BARN, HURSTBOURNE TARRANT

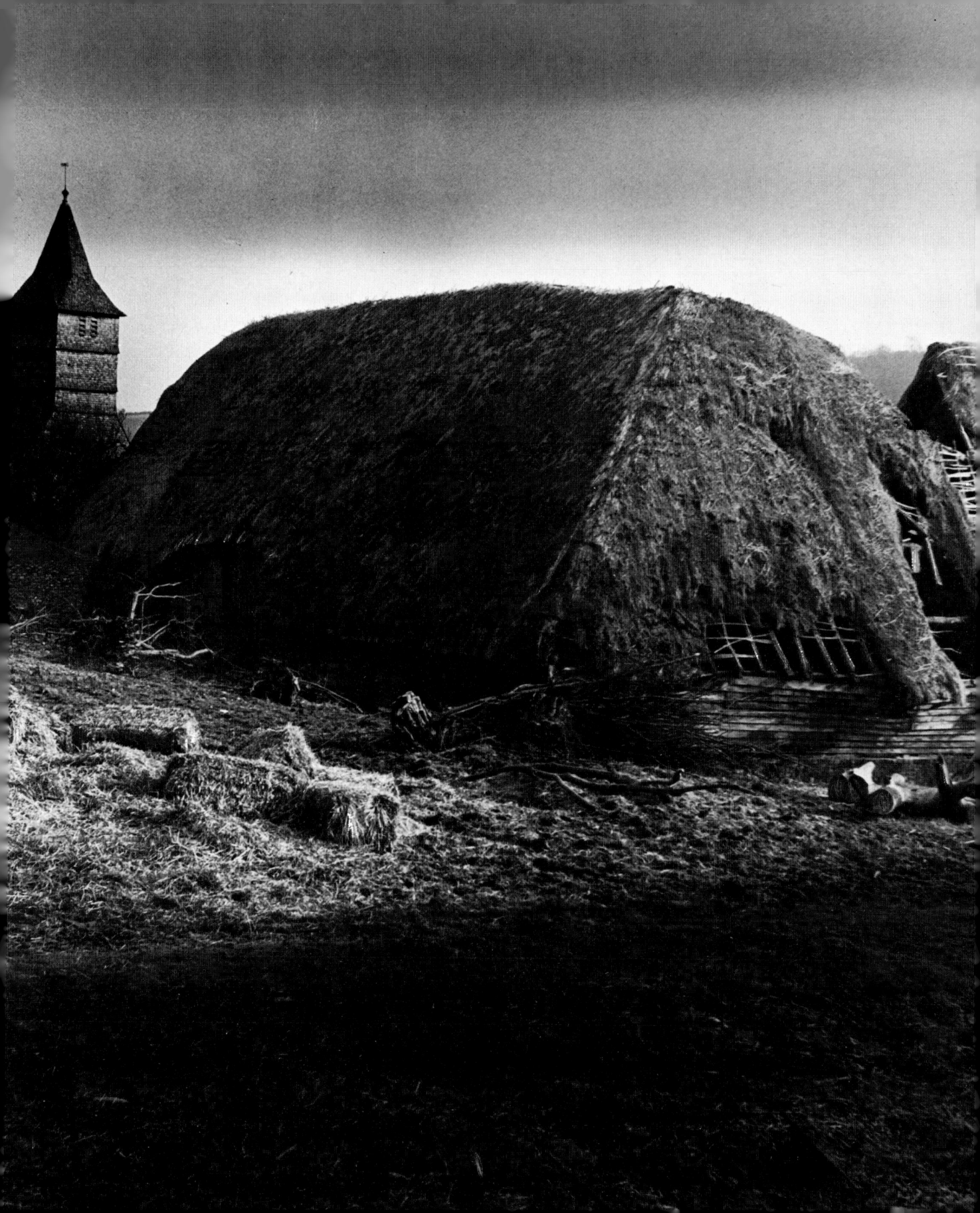

SAMUEL TAYLOR COLERIDGE

Born: *Ottery St Mary, Devon, 21 October, 1772*
Died: *Highgate, 25 July, 1834*

In a letter to Southey, dated from Greta Hall, 13 April, 1801, Coleridge wrote: 'Our house stands on a low hill, the whole front of which is one field and an enormous garden, nine-tenths of which is a nursery garden. Behind the house is an orchard, and a small wood on a steep slope, at the foot of which flows the River Greta, which winds round and catches the evening lights in the front of the house. In front we have a giant's camp – an encamped army of tent-like mountains, which by an inverted arch gives a view of another vale. On our right the lovely vale and the wedge-shaped lake of Bassenthwaite; and on our left Derwentwater and Lodore in full view, and the fantastic mountains of Borrowdale. Behind us the massy Skiddaw, smooth, green, high, with two chasms and a tent-like ridge in the larger. A fairer scene you have not seen in all your wanderings. Without going from our grounds we have all that can please a human being. . . .

'The house is full twice as large as we want; it hath more rooms in it than Allfoxen; you might have a bedroom, parlour, study, etc., etc., and there would always be rooms to spare for your or my visitors. In short for situation and convenience, – and when I mention the name of Wordsworth, for society of men of intellect – I know no place in which you and Edith would find yourselves so well suited.'

18. GRETA HALL, KESWICK

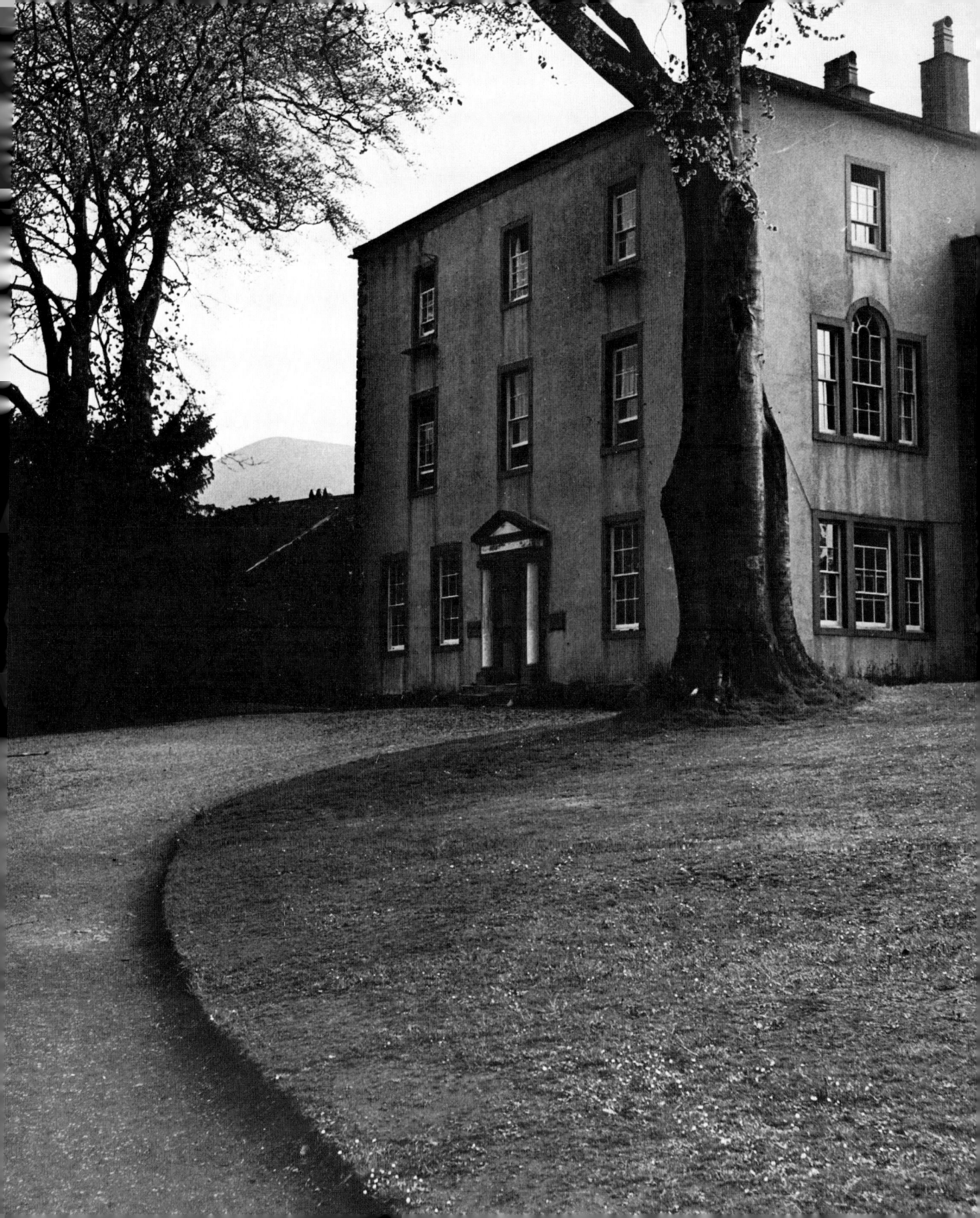

GEORGE CRABBE

Born: *Aldeburgh*, 24 December, 1754
Died: *Trowbridge*, 3 February, 1832

Thus by himself compell'd to live each day,
To wait for certain hours the tide's delay;
At the same times the same dull views to see,
The bounding marsh-bank and the blighted tree;
The water only, when the tides were high,
When low, the mud half-cover'd and half-dry;
The sun-burnt tar that blisters on the planks,
And bank-side stakes in their uneven ranks;
Heaps of entangled weeds that slowly float,
As the tide rolls by the impeded boat.
    When tides were neap, and, in the sultry day,
Through the tall bounding mud-banks made their way,
Which on each side rose swelling, and below
The dark warm flood ran silently and slow;
There anchoring, Peter chose from man to hide,
There hang his head, and view the lazy tide
In its hot slimy channel slowly glide;
Where the small eels that left the deeper way
For the warm shore, within the shallows play;
Where gaping mussels, left upon the mud,
Slope their slow passage to the fallen flood . . .

The Borough

19. ALDEBURGH

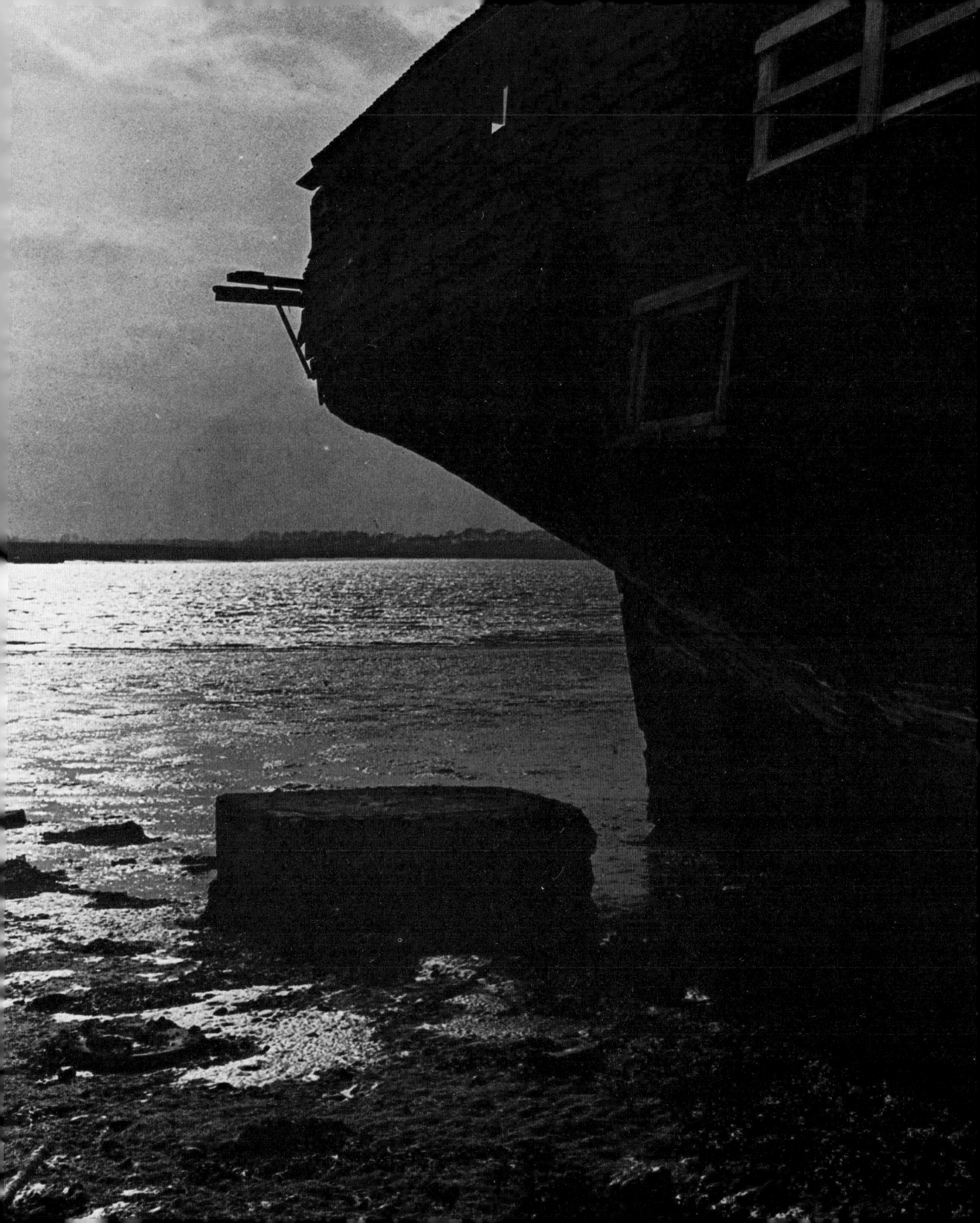

GEORGE CRABBE

Be it the summer noon: a sandy space
The ebbing tide has left upon its place;
Then just the hot and stony beach above,
Light twinkling streams in bright confusion move;
(For heated thus, the warmer air ascends,
And with the cooler in its fall contends) –
Then the broad bosom of the ocean keeps
An equal motion; swelling as it sleeps,

    .   .   .   .

Art thou not present, this calm scene before,
Where all beside is pebbly length of shore,
And far as eye can reach, it can discern no more?

The Borough

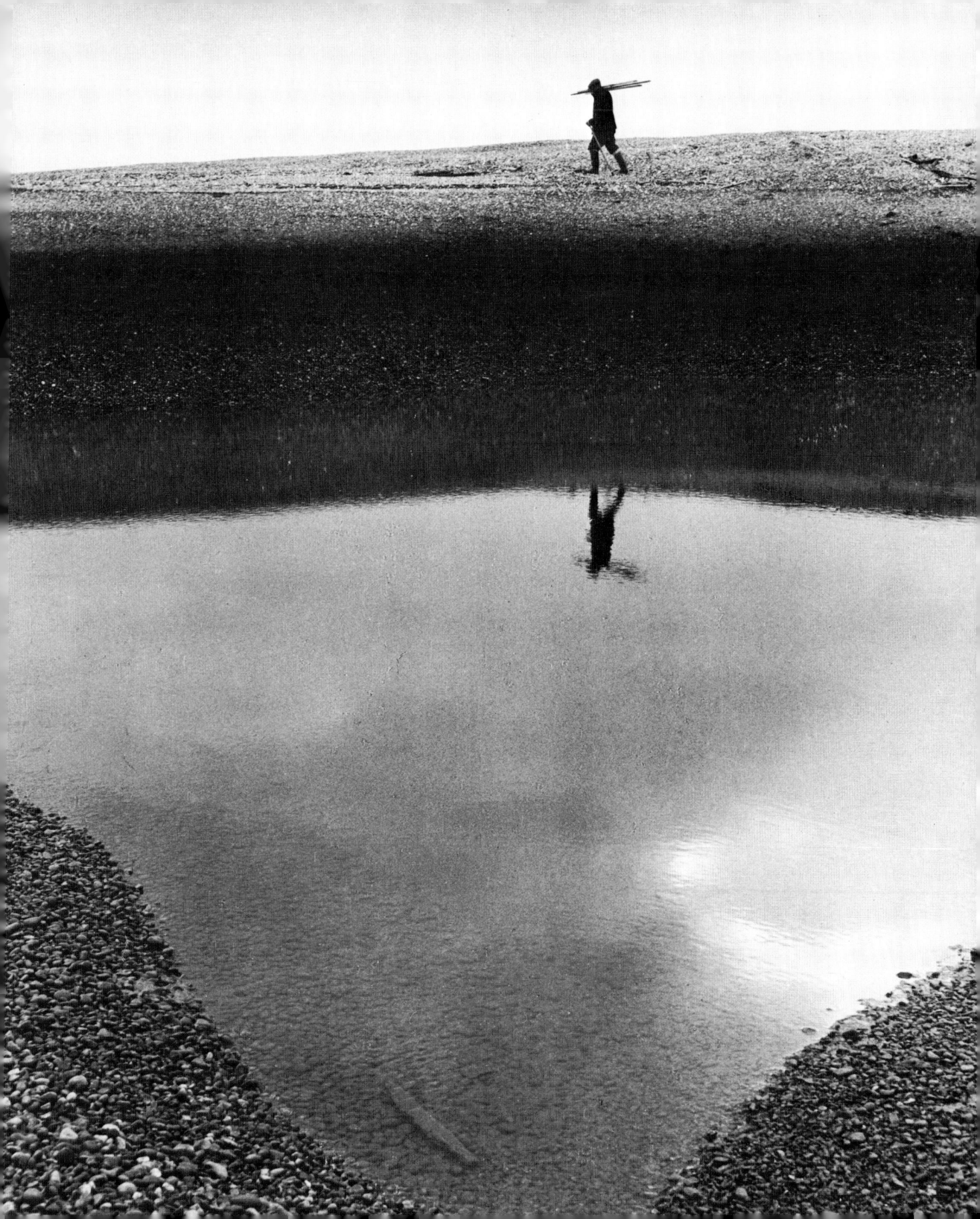

GEORGE CRABBE

Where hang at open doors the net and cork
While squalid sea-dames mend the meshy work.
Till comes the hour when fishing through the tide
The weary husband throws his freight aside.

The Borough

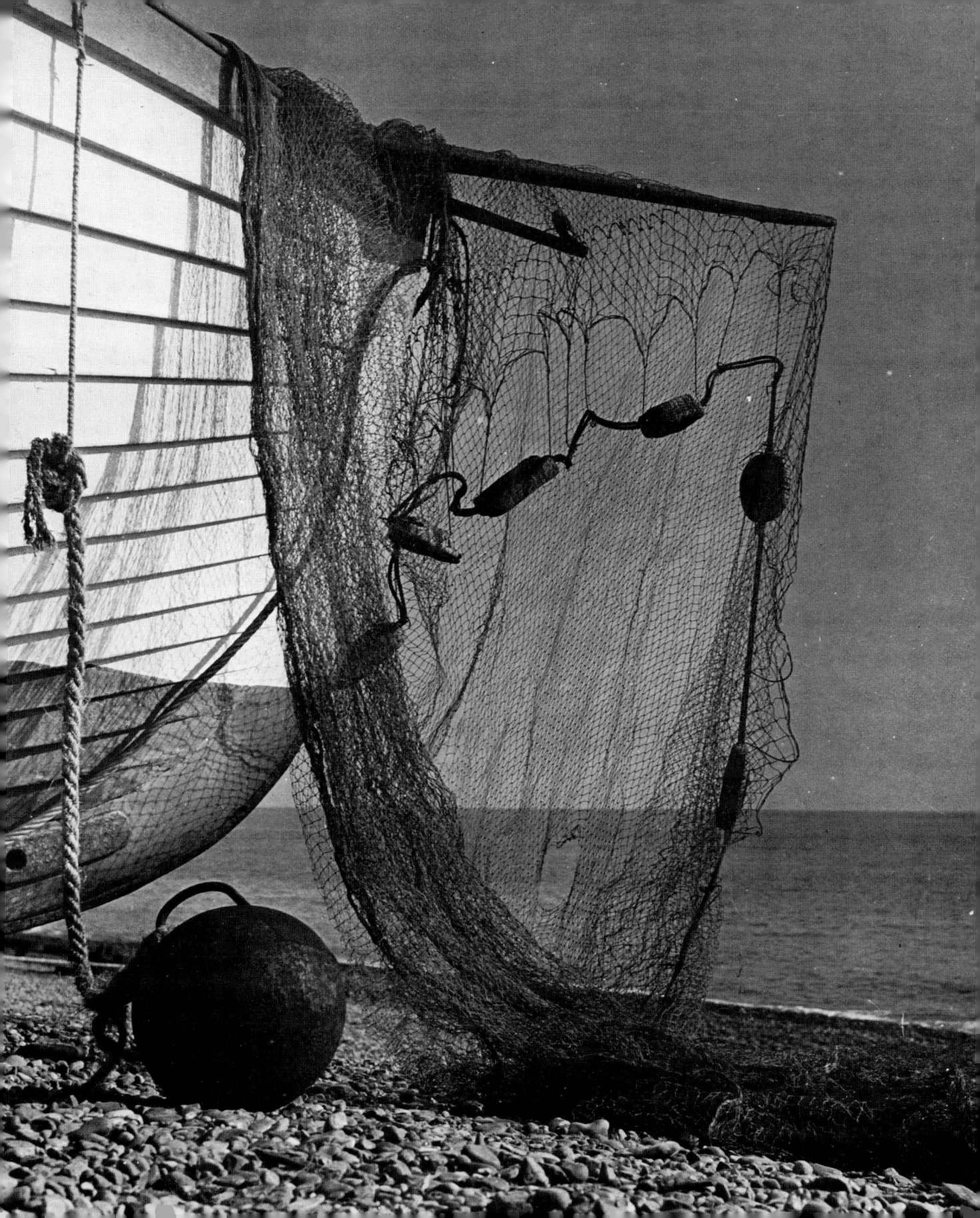

CHARLES DICKENS

Born: *Portsmouth, 7 February,* 1812
Died: *Gad's Hill Place, Kent, 9 June,* 1870

Gad's Hill Place, some two miles from Rochester, was bought by Dickens in 1856 and after spending a considerable sum on improvements he took up his permanent residence there in 1860. While staying there in July, 1858, he wrote to his French friend De Cerjat:

'At this present moment I am on my little Kentish freehold looking on as pretty a view out of my study window as you will find in a long day's English ride. My little place is a grave red brick house (time of George the First, I suppose) which I have added to and stuck bits upon in all manner of ways, so that it is pleasantly irregular, and as violently opposed to all architectural ideas, as the most hopeful man could possibly desire. It is on the summit of Gad's Hill. The robbery was committed before the door, on the man with the treasure, and Falstaff ran away from the identical spot of ground now covered by the room in which I write. A little rustic alehouse, called the Sir John Falstaff, is over the way – has been over the way ever since, in honour of the event. Cobham Woods and Park are behind the house; the distant Thames in front; the Medway, with Rochester, and its old castle and cathedral on one side. The whole stupendous property is on the old Dover Road, so when you come, come by the North Kent Railway (not the South Eastern) to Strood or Higham, and I'll drive over to fetch you.'

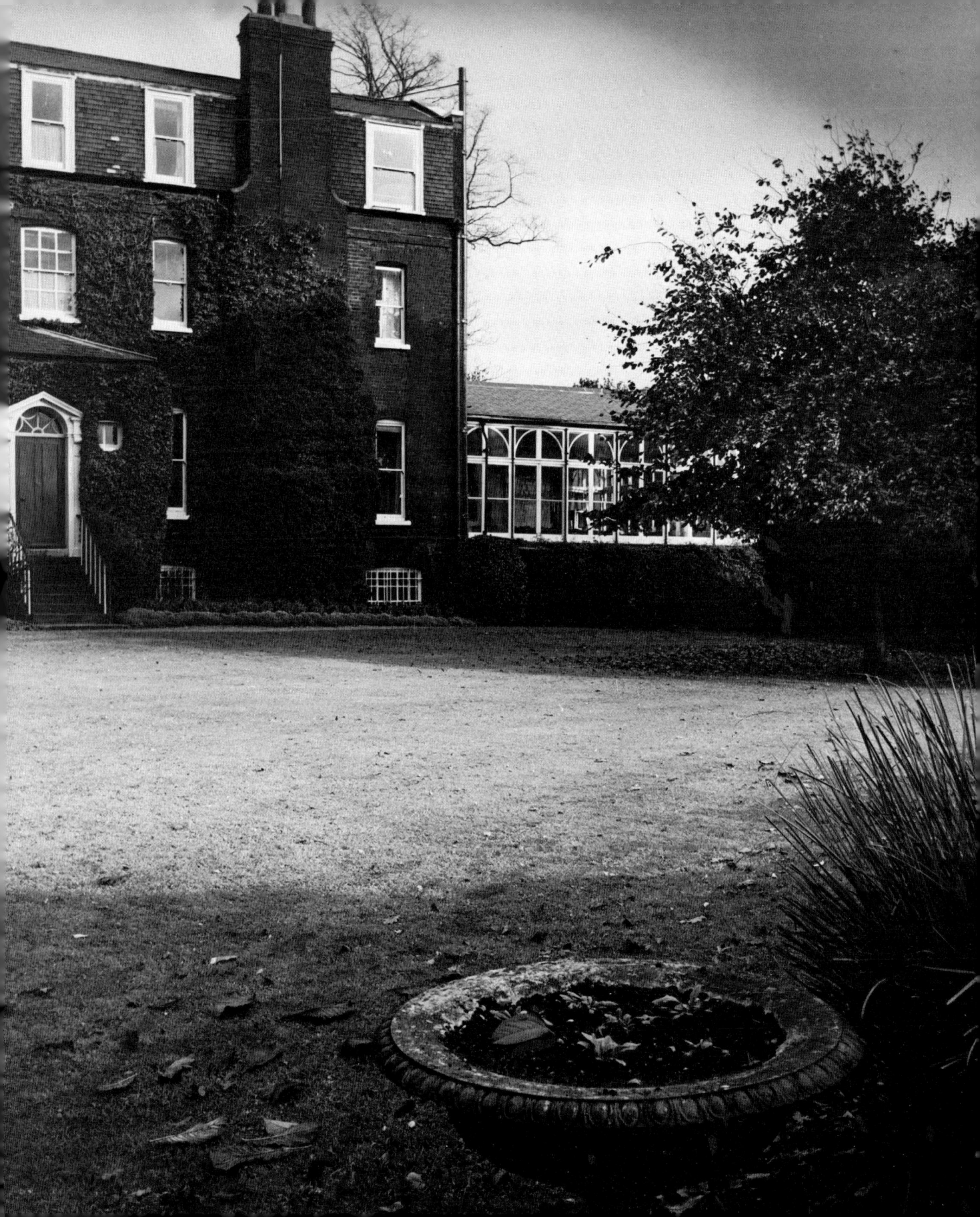

CHARLES DICKENS

'Ours was the marsh country, down by the river, within, as the river wound, twenty miles of the sea. My first most vivid and broad impression of the identity of things, seems to me to have been gained on a memorable raw afternoon towards evening. At such a time I found out for certain, that this bleak place overgrown with nettles was the churchyard; and that Philip Pirrip, late of this parish, and also Georgiana wife of the above, were dead and buried; and that Alexander, Bartholomew, Abraham, Tobias, and Roger, infant children of the aforesaid, were also dead and buried; and that the dark flat wilderness beyond the churchyard, intersected with dykes and mounds and gates, with scattered cattle feeding on it, was the marshes; and that the low leaden line beyond was the river; and that the distant savage lair from which the wind was rushing, was the sea . . .'

Great Expectations

23. COOLING GRAVEYARD

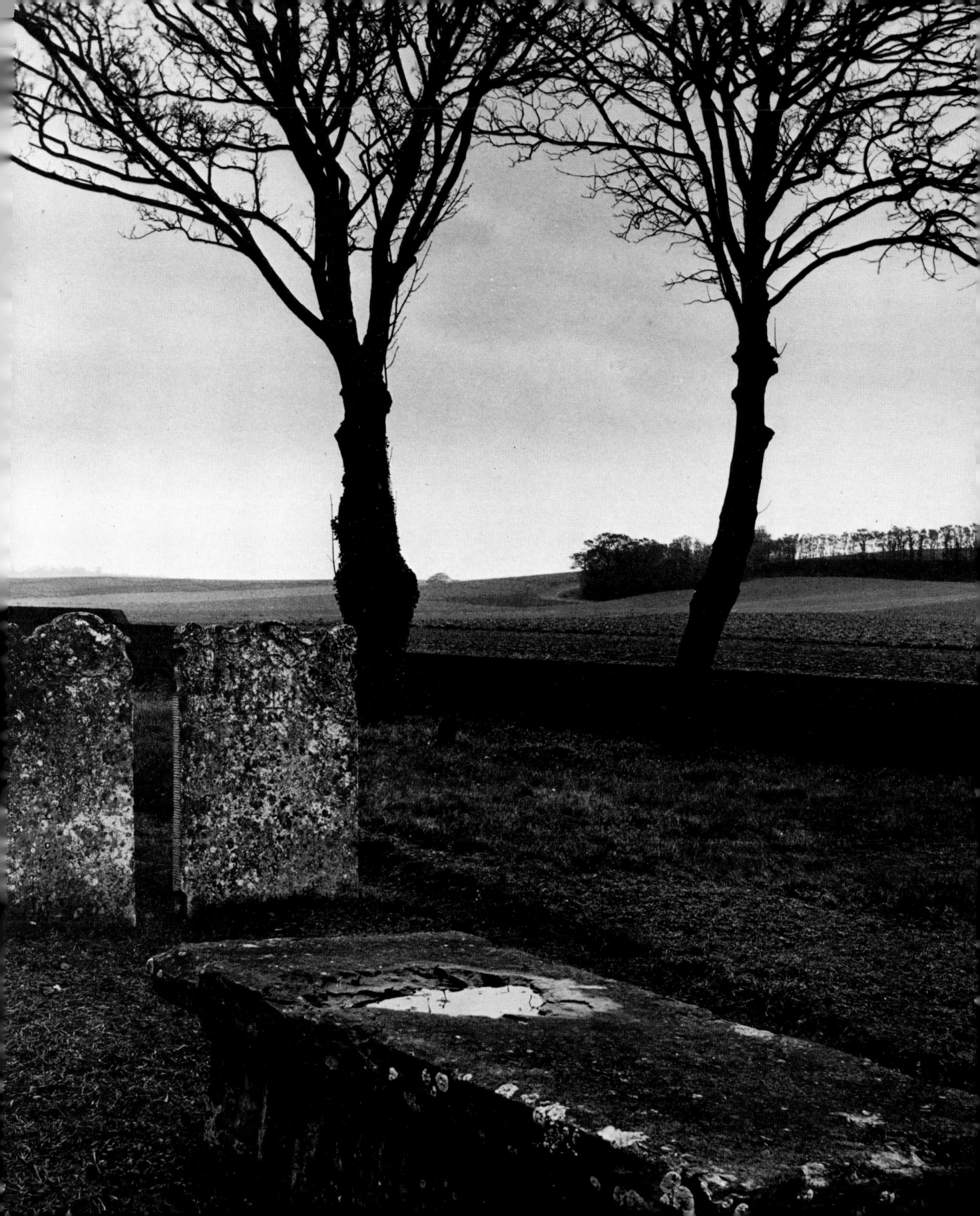

CHARLES DICKENS

In 1859 the actor Charles Fechter presented Dickens with a Swiss chalet which arrived from Paris in ninety-four pieces, fitting together, as Forster says, like the joints of a puzzle. It was erected in the shrubbery, and in the summer months much of Dickens's work was done there. 'I have put five mirrors in the chalet,' he wrote to an American friend, 'and they reflect and refract in all kinds of ways, the leaves that are quivering at the windows, and the great fields of waving corn, and the sail-dotted river. My room is up among the branches of the trees; and the birds and the butterflies fly in and out, and the green branches shoot in at the open windows, and the lights and shadows of the clouds come and go with the rest of the company.'

Great Expectations, *A Tale of Two Cities*, *Our Mutual Friend* and many smaller works and articles were written in the Chalet, and Dickens was working there on *Edwin Drood* on the day of his final seizure.

24. THE CHALET, GAD'S HILL

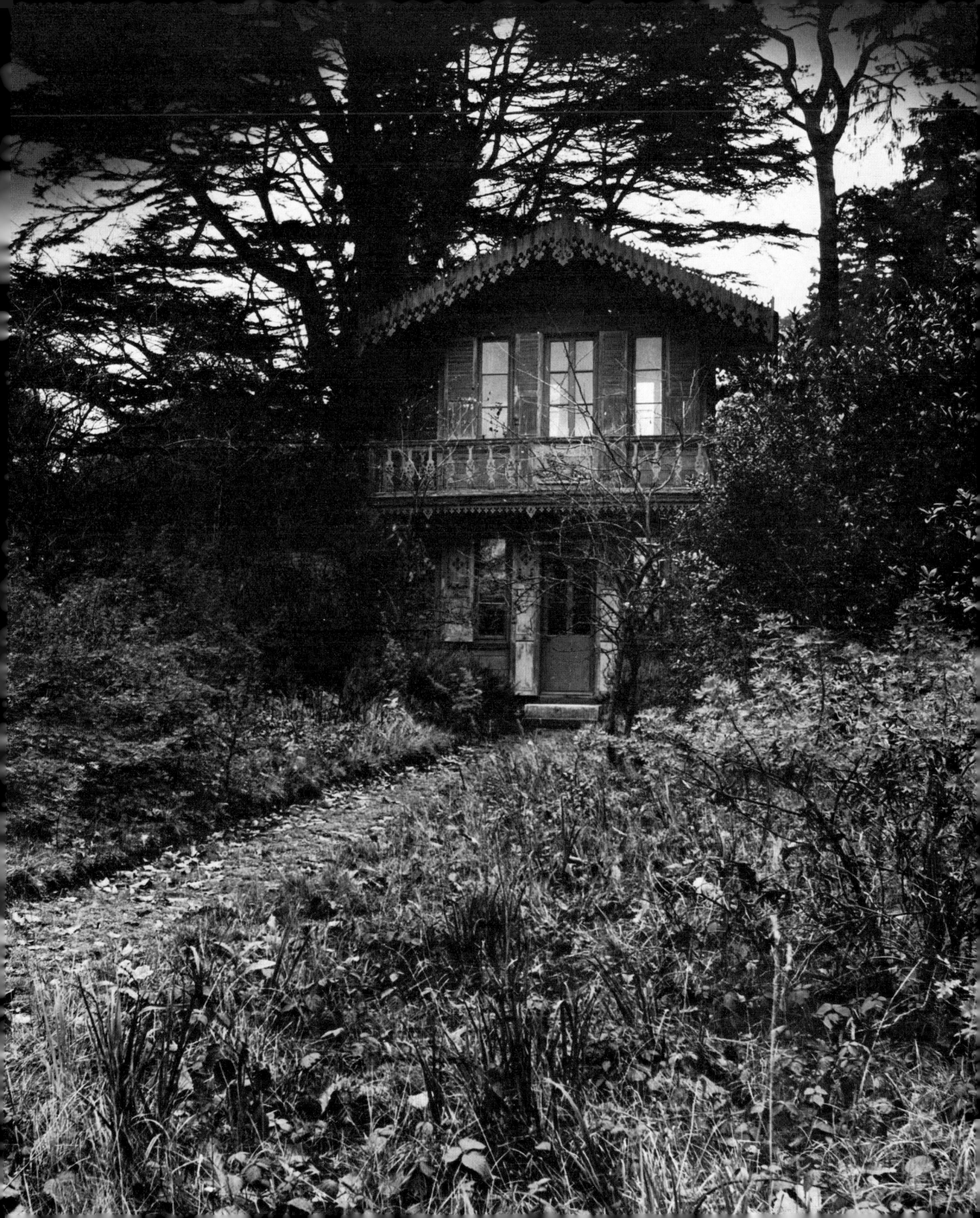

CHARLES DICKENS

'Joe's forge adjoined our house, which was a wooden house, as many of the dwellings in our country were most of them, at that time. When I ran home from the churchyard, the forge was shut up, and Joe was sitting alone in the kitchen. Joe and I being fellow-sufferers, and having confidences as such, Joe imparted a confidence to me, the moment I raised the latch of the door and peeped in at him opposite to it, sitting in the chimney corner.'

Great Expectations

25. THE FORGE, CHALK

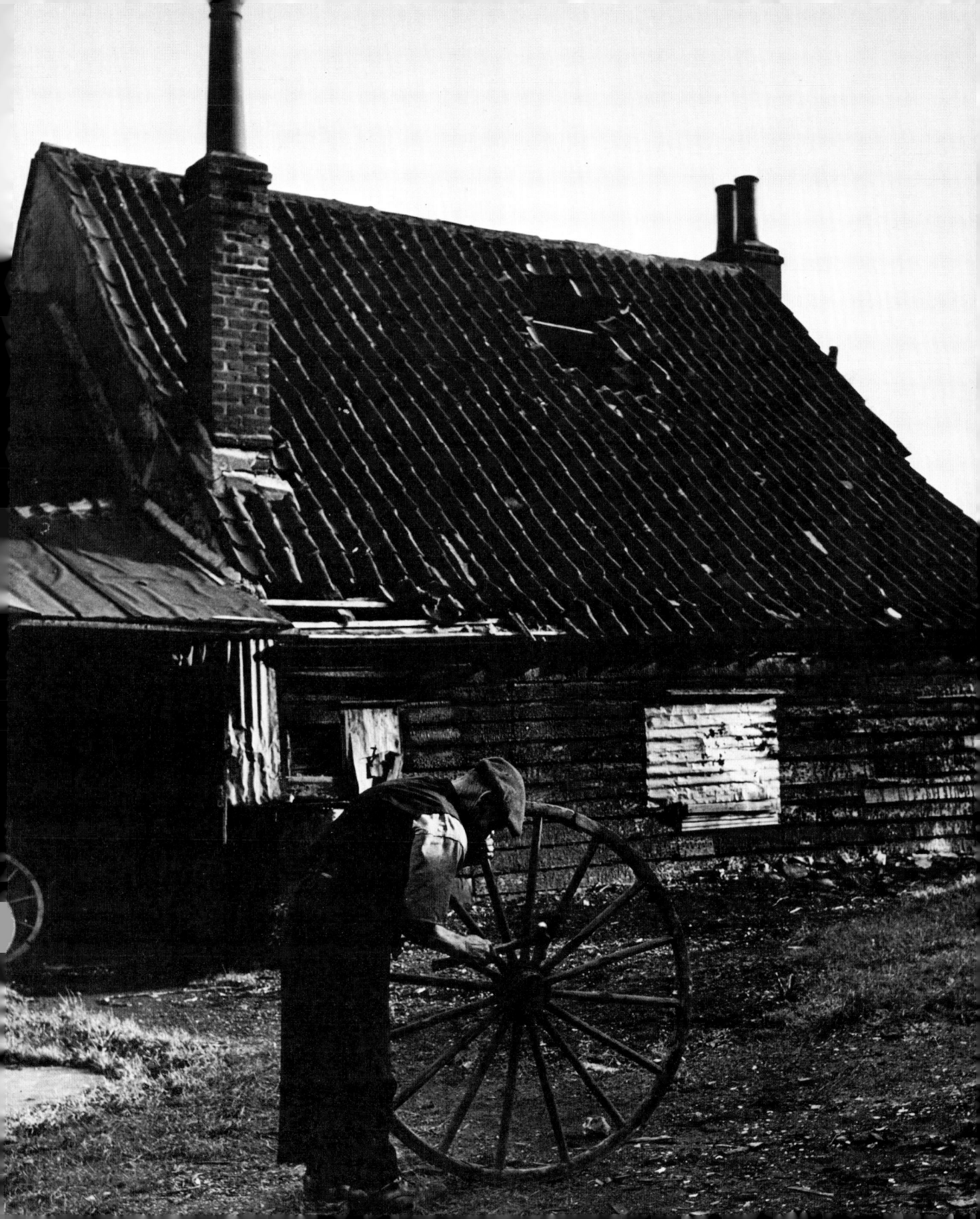

HENRY FIELDING

Born: *Sharpham Park, Glastonbury, 23 April,* 1701
Died: *Lisbon, 8 October,* 1754

Prior Park was the home of Ralph Allen, Fielding's benefactor, whose excellent goodness is portrayed in the character of Tom Jones. During the time after 1742 when Fielding was living in or visiting Bath, he spent many a happy hour at Prior Park.

'At Esher, at Stowe, at Wilton, at Estbury, and at Prior's Park, days are too short for the ravished imagination; while we admire the wondrous power of art in improving nature. In some of these, art chiefly engages our admiration; in others, nature and art contend for our applause; but, in the last, the former seems to triumph. Here nature appears in her richest attire, and art, dressed with the modestest simplicity, attends her benignant mistress.'

Letters

26. PRIOR PARK, NR BATH

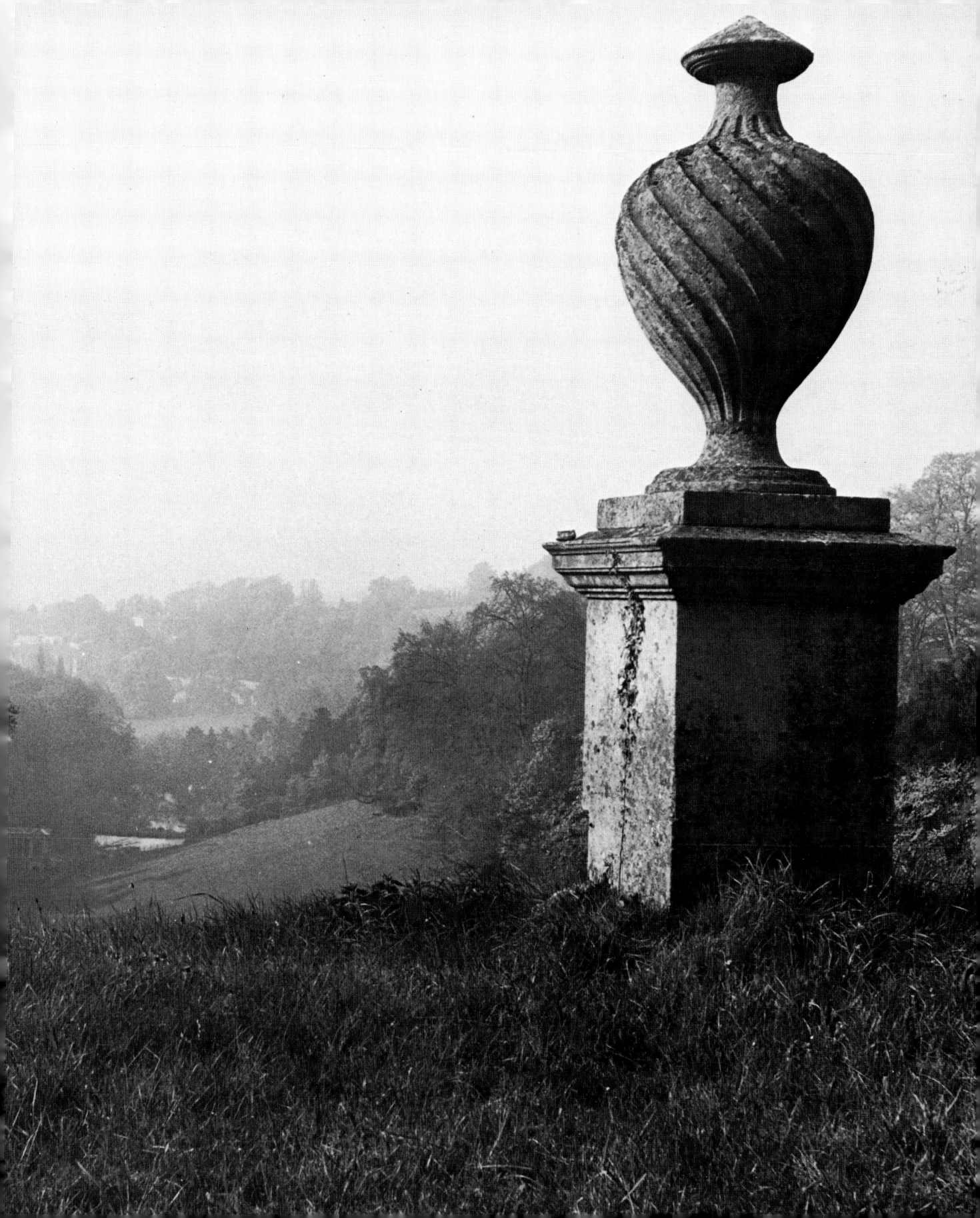

THOMAS GRAY

Born: *London, 26 December*, 1716
Died: *Cambridge, 30 July*, 1771

Beneath those rugged elms, that yew-tree's shade,
Where heaves the turf in many a mould'ring heap,
Each in his narrow cell for ever laid,
The rude Forefathers of the hamlet sleep.

Elegy written in a Country Churchyard

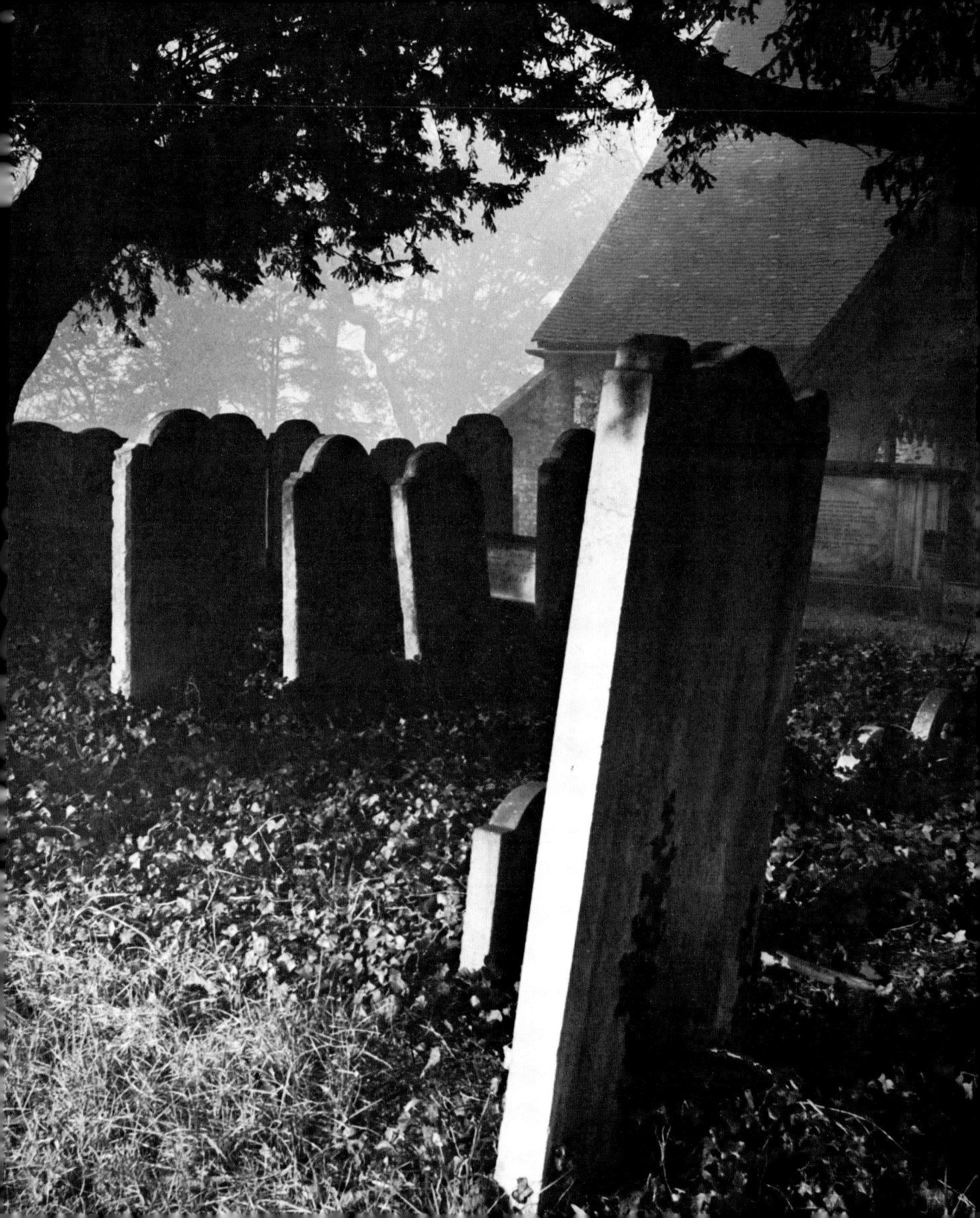

THOMAS HARDY

Born: *Bockhampton, Dorset, 2 June, 1840*
Died: *Max Gate, Dorchester, 11 January, 1928*

Abbotsbury, with its hill-top chapel dedicated to St Catherine, is 'Abbotsea' in Wessex nomenclature. 'Abbotsea Beach' is mentioned in *The Trumpet Major* and the great barn in *Far from the Madding Crowd* is really a description of the monastic barn of Abbotsbury.

THOMAS HARDY

'The band of silver paleness along the east horizon made even the distant parts of the Great Plain appear dark and near; and the whole enormous landscape bore that impress of reserve, taciturnity and hesitation which is usual just before day. The eastward pillars and their architraves stood up blackly against the light, and the great flame-shaped Sun-stone beyond them.'

Tess of the D'Urbervilles

29. STONEHENGE

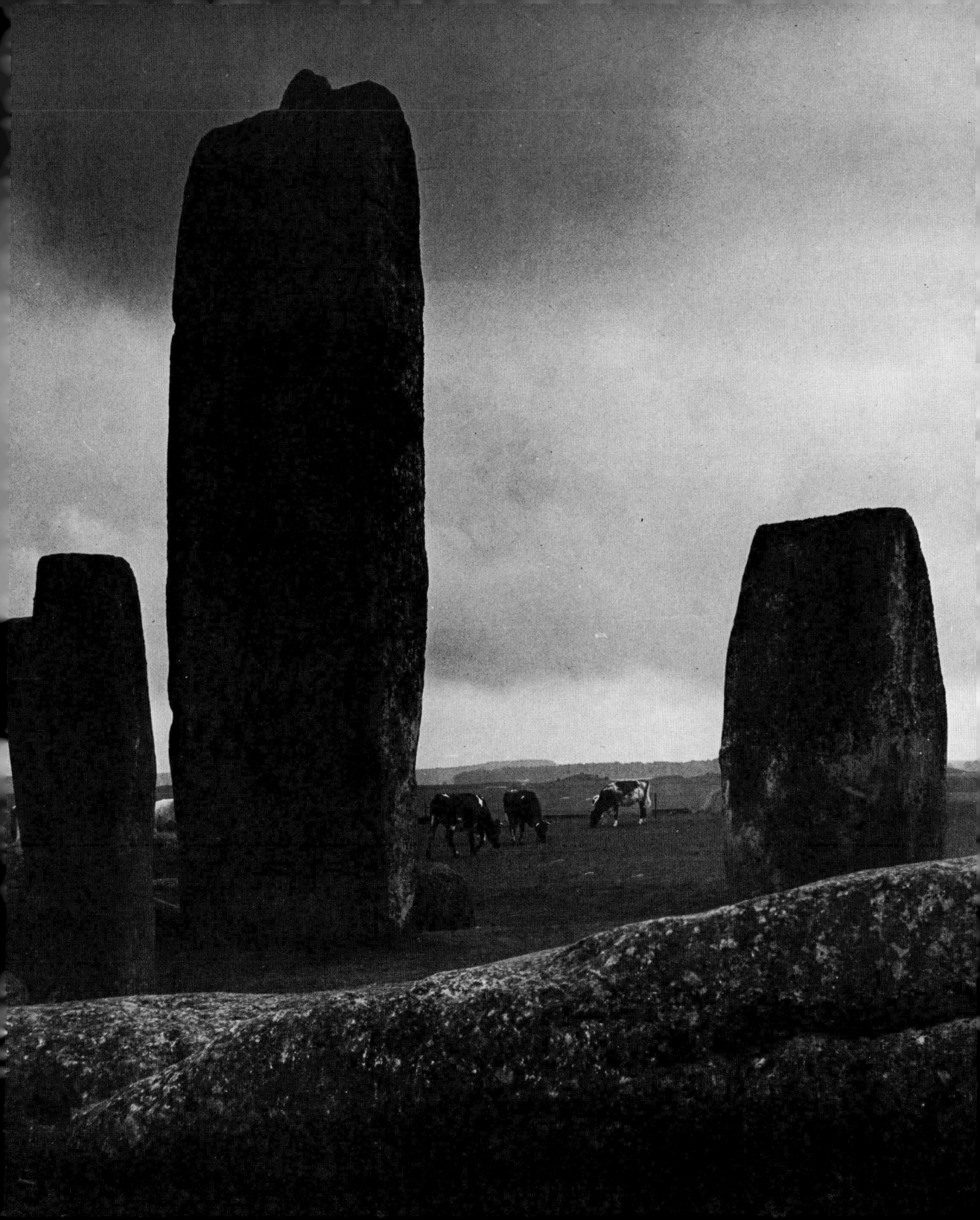

THOMAS HARDY

'The face of the heath by its mere complexion added half-an-hour to eve; it could in like manner retard the dawn, sadden noon, anticipate the frowning of storms scarcely generated, and intensify the opacity of a moonless midnight to a cause of shaking and dread. In fact, precisely at this transitional point of its nightly roll into darkness the great and particular glory of the Egdon waste began, and nobody could be said to understand the heath who had not been there at such a time. . . . The sport was, indeed, a near relation of night, and when night showed itself an apparent tendency to gravitate together could be perceived in its shades and the scene. The sombre stretch of rounds and hollows seemed to rise and meet the evening gloom in pure sympathy, the heath exhaling darkness as rapidly as the heavens precipitated it.'

The Return of the Native

30. EGDON HEATH

THOMAS HARDY

'The village of Marlott lay amid the north-eastern undulation of the beautiful Vale of Blakemore or Blackmoor aforesaid, an engirdled and secluded region, for the most part untrodden as yet by tourist or landscape painter, though within a four-hours' journey from London. It is a vale whose acquaintance is best made by viewing it from the summits of the hills that surround it – except perhaps during the droughts of summer ... This fertile and sheltered tract of country, in which the fields are never brown and the springs never dry, is bounded on the south by the bold chalk ridge that embraces the prominences of Hambledon Hill, Bulbarrow, Nettlecombe-Tout, Dogbury, High Stoy, and Bubb Down.'

Tess of the D'Urbervilles

31. TESS'S COTTAGE

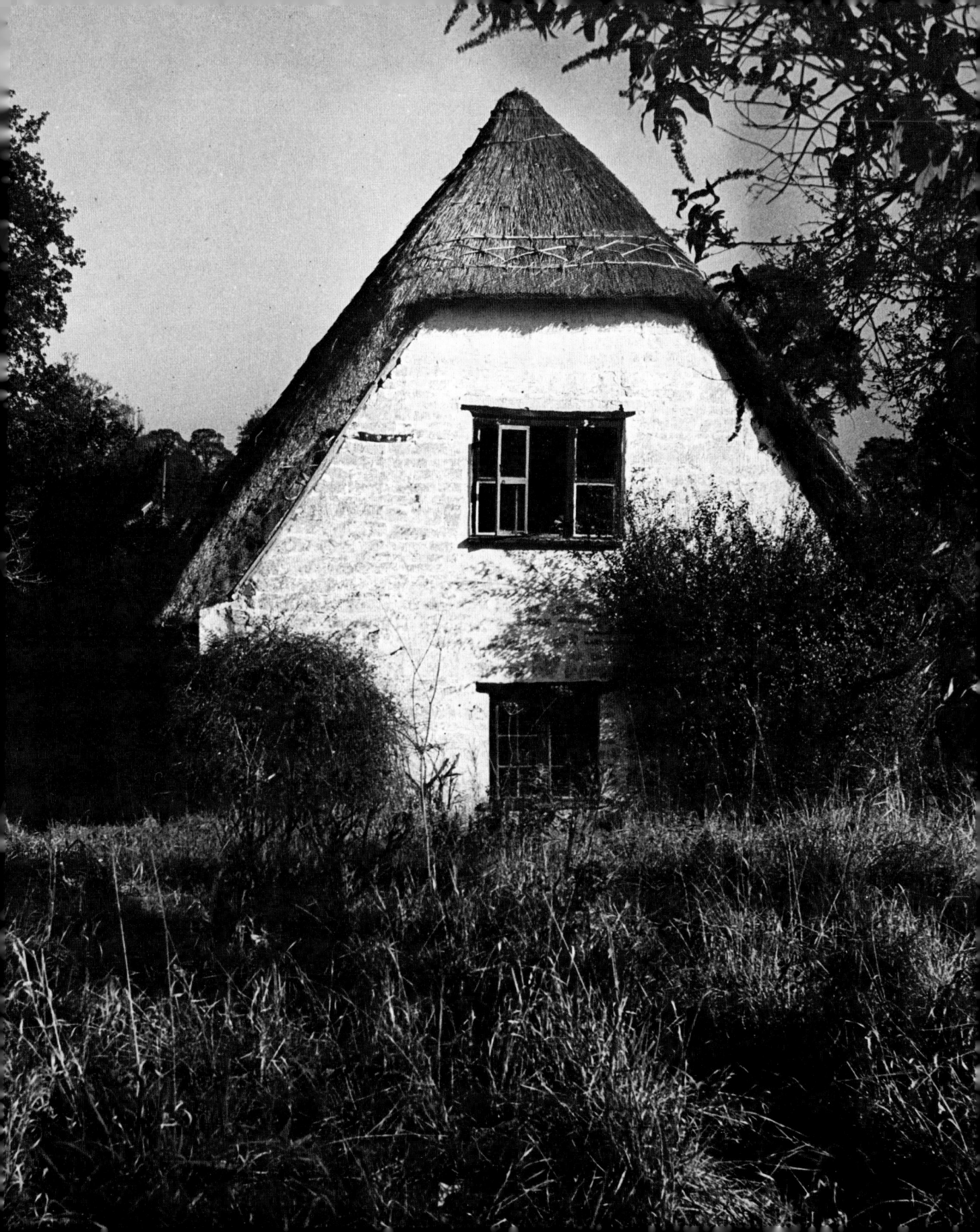

THOMAS HARDY

'It was thought and always said by my uncle Job, sergeant of foot (who used to know all about these matters), that Bonaparte meant to cross with oars on a calm night. The grand query with us was, Where would my gentleman land? Many of the common people thought it would be at Dover; others, who knew how unlikely it was that any skilful general would make a business of landing just where he was expected, said he'd go either east into the River Thames, or west'ard to some convenient place, most likely one of the little bays inside the Isle of Portland, between Beal and St Alban's Head – and for choice the three-quarter-round Cove screened from mortal eye, that seemed made o' purpose, out by where we lived, and which I've climmed up with two tubs of brandy across my shoulders on scores o' dark nights in my younger days'.

Life's Little Ironies

32. STAIR HOLE, LULWORTH COVE

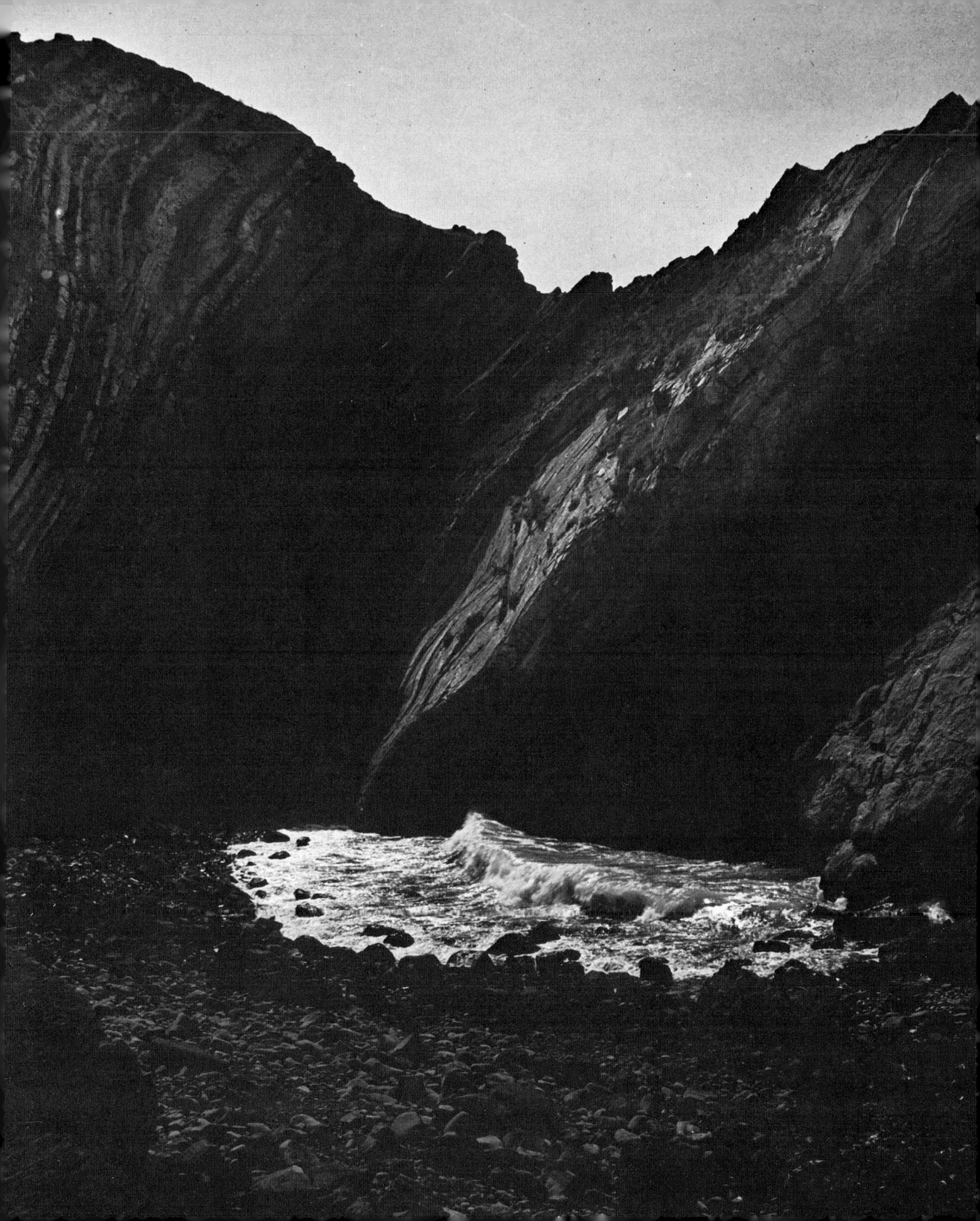

THOMAS HARDY

I mark the months in liveries dank and dry
    The noontides many-shaped and hued;
    I see the nightfall shades subtrude,
And hear the monotonous hours clang negligently by.

I view the evening bonfires of the sun
    On hills where morning rains have hissed;
    The eyeless countenance of the mist
Pallidly rising when the summer droughts are done . . .

Wessex Poems

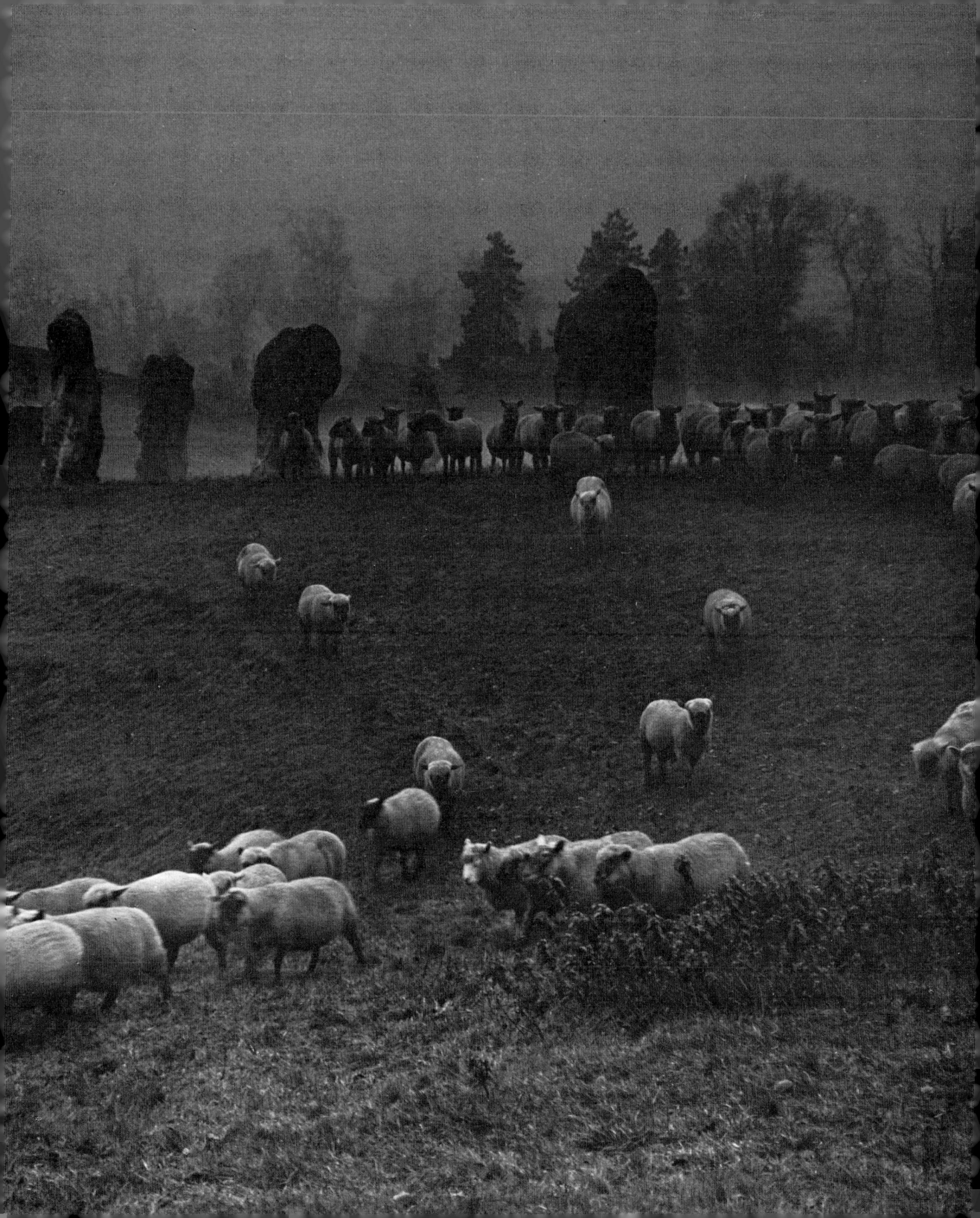

WILLIAM HENRY HUDSON

Born: *Quilmas, near Buenos Aires, 4 August,* 1841
Died: *London,* 18 *August,* 1922

'I don't say that I want to have my life again because 'twould be sinful. We must take what is sent. But if 'twas offered to me and I was told to choose my work, I'ld say, Give me my Wiltsheer Downs again and let me be a shepherd there all my life long.'

A Shepherd's Life

34. THE WILTSHIRE DOWNS

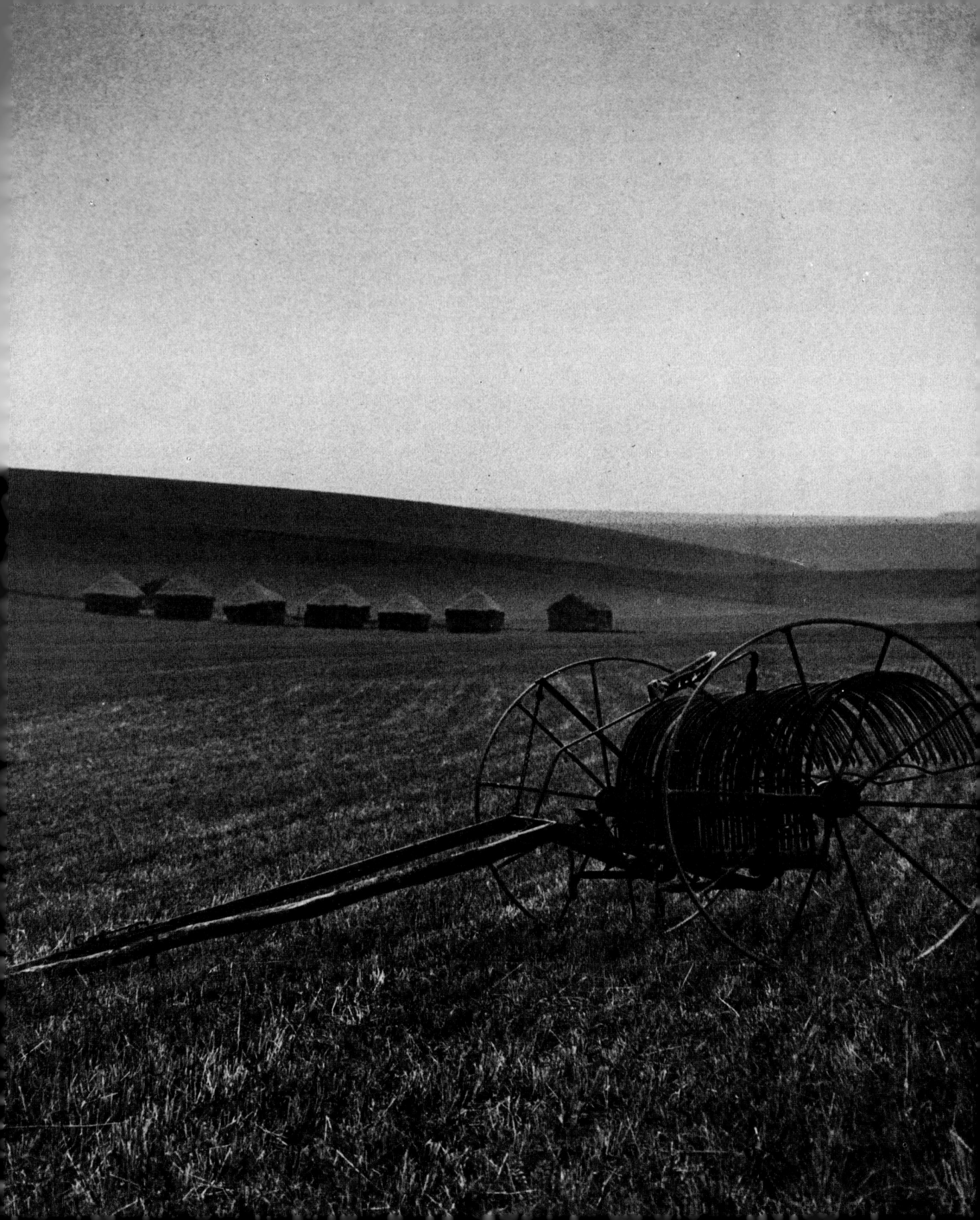

HENRY JAMES

Born: *New York*, 15 *April*, 1843
Died: *London*, 28 *February*, 1916

'The Club question has become serious and difficult; a club was indispensable, but I had, of course, none of my own. I went through Gaskell's (and I think Locker's) kindness for some time to the Travellers' . . . At last, I forget exactly when, I was elected to the Reform; I think it was about April, 1878 . . . This was an excellent piece of good fortune, and the Club has ever since been, to me, a convenience of the first order. I could not have remained in London without it, and I have become extemely fond of it, a deep local attachment.'

The Notebooks of Henry James

Henry James lived for over twenty years in the Reform Club.

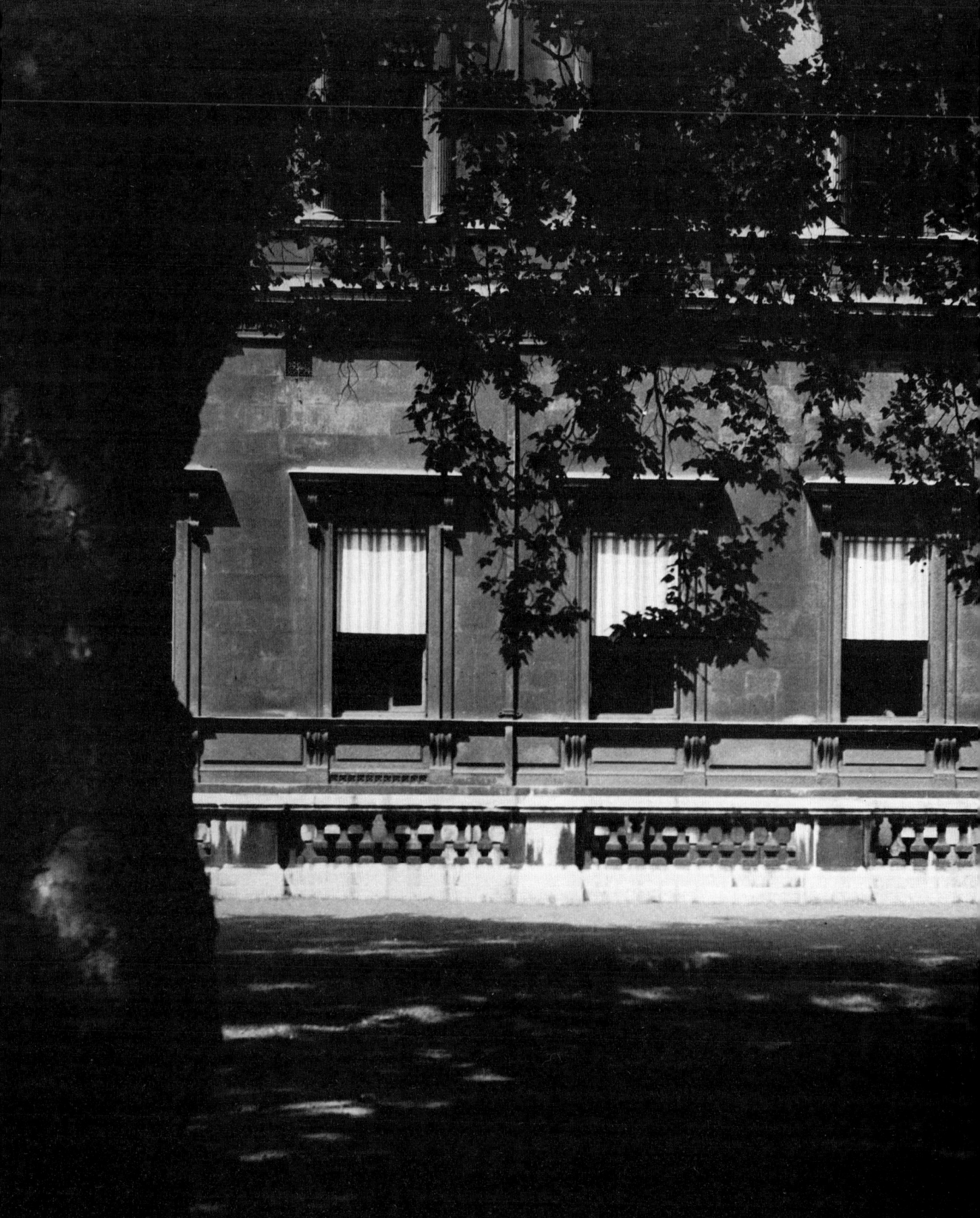

RICHARD JEFFERIES

Born: *Swindon, 6 November, 1848*
Died: *Goring, 14 August, 1887*

'The most commanding down is crowned with the grassy mound and trenches of an ancient earthwork, from whence there is a noble view of hill and plain. . . . A faint sound as of a sea heard in a dream – sibilant "sish, sish" – passes along outside, dying away and coming again as a fresh wave of the wind rushes through the bennets and the dry grass. Behind the fosse sinks, and the rampart rises high and steep; two butterflies are wheeling in uncertain flight over the summit.'

Wild Life in a Southern County

36. BARBARY CASTLE, MARLBOROUGH DOWNS

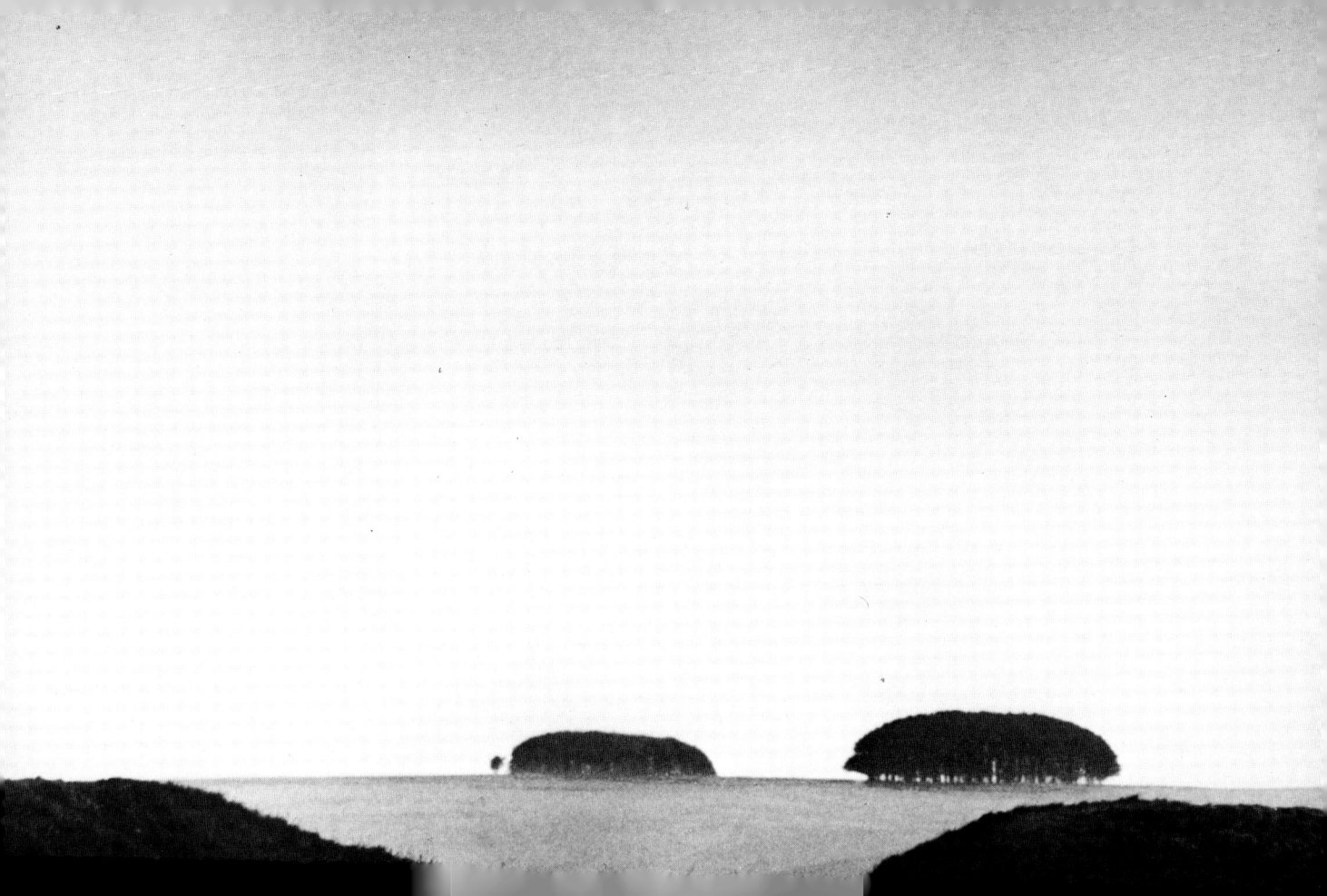

DR SAMUEL JOHNSON

Born: *Lichfield*, 18 *September*, 1709
Died: *London*, 13 *December*, 1784

'Samuel Johnson was born at Lichfield, in Staffordshire, on the 18th September, N.S. 1709; and his initiation into the Christian church was not delayed; for his baptism is recorded, in the register of St Mary's parish in that city, to have been performed on the day of his birth: his father is there styled "Gentleman", a circumstance of which an ignorant panegyrist has praised him for not being proud; when the truth is, that the appellation of Gentleman, though now lost in the indiscriminate assumption of "Esquire", was commonly taken by those who could not boast of gentility. His father was Michael Johnson, a native of Derbyshire, of obscure extraction, who settled in Lichfield as a bookseller and stationer. His mother was Sarah Ford, descended of an ancient race of substantial yeomanry in Warwickshire. They were well advanced in years when they married, and never had more than two children, both sons; Samuel, their first-born, who lived to be the illustrious character whose various excellence I am to endeavour to record, and Nathanael, who died in his twenty-fifth year.'

Boswell's *Life of Johnson*

37. THE HOUSE WHERE JOHNSON WAS BORN

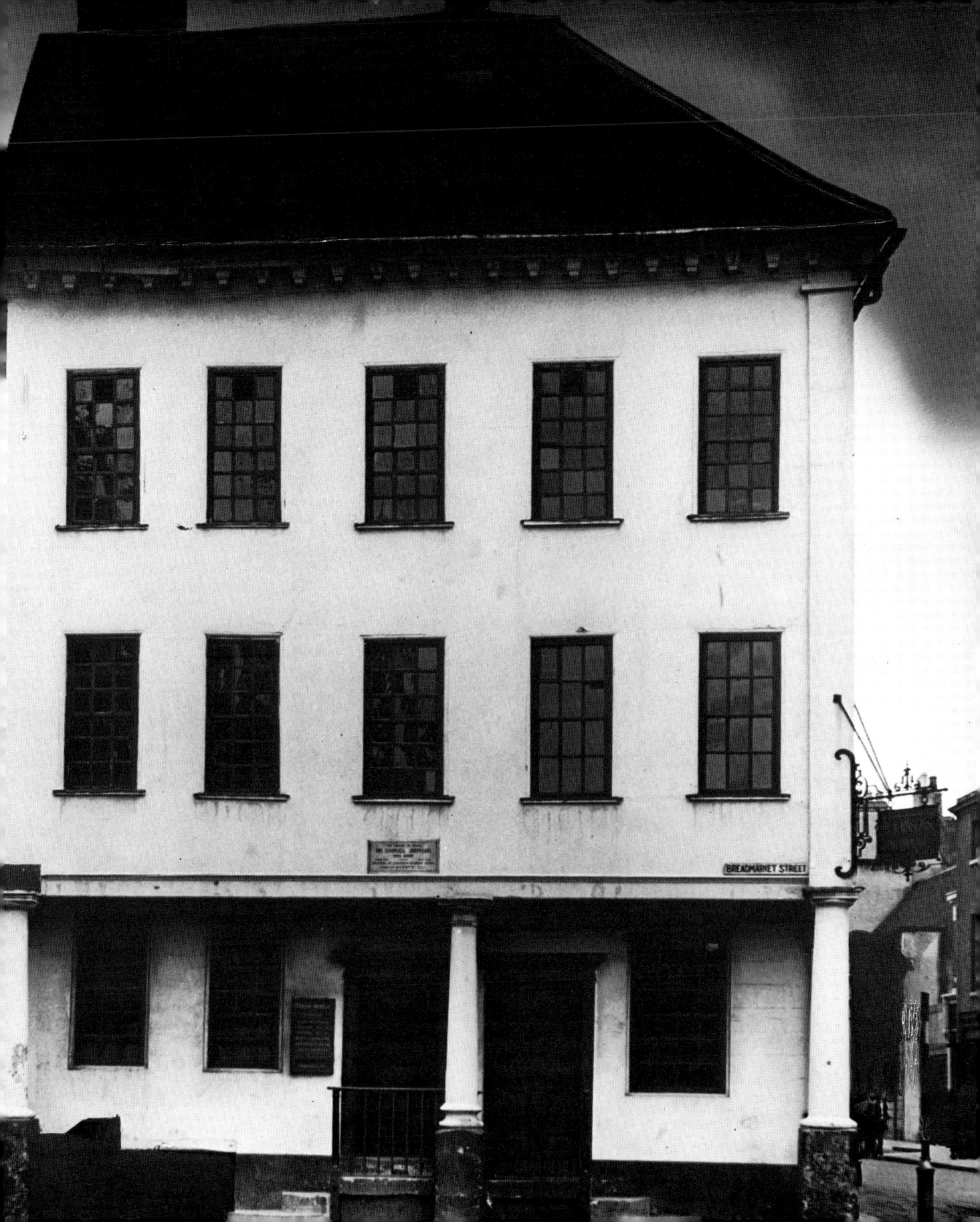

DR SAMUEL JOHNSON

'It is natural, in traversing this gloom of desolation, to inquire, whether something may not be done to give nature a more cheerful face, and whether those hills and moors that afford heath cannot with a little care and labour bear something better? The first thought that occurs is to cover them with trees. . . . Sir James Macdonald, in part of the wastes of his territory, set or sowed trees, to the number, as I have been told, of several millions, expecting, doubtless, that they would grow up into future navies and cities; but for want of enclosure, and of that care which is always necessary, and will hardly ever be taken, all his cost and labour have been lost, and the ground is likely to continue an useless heath.'

A Journey to the Western Islands

38. LORD MACDONALD'S FOREST, SKYE

DR SAMUEL JOHNSON

'To abstract the mind from all local emotion would be impossible, if it were endeavoured, and would be foolish, if it were possible. Whatever withdraws us from the power of our senses; whatever makes the past, the distant, or the future predominate over the present, advances us in the dignity of thinking beings. Far from me and my friends, be such frigid philosophy as may conduct us indifferent and unmoved over any ground which has been dignified by wisdom, bravery, or virtue. That man is little to be envied, whose patriotism would not gain force upon the plain of Marathon, or whose piety would not grow warmer among the ruins of Iona!'

A Journey to the Western Islands of Scotland

39. THE GRAVEYARD AT STRATH

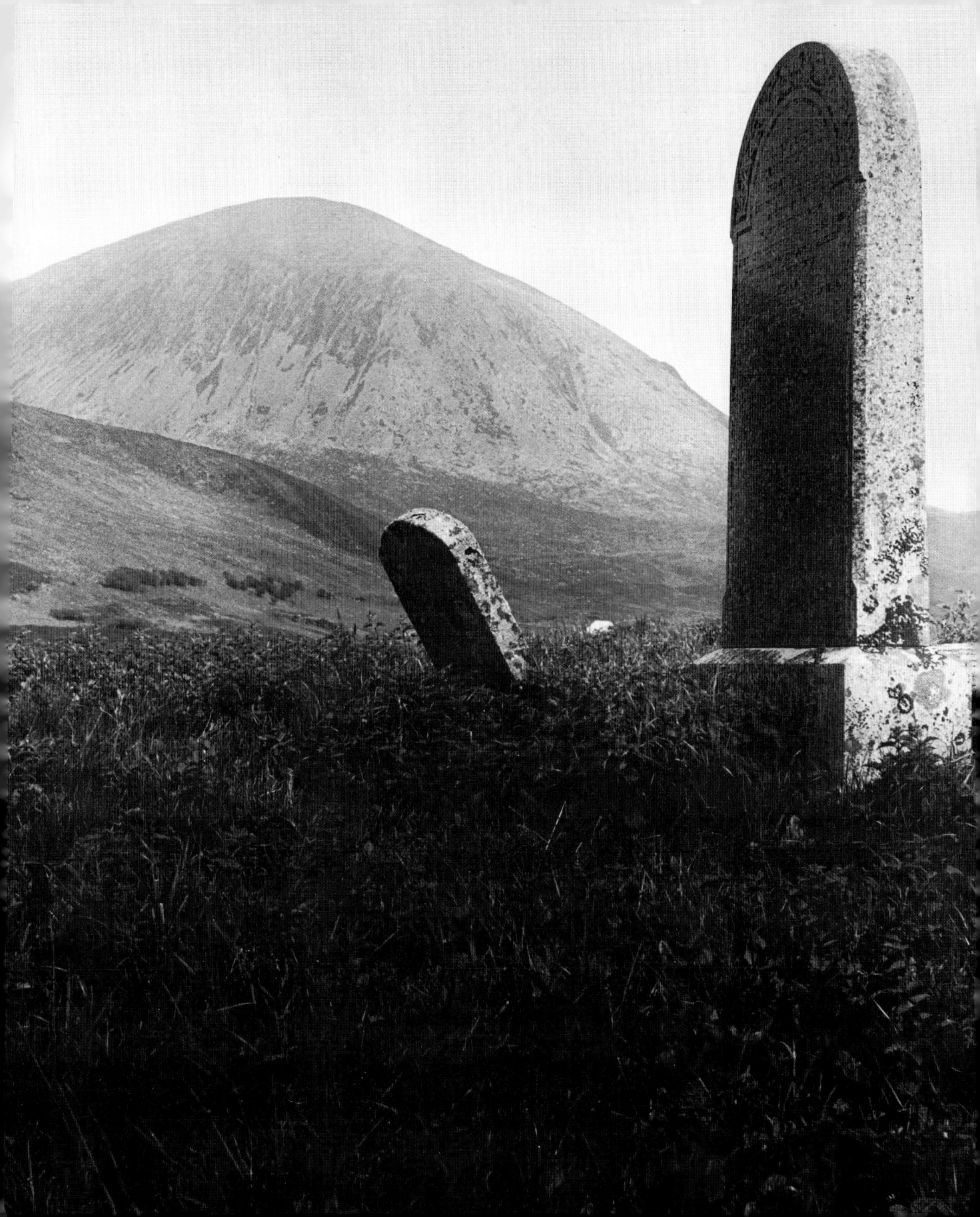

DR SAMUEL JOHNSON

'The evening was now approaching, and we were yet at a considerable distance from the end of our expedition. We could therefore stop no more to make remarks in the way, but set forward with some degree of eagerness. The day soon failed us, and the moon presented a very solemn and pleasing scene. The sky was clear, so that the eye commanded a wide circle: the sea was neither still nor turbulent: the wind neither silent nor loud. We were never far from one coast or another, on which, if the weather had become violent, we could have found shelter, and therefore contemplated at ease the region through which we glided in the tranquillity of the night, and saw now a rock and now an island grow gradually conspicuous and gradually obscure.'

A Journey to the Western Islands of Scotland

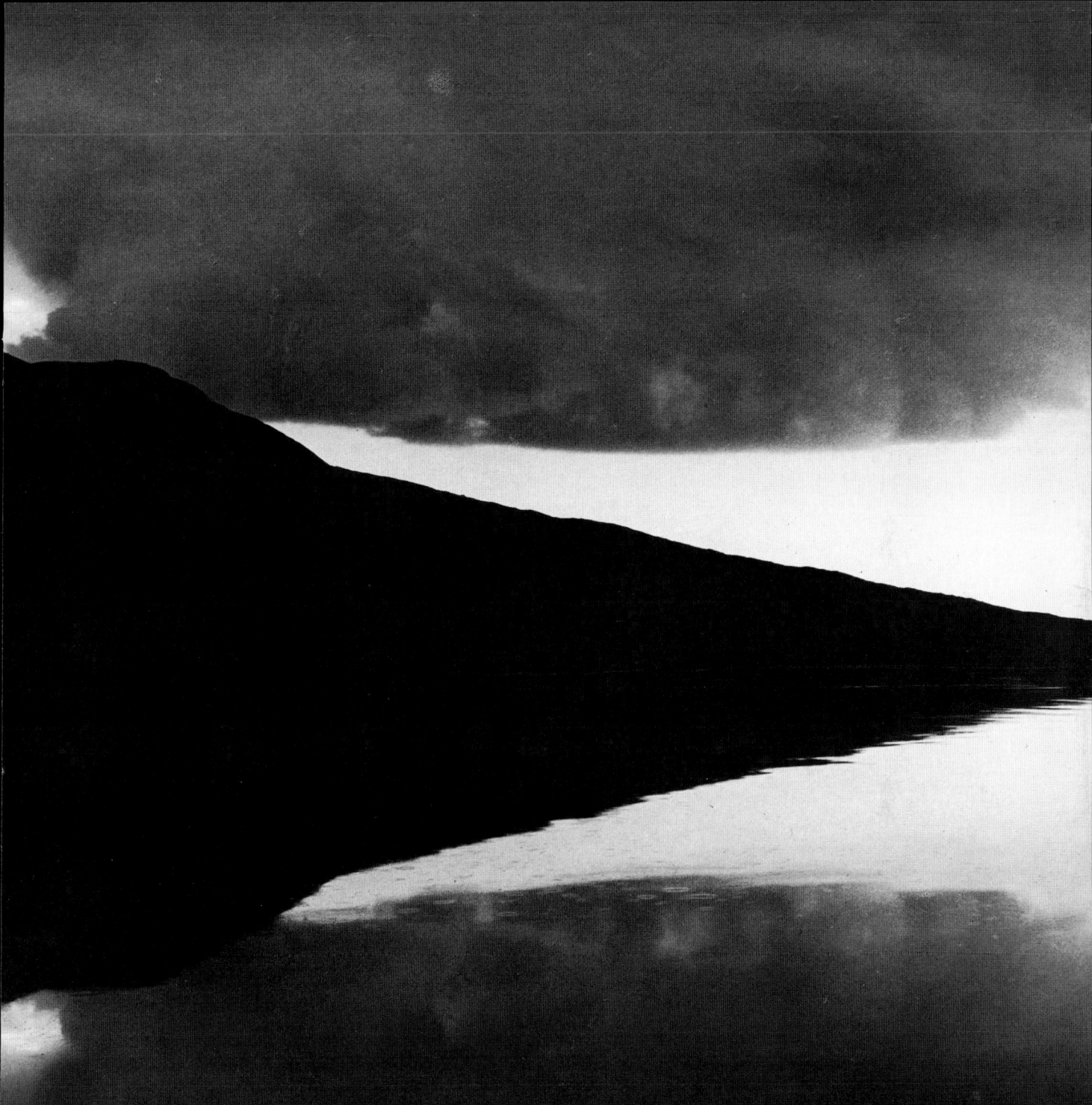

JOHN KEATS

Born: *London, 31 October, 1795*
Died: *Rome, 23 February, 1821*

And in the midst of this wide quietness
A rosy sanctuary will I dress
With the wreath'd trellis of a working brain,
With buds, and bells, and stars without a name.
With all the gardener Fancy e'er could feign,
Who breeding flowers, will never breed the same:
And there shall be for thee all soft delight
That shadowy thought can win,
A bright torch, and a casement ope at night,
To let the warm Love in!

Ode to Psyche

In a letter to Fanny Brawn, Keats wrote: 'You will have a pleasant walk to-day. I shall see you pass. I shall follow you with my eyes over the Heath. Will you come towards evening instead of before dinner? When you are gone, 'tis past – if you do not come till the evening I have something to look forward to all day. Come round to my window for a moment when you have read this.'

41. WENTWORTH PLACE, HAMPSTEAD
(The room in which the light is on was Keats's room.)

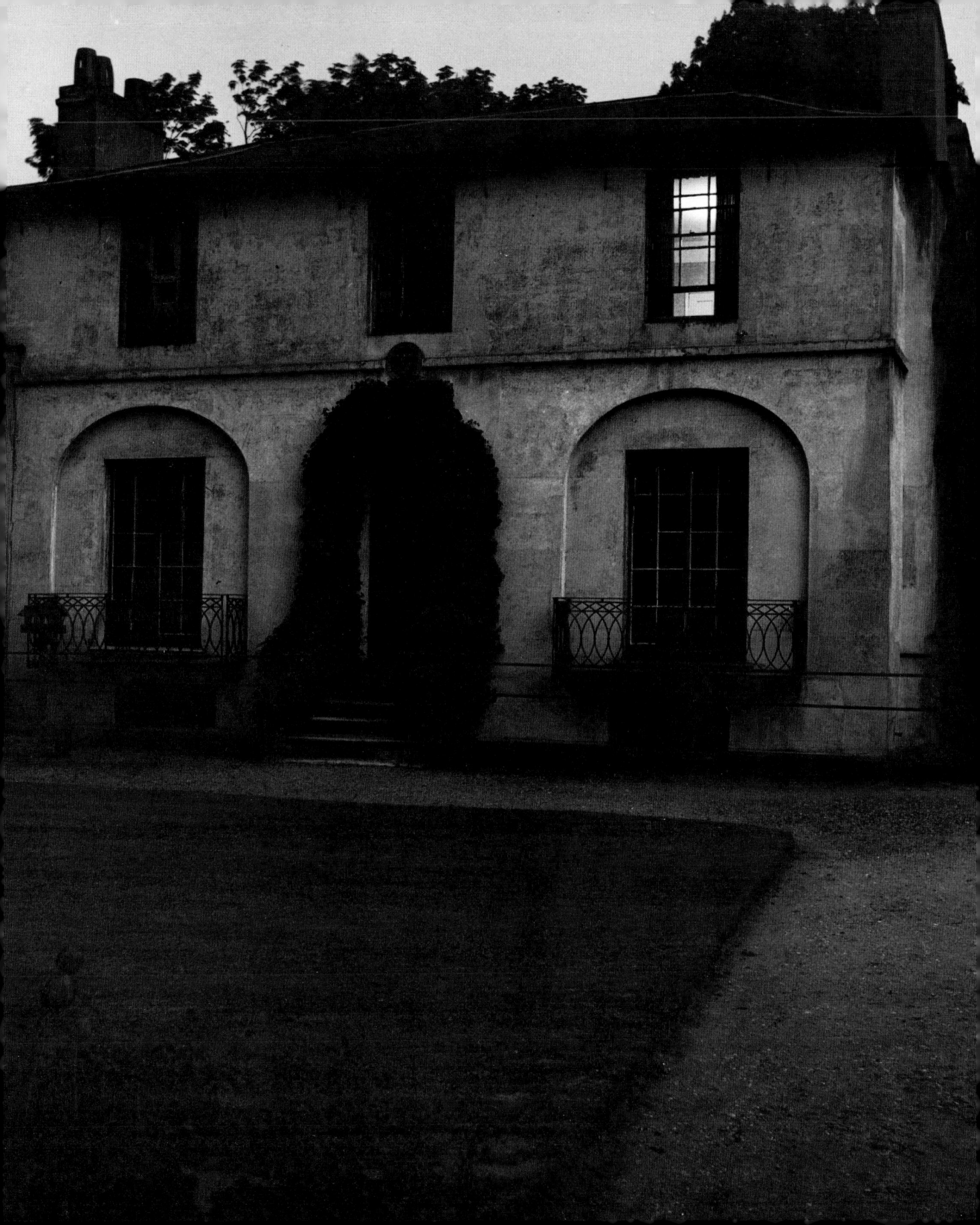

RUDYARD KIPLING

Born: *Bombay*, 30 December, 1865
Died: *London*, 18 January, 1936

'It is *the* Wall. Along the top are towers with guard-houses, small towers, between. Even on the narrowest part of it three men with shields can walk abreast, from guard-house to guard-house. A little curtain wall, no higher than a man's neck, runs along the top of the thick wall, so that from a distance you see the helmets of the sentries sliding back and forth like beads. Thirty feet high is the Wall, and on the Picts' side, the North, is a ditch, strewn with blades of old swords and spear-heads set in wood, and tyres of wheels joined by chains.'

Puck of Pook's Hill

42. THE ROMAN WALL
(Looking eastward across Crag Loch to Hotbank)

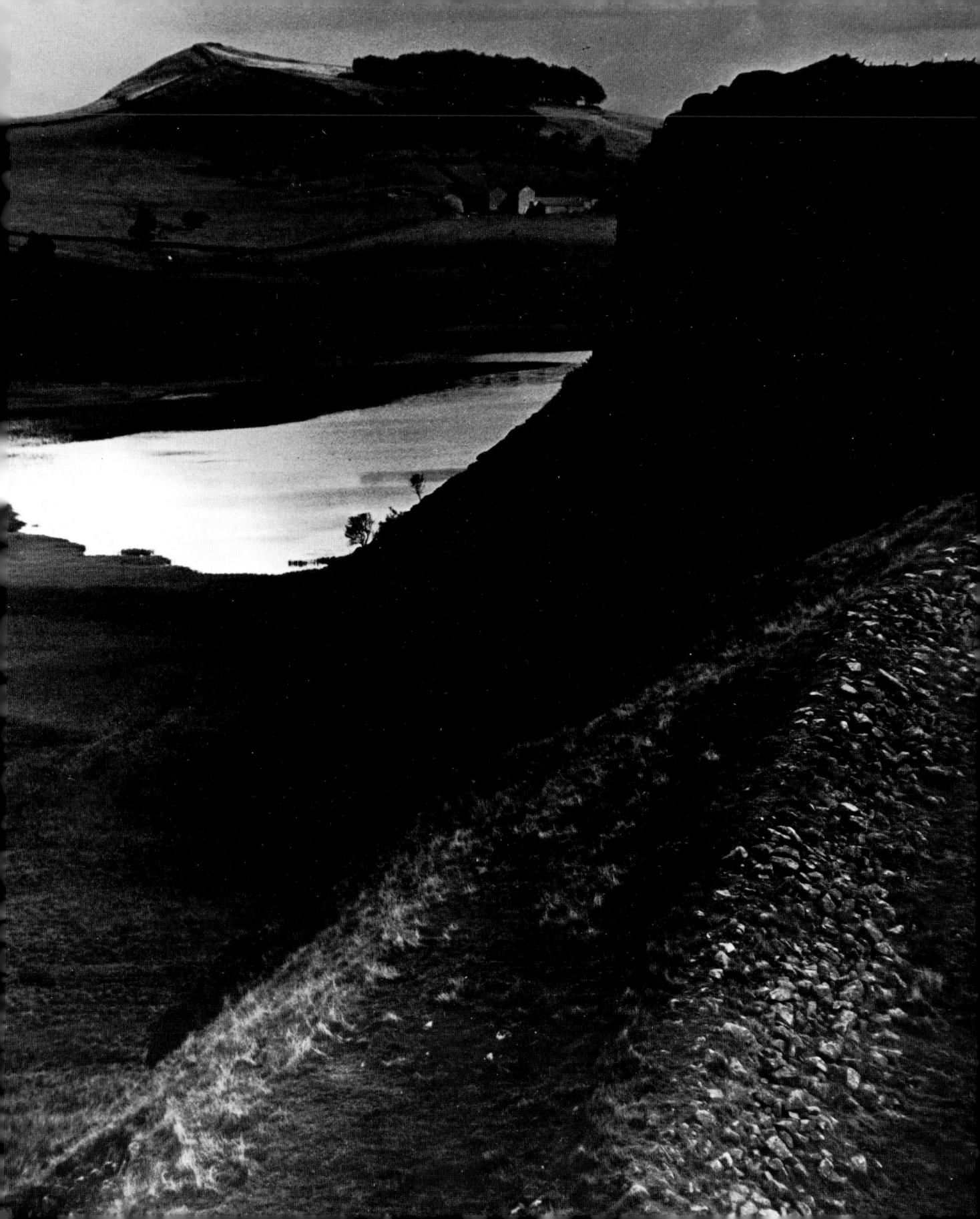

WILLIAM LANGLAND

Born and Died: *c.* 1330–1400

In a somer seson whan soft was the sonne,
I shope me in shroudes as I a shepe were,
In habite as a hermite unholy of workes,
Went wyde in this world wondres to here.
Ac on a May mornynge on Malverne hulles,
Me byfel a ferly of fairy me thoughte;
I was wery forwandred and went me to reste
Under a brode banke bi a bornes side.

The Vision of Piers Plowman

43. THE MALVERN HILLS

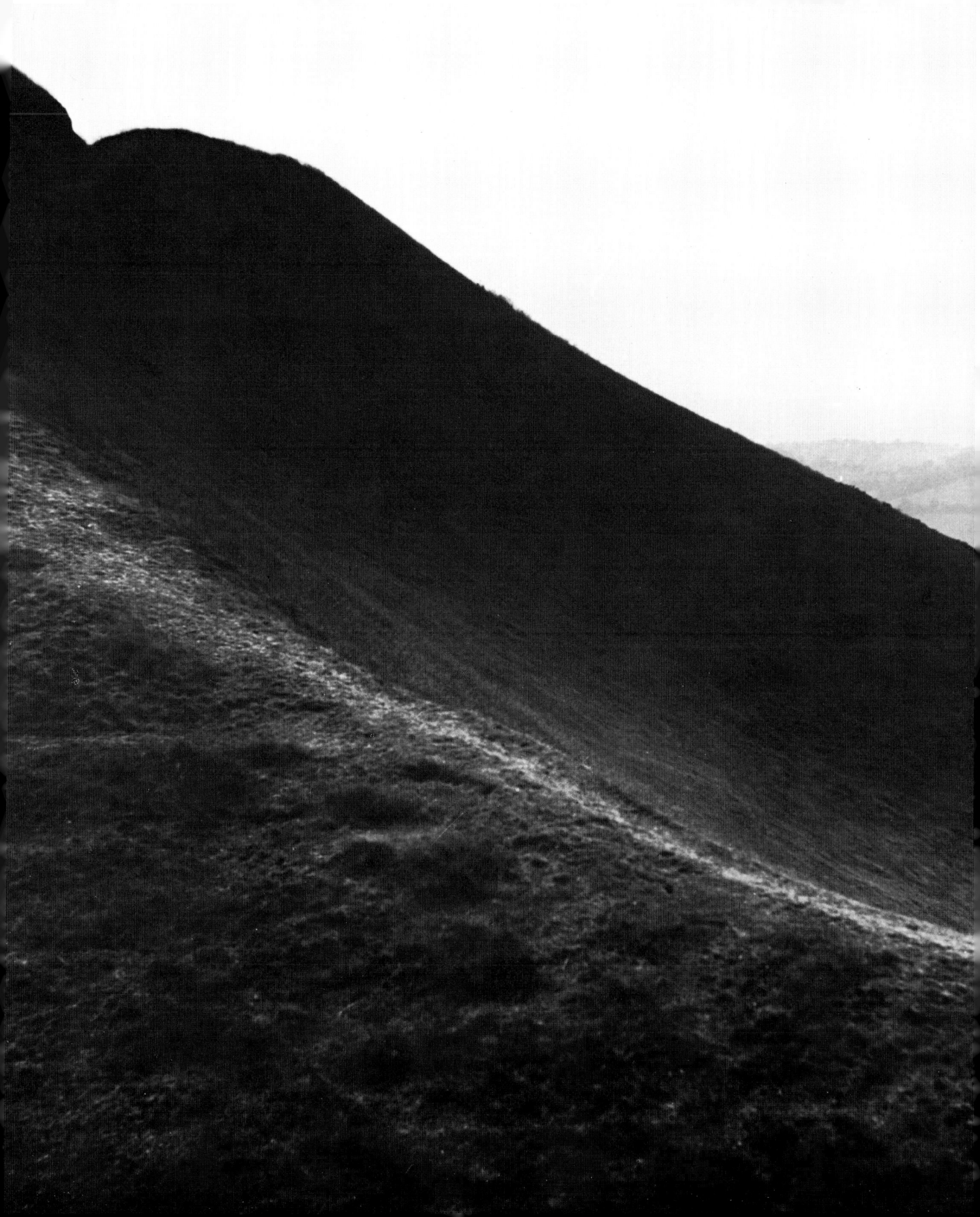

DAVID HERBERT LAWRENCE

Born: *Eastwood, Nottinghamshire,* 11 *September,* 1885
Died: *Vence, Nice, France,* 2 *March,* 1930

D. H. Lawrence was born in Victoria Street, Eastwood, where his father was a 'butty' or man in charge of a section of the coalface in the Brinsley Colliery. When D. H. was ten years old the family moved to the Breach – 'The Bottoms' of *Sons and Lovers,* described by his sister Ada: 'The Breach consisted of blocks of houses belonging to Barber, Walker and Co., the pit-owners. Our house was at the end of the row, with a garden on three sides. I remember so well the white currant bushes by the house and the old-fashioned white rose trees in the little front garden. My mother never liked being there, partly because the houses were in a hollow, principally because the backs looked out on to drab patches of garden with ashpits at the bottom.'

44. LAWRENCE'S BIRTHPLACE

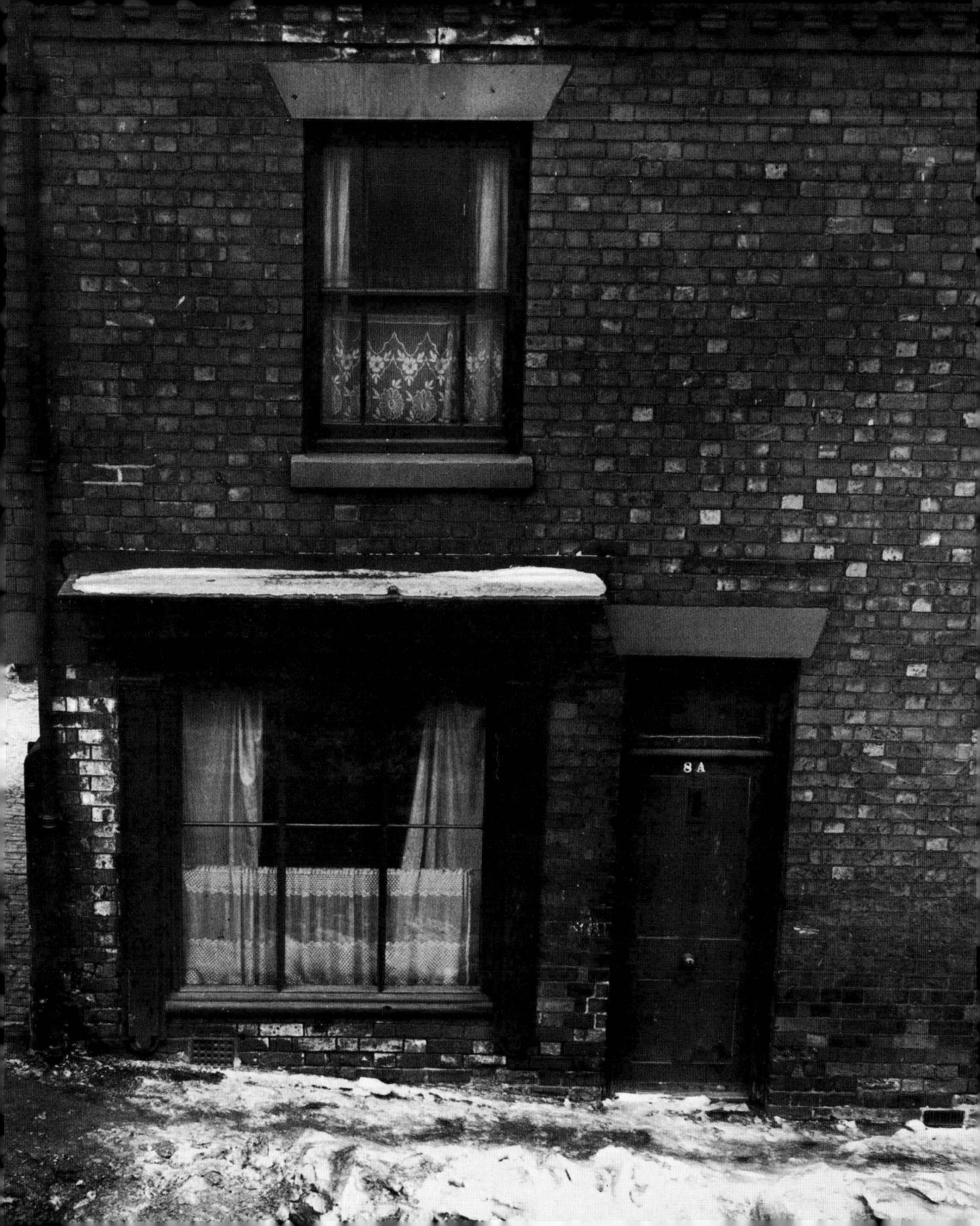

DAVID HERBERT LAWRENCE

D. H. Lawrence wrote to Lady Ottoline Morrell, who offered him Garsington Manor for a holiday: 'It is like the Boccacio Place where they told all the Decamerone. That wonderful lawn under the ilex trees, with the old house and its exquisite old front – it is so remote, so perfectly a small world to itself, where one can get away from the temporal things to consider the big things . . .'

45. THE GARDEN OF GARSINGTON MANOR

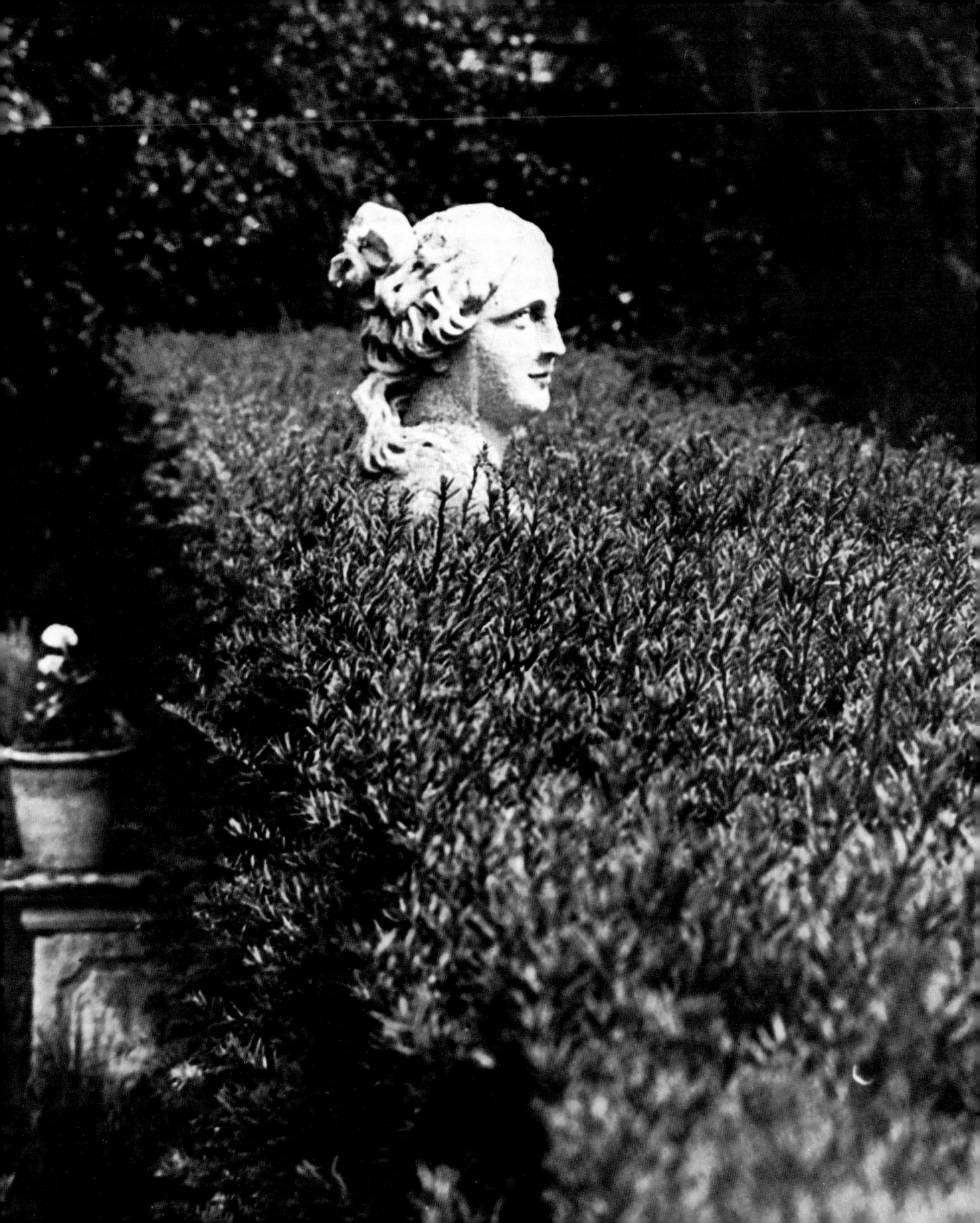

CHRISTOPHER MARLOWE

Born: *Canterbury*, 6 *February*, 1564
Died: *Deptford*, 1 *June*, 1593

EDWARD II: This dungeon where they keep me is the sink
Wherein the filth of all the castle falls.

.   .   .   .

And there, in mire and puddle, have I stood
This ten days' space; and, lest that I should sleep,
One plays continually upon a drum;
They give me bread and water, being a king;
So that, for want of sleep and sustenance,
My mind's distempered, and my body's numb'd,
And whether I have limbs or no I know not.
O, would my blood dropp'd out from every vein,
As doth this water from my tatter'd robes!
Tell Isabel the queen, I look'd not thus,
When for her sake I ran at tilt in France,
And there unhors'd the Duke of Cleremont.

Edward the Second, V. 5

46. BERKELEY CASTLE

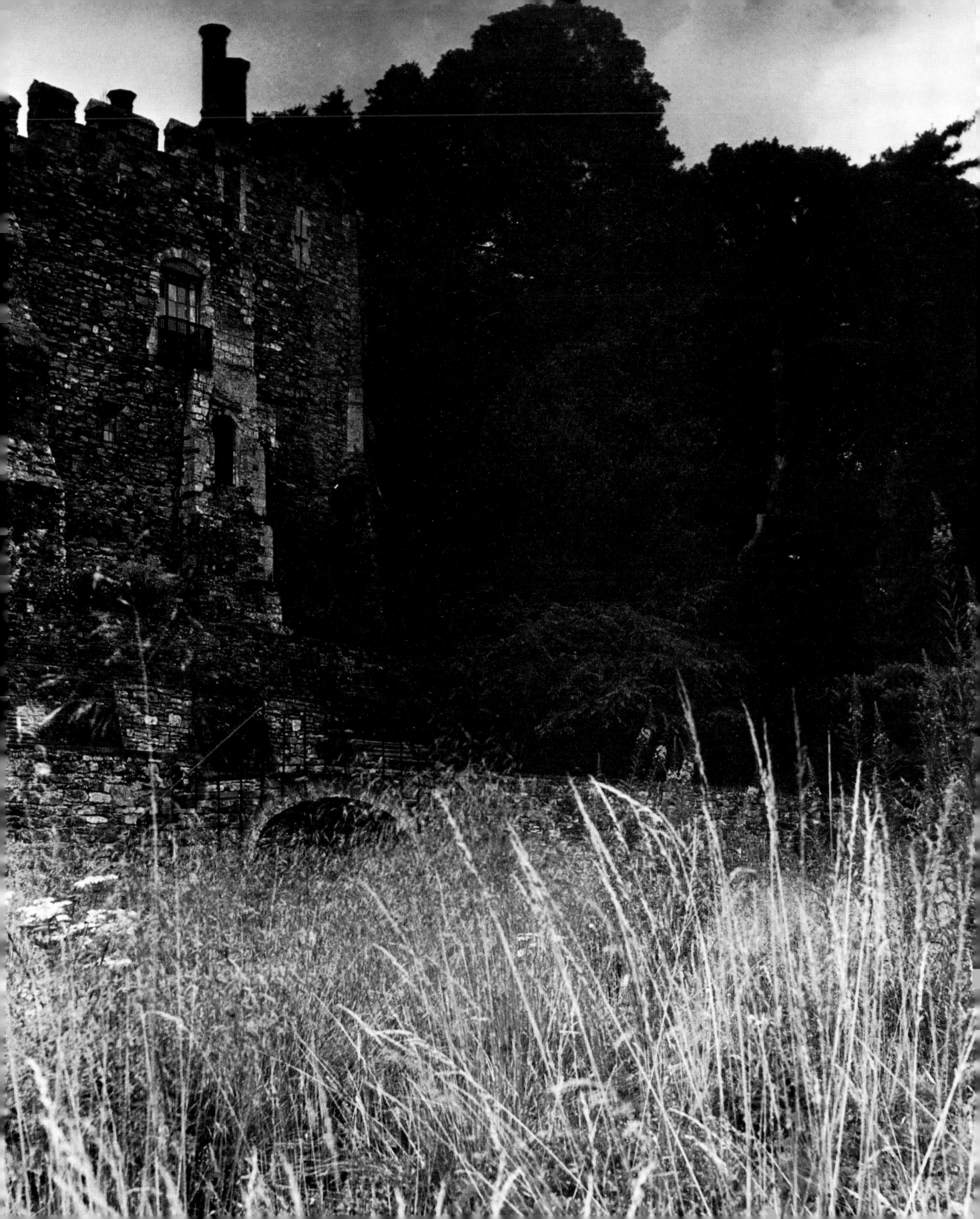

GEORGE MEREDITH

Born: *Portsmouth*, 12 *February*, 1828
Died: *Flint Cottage, Boxhill, Surrey*, 18 *May*, 1909

In a letter to John Morley, dated 25 April, 1877, Meredith wrote: '. . . All I can say is, that the nightingale is now in sweet song; there's not a ghost of a harvester to bite you even in fancy. I want you to see my study; I want to see you. We have a bedroom and dressing room for you. You will be here upon the opening of the beeches. Really the sweet o' the year.'

47. FLINT COTTAGE, BOXHILL

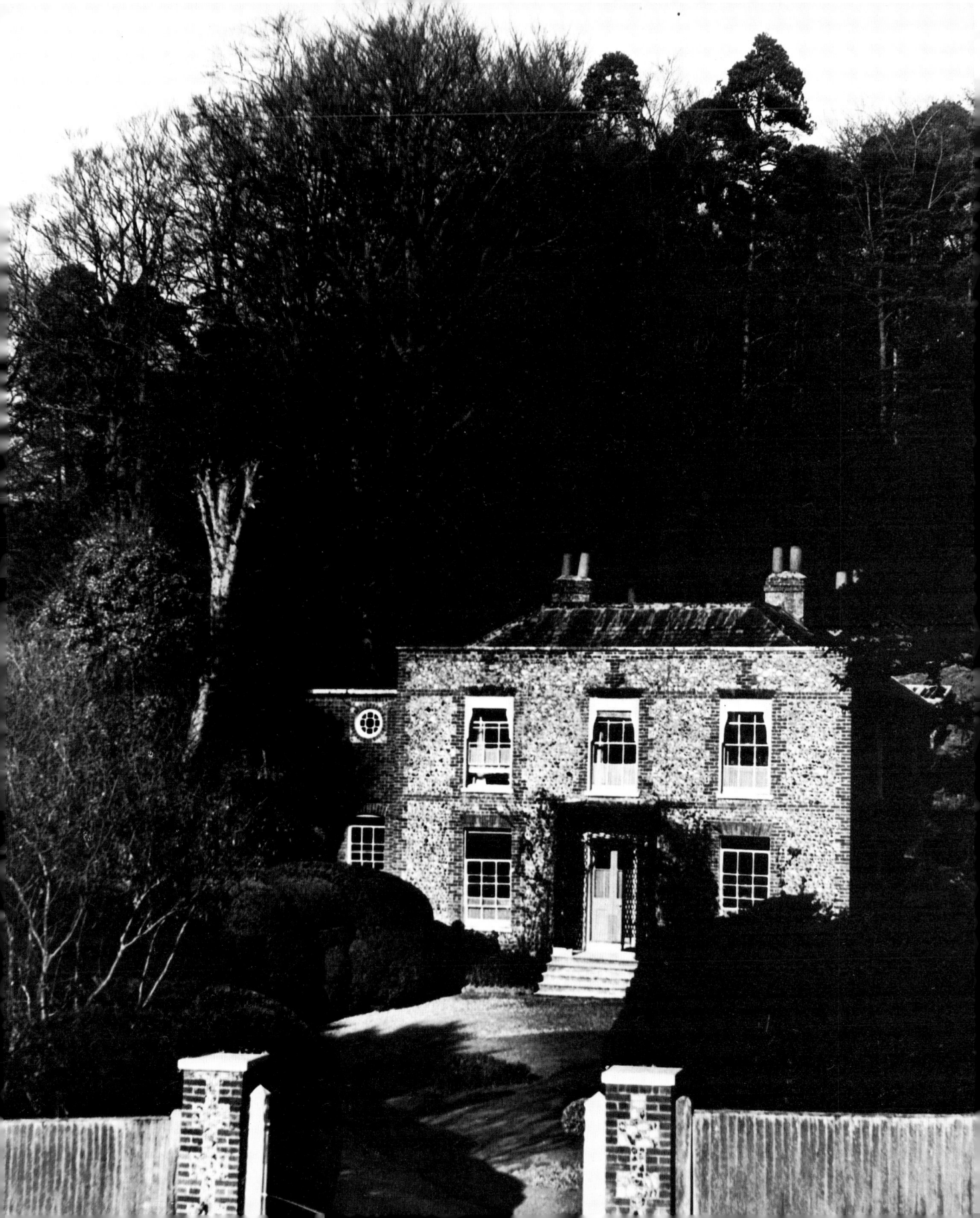

JOHN MILTON

Born: *London, 9 December, 1608*
Died: *London, 8 November, 1674*

Dr Johnson, in his *Lives of the English Poets*, writes this of Milton's career at Christ's College, Cambridge, which lasted for seven years from 1625 to 1632: '. . . there is reason to suspect that he was regarded in his college with no great fondness. That he obtained no fellowship is certain; but the unkindness with which he was treated was not merely negative. I am ashamed to relate what I fear is true, that Milton was one of the last students in either university that suffered the publick indignity of corporal correction . . . He took both the usual degrees; that of Bachelor in 1628, and that of Master in 1632; but he left the university with no kindness for its institution, alienated either by the injudicious severity of his governors, or his own captious perverseness.'

But Milton himself said in 1652 of his time at the university: 'There for seven years I studied the learning and arts wont to be taught, far from all vice and approved by all good men, even till having taken what they call the Master's degree, and that with praise, I . . . of my own accord went home, leaving even a sense of my loss among most of the Fellows of my College, by whom I had in no ordinary degree been regarded.'

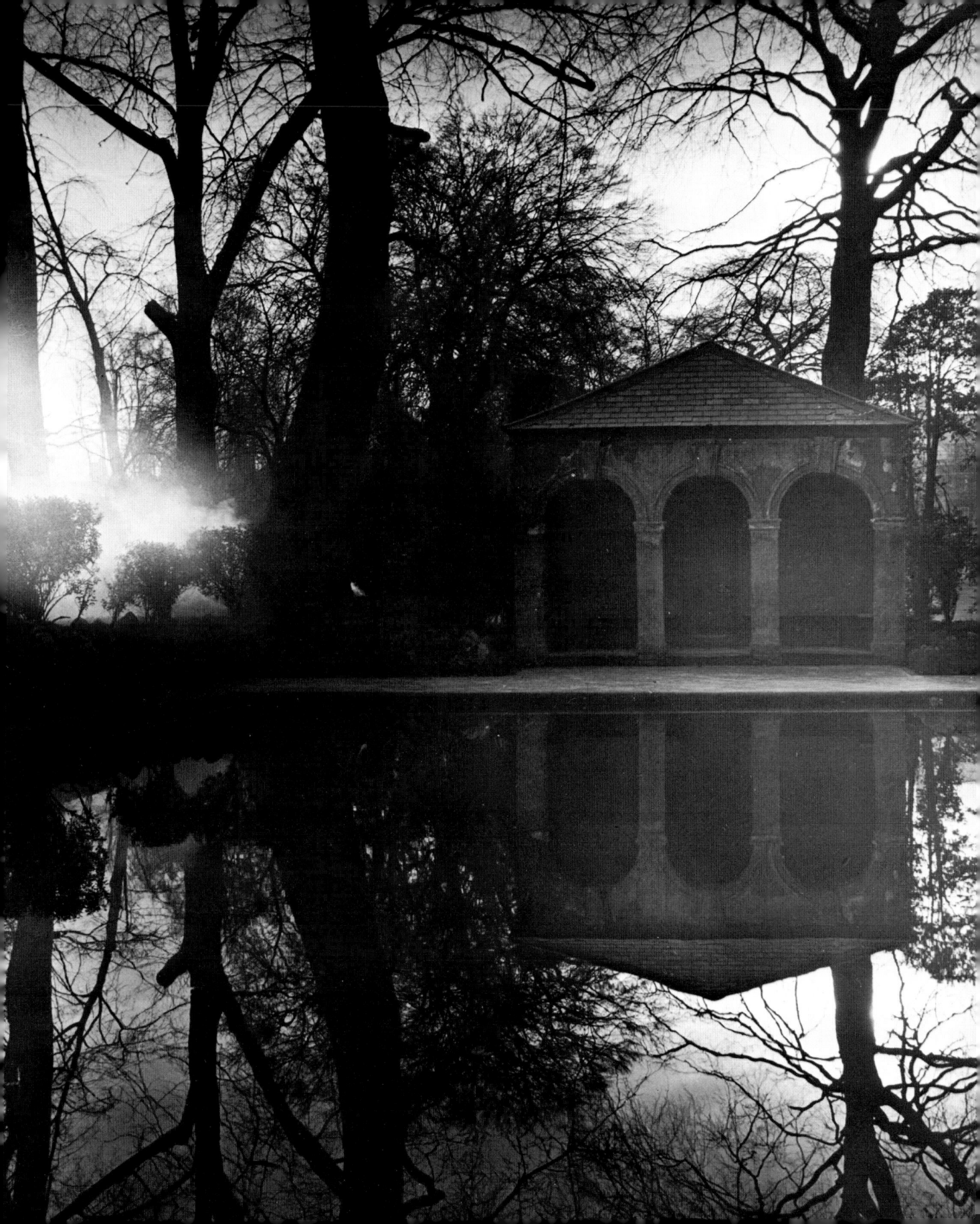

THE PASTONS

JOHN (1421–66), his wife MARGARET (d.1484) and their son SIR JOHN (1442–79).

These Pastons, writers of most of the Paston Letters, inherited Caister Castle, three miles from Yarmouth, from its builder, Sir John Fastolf. Their tenure of the castle was much disputed by the Dukes of Norfolk for many years and the endless litigation on one occasion even swelled into a siege of the castle by Margaret after her husband's death.

49. CAISTER CASTLE, NORFOLK

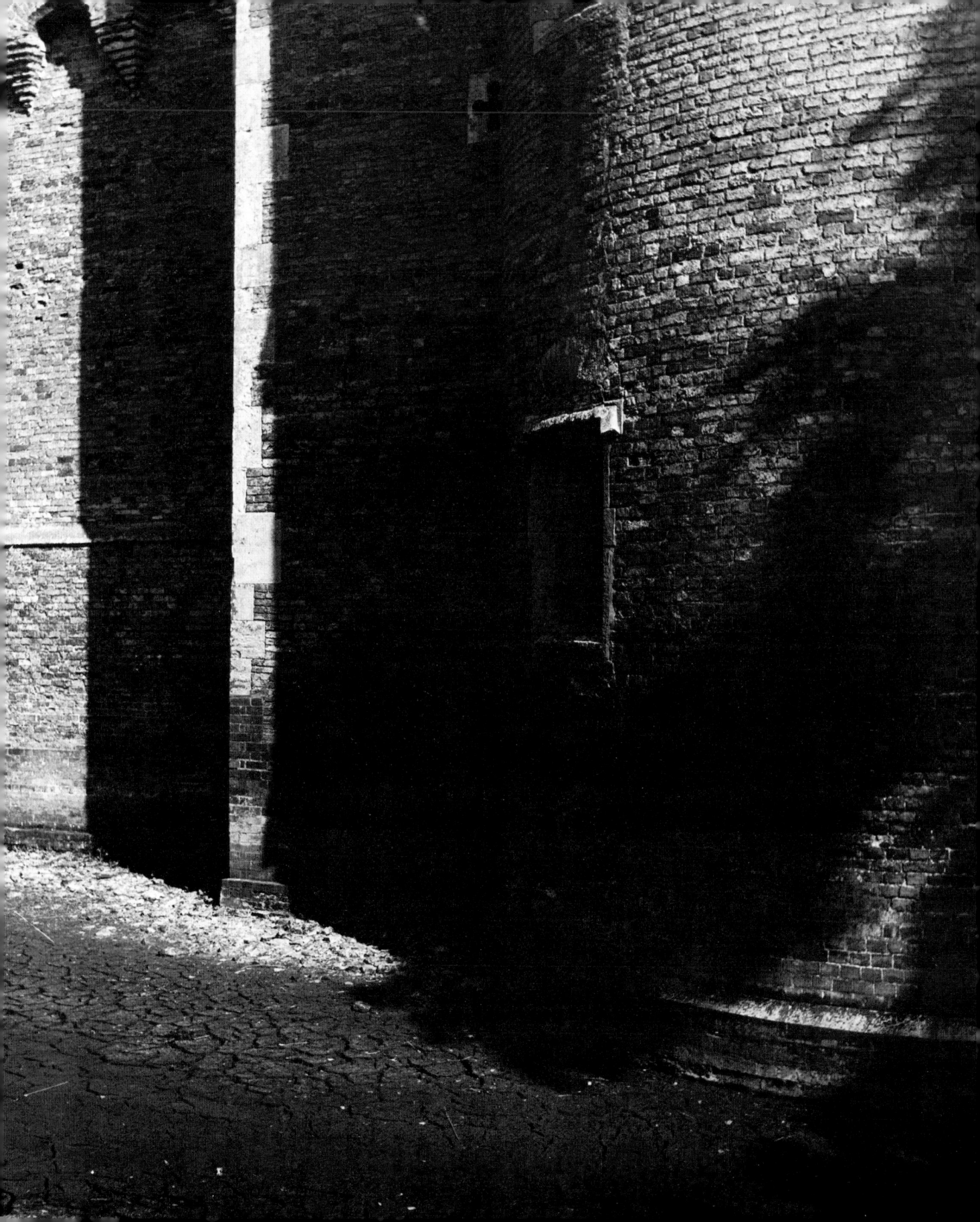

SAMUEL PEPYS

Born: *probably at Brampton*, 23 *February*, 1663
Died: *Clapham*, 26 *May*, 1703

'. . . come to Brampton at about noon, and there find my father and sister and brother all well: and here laid up our things, and up and down to see the garden with my father, and the house, and do altogether find it very pretty; especially the little parlour and the summer-houses in the garden, only the wall do want greens upon it, and the house is too low-roofed; but that is only because of my coming from a house with higher ceilings. But altogether is very pretty; and I bless God that I am like to have such a pretty place to retire to: and I did walk with my father without doors, and do find a very convenient way of laying out money there in building, which will make a very good seat, and the place deserves it, I think, very well.'

Diary, 9 October, 1667

50. BUCKDEN COTTAGE, BRAMPTON

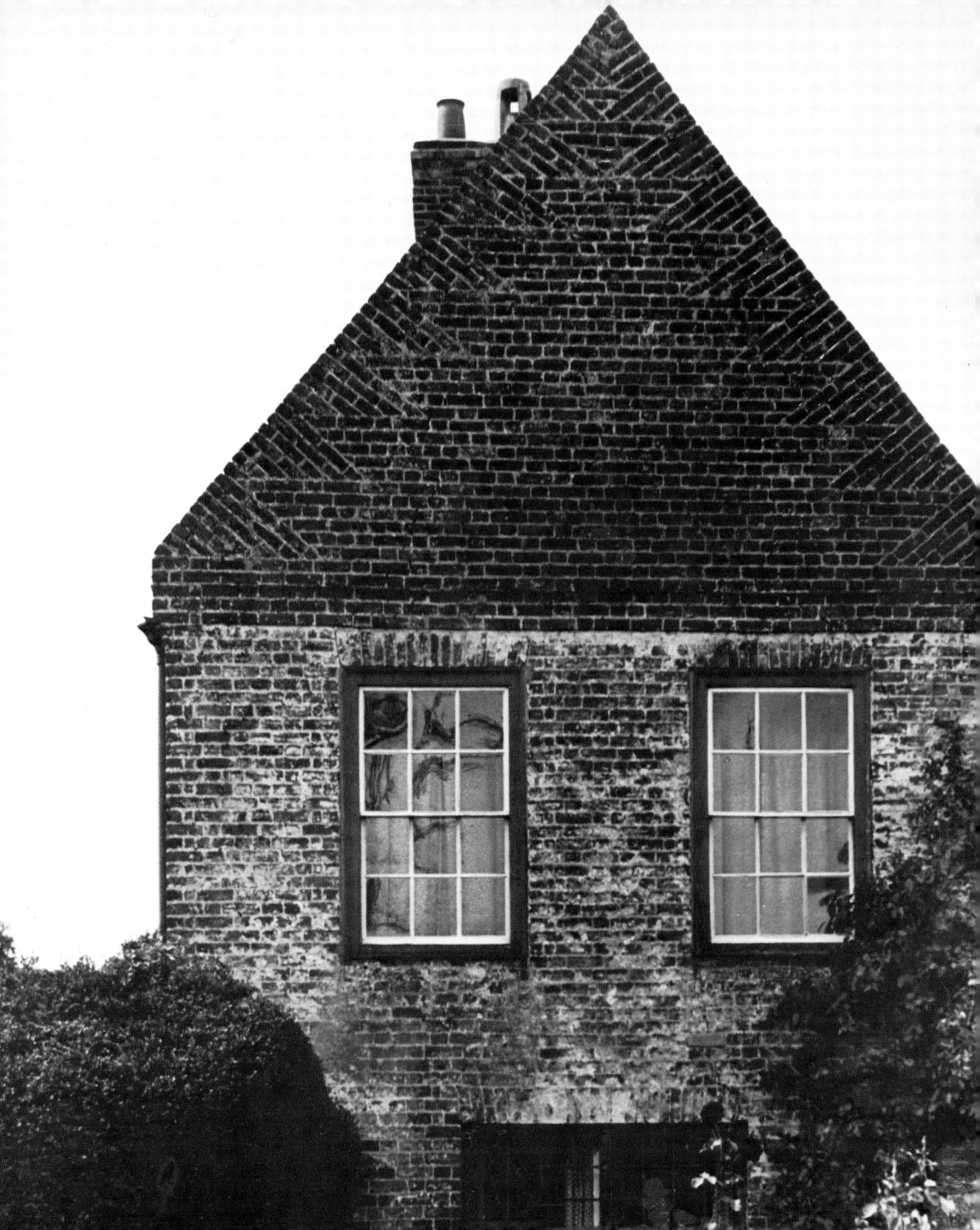

ALEXANDER POPE

Born: *London*, 21 *May*, 1688
Died: *Twickenham*, 30 *May*, 1744

It was to this statue that Pope wrote the lines:

Nymph of the grot, these sacred springs I keep
And to the murmur of these waters sleep;
Ah! spare my slumbers, gently tread the cave
And drink in silence or in silence leave.

51. IN THE GARDENS OF STOURHEAD WILTSHIRE

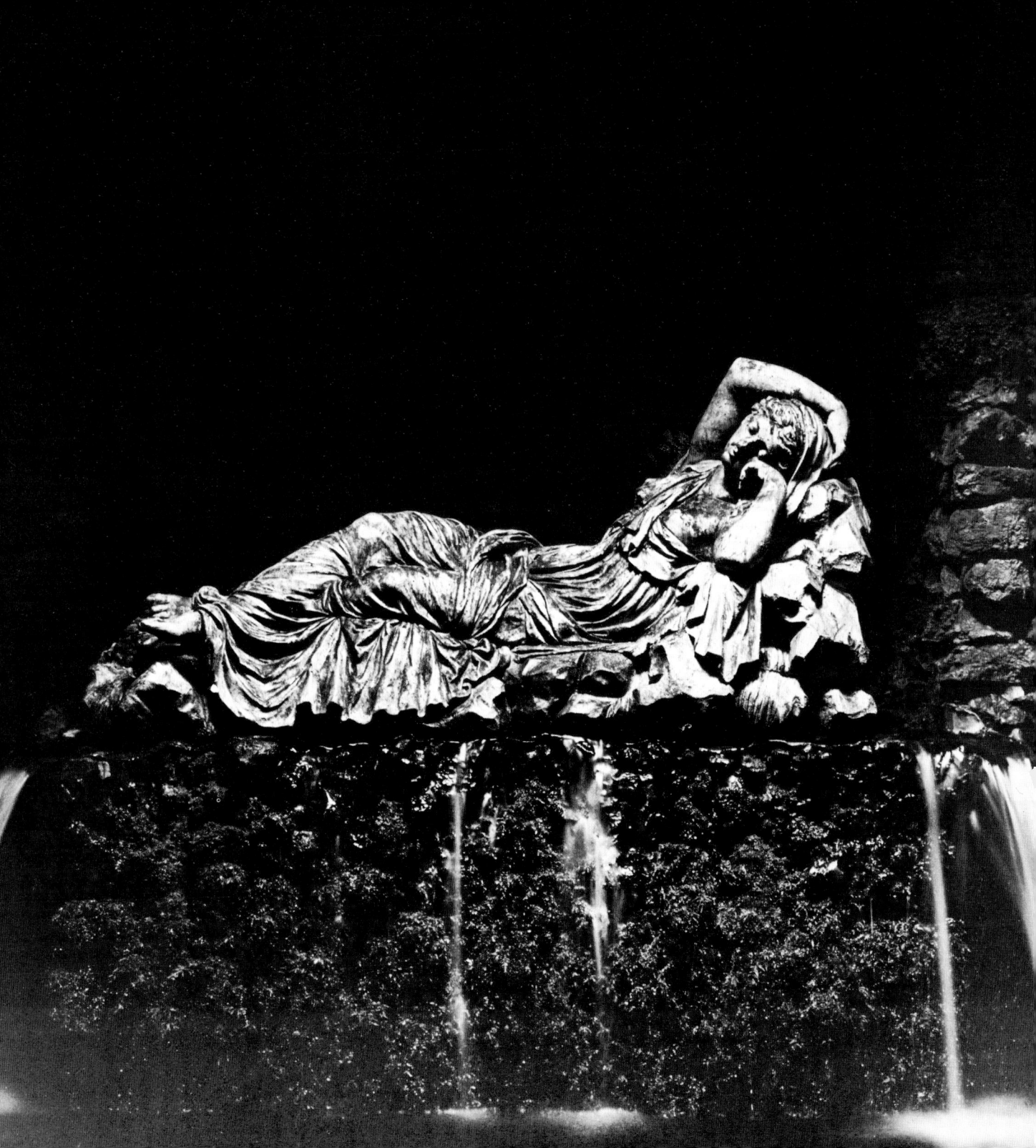

SAMUEL RICHARDSON

Born: *Derbyshire*, 1689
Died: *London*, 4 *July*, 1761

Samuel Richardson lived over his business premises in Salisbury Square, Fleet Street, but he had his country home at The Grange, North End, Hammersmith, where he spent Saturdays and Sundays. It was there that he wrote *Clarissa* and *Sir Charles Grandison*.

Sir Richard Phillips used to relate with glee the following anecdote respecting his inquiries in the neighbourhood: – 'A widow kept a public-house near the corner of North End Lane, about two miles from Hyde Park Corner, where she had lived about fifty years; and I wanted to determine the house in which Samuel Richardson, the novelist, had resided in North End Lane. She remembered his person, and described him as "a round, short gentleman, who most days passed her door", and she said she used to serve his family with beer. "He used to live and carry on his business," said I, "in Salisbury Square." "As to that," said she, "I know nothing, for I never was in London." "Never in London!" said I, "and in health, with the free use of your limbs!" "No," replied the woman; "I had no business there, and had enough to do at home." "Well, then," I observed, "you know your own neighbour-hood the better – which was the house of Mr Richardson, in the next lane?" "I don't know," she replied; "I am, as I told you, no traveller. *I never was up the lane* – I only know that he did live somewhere up the lane." "Well," said I, "but living in Fulham, you go to church?" "No," said she, "I never had time; on a Sunday our house is always full – I never was at Fulham but once, and that was when I was married, and many people say that was once too often, though my husband was as good a man as ever broke bread – God rest his soul!" *Sic transit gloria.*'

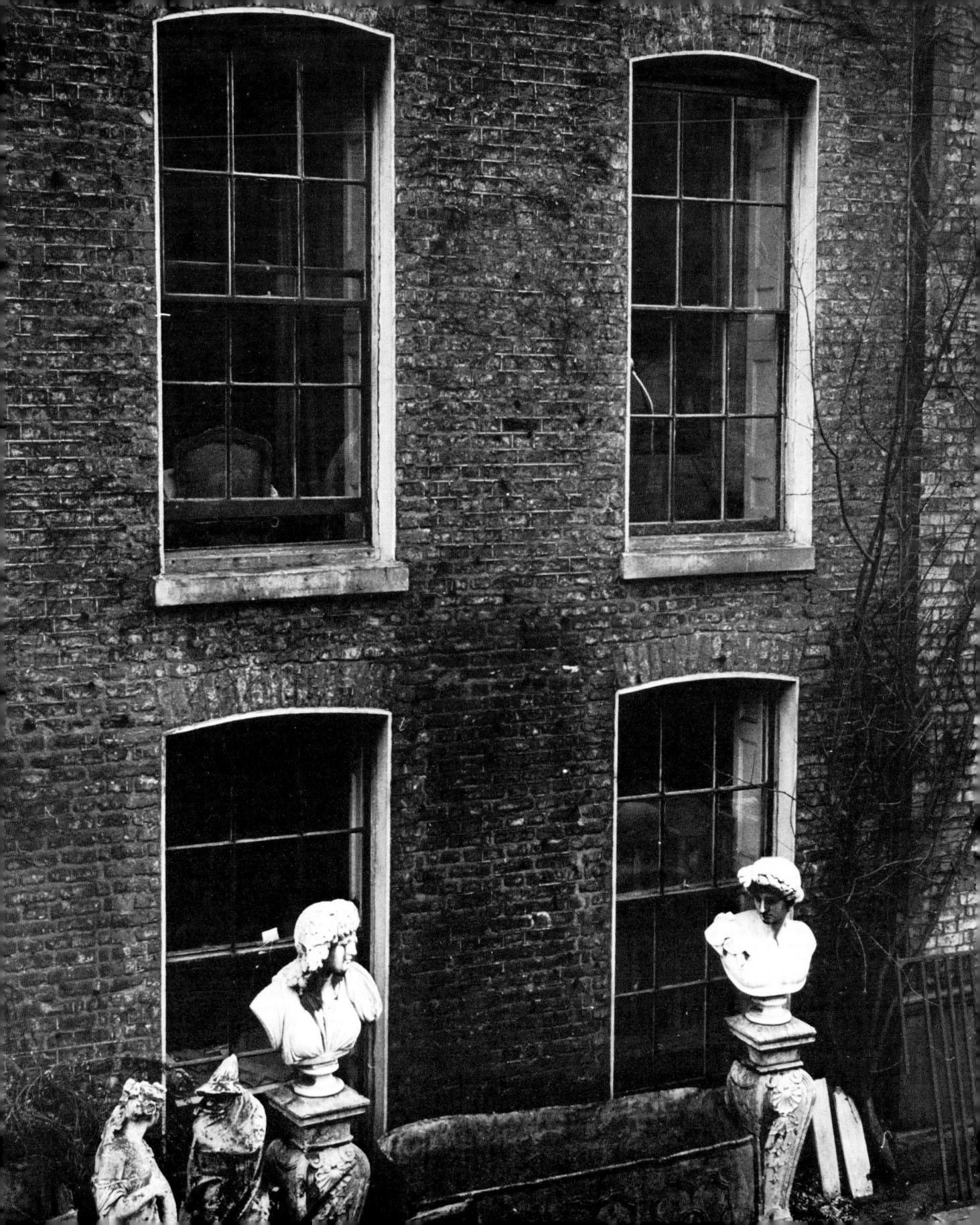

SIR WALTER SCOTT

Born: *Edinburgh*, 15 *August*, 1771
Died: *Abbotsford*, 21 *September*, 1832

If thou wouldst view fair Melrose aright,
Go visit it by the pale moonlight;
For the gay beams of lightsome day
Gild, but to flout, the ruins grey.
When the broken arches are black in night,
And each shafted oriel glimmers white;
When the cold light's uncertain shower
Streams on the ruined central tower;
When buttress and buttress, alternately,
Seem framed of ebon and ivory;
When silver edges the imagery,
And the scrolls that teach thee to live and die;
When distant Tweed is heard to rave,
And the owlet to hoot o'er the dead man's grave,
Then go – but go alone the while –
Then view St David's ruined pile;
And, home returning, soothly swear,
Was never scene so sad and fair!

Lay of the Last Minstrel

53. MELROSE ABBEY

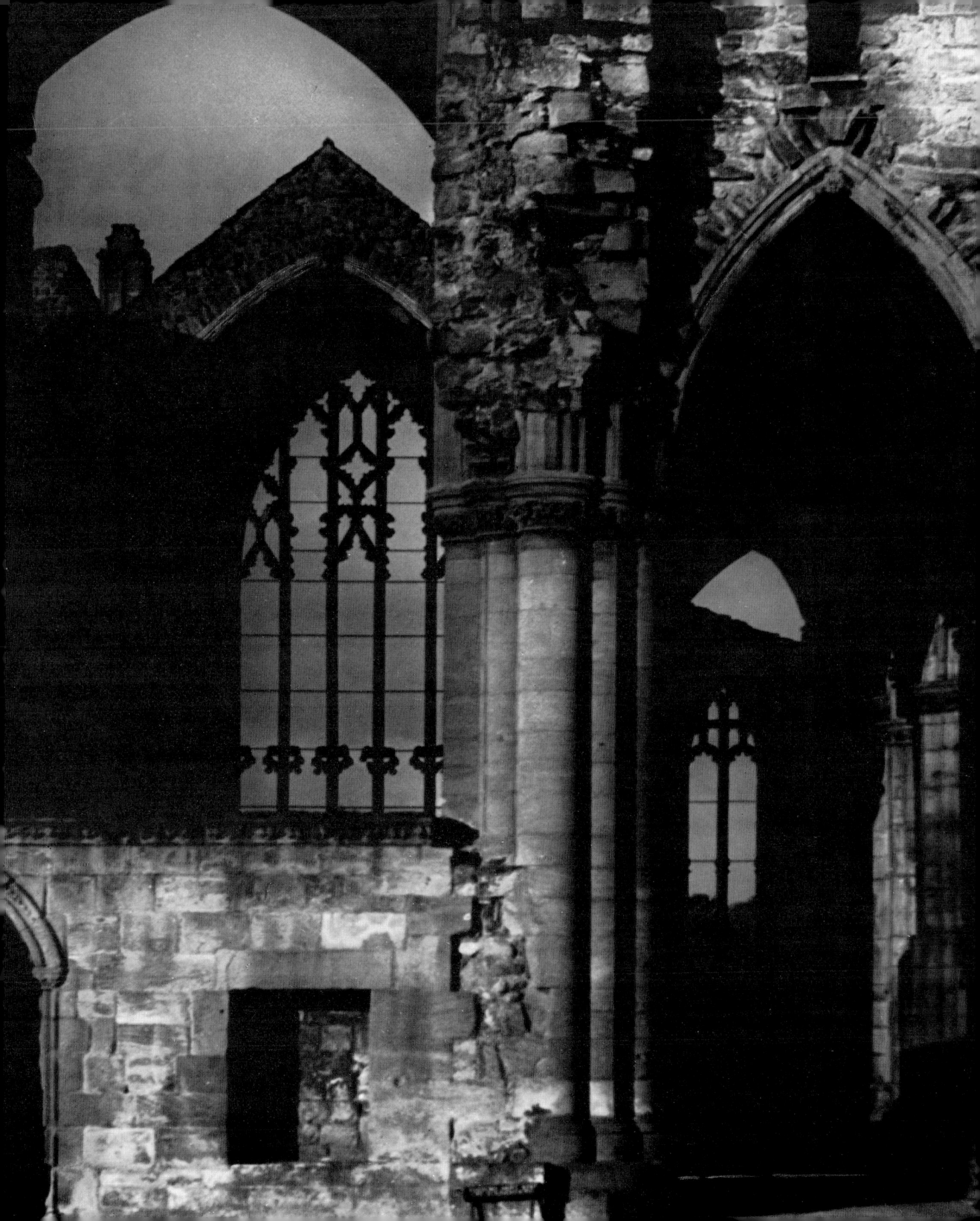

WILLIAM SHAKESPEARE

Born: *Stratford-on-Avon*, 22 or 23 *April*, 1564
Died: *Stratford-on-Avon*, 23 *April*, 1616

MESSENGER: As I did stand my watch upon the hill,
I look'd toward Birnam, and anon, methought,
The wood began to move.

MACBETH: Liar and slave!

MESSENGER: Let me endure your wrath, if't be not so:
Within this three mile may you see it coming;
I say, a moving grove.

MACBETH: If thou speak'st false,
Upon the next tree shalt thou hang alive,
Till famine cling thee: if thy speech be sooth,
I care not if thou dost for me as much. –
I pull in resolution; and begin
To doubt th' equivocation of the fiend,
That lies like truth: 'Fear not, till Birnam wood
Do come to Dunsinane'; – and now a wood
Comes toward Dunsinane. – Arm, arm, and out!
If this which he avouches does appear,
There is nor flying hence nor tarrying here.
I 'gin to be a-weary of the sun,
And wish th' estate o' th' world were now undone. –
Ring the alarum-bell! – Blow, wind! come, wrack!
At least we'll die with harness on our back.

Macbeth, V. 5

54. FROM GLAMIS CASTLE

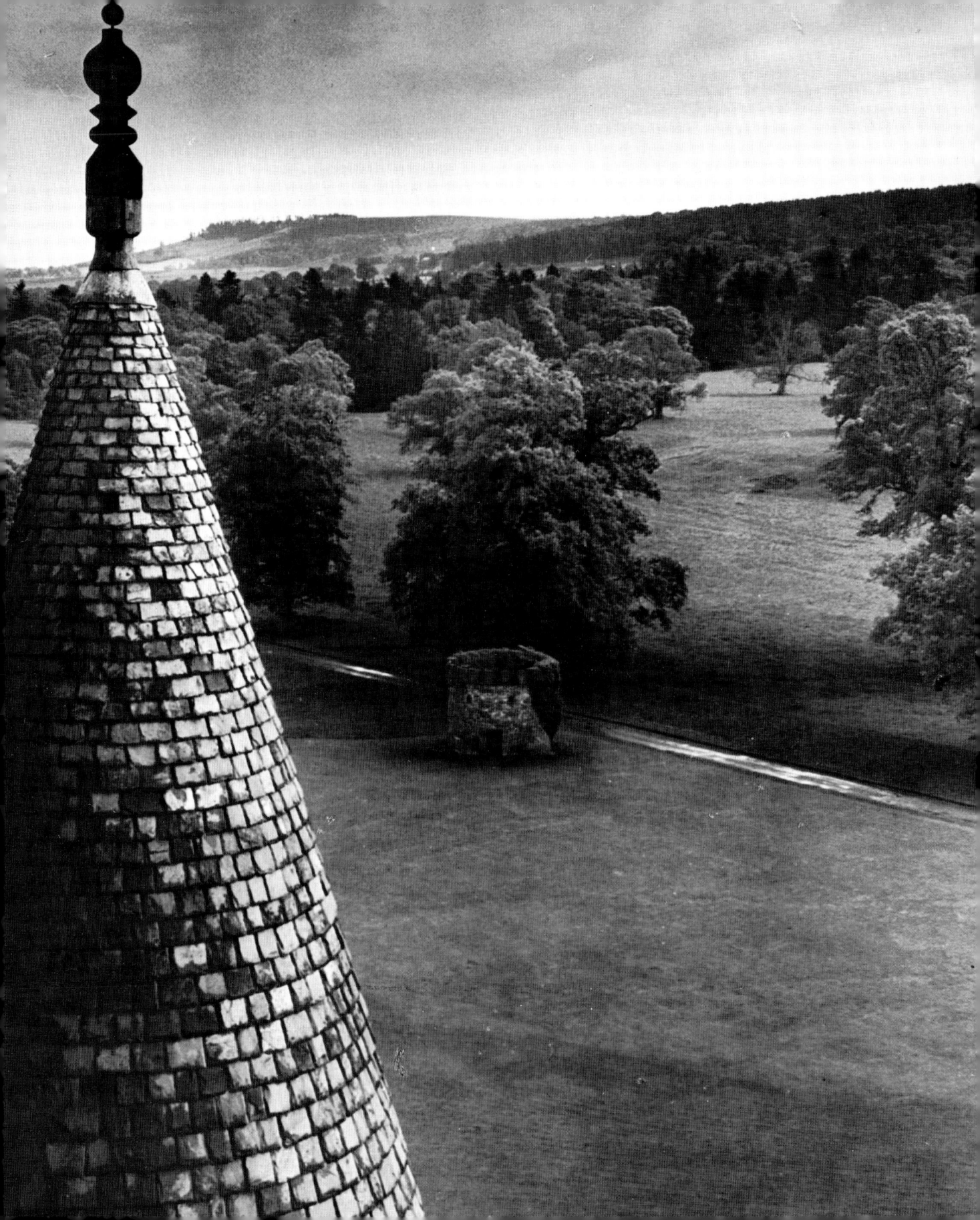

WILLIAM SHAKESPEARE

BOLINGBROKE: (*to Northumberland*): Noble lord,
Go to the rude ribs of that ancient castle;
Through brazen trumpet send the breath of parley
Into his ruin'd ears, and thus deliver: —
Henry Bolingbroke
On both his knees doth kiss King Richard's hand,
And sends allegiance and true faith of heart
To his most royal person; hither come
Even at his feet to lay my arms and power,
Provided that my banishment repeal'd
And lands restored again be freely granted:
If not, I'll use th' advantage of my power,
And lay the summer's dust with showers of blood
Rain'd from the wounds of slaughter'd Englishmen:
The which, how far off from the mind of Bolingbroke
It is, such crimson tempest should bedrench
The fresh green lap of fair King Richard's land,
My stooping duty tenderly shall show.
Go, signify as much, while here we march
Upon the grassy carpet of this plain.
Let's march without the noise of threatening drum,
That from this castle's tatter'd battlements
Our fair appointments may be well purused.

King Richard II, III. 3

55. FLINT CASTLE

GEORGE BERNARD SHAW

Born: *Dublin, 26 July, 1856*
Died: *Ayot St Lawrence, Hertfordshire, 2 November, 1950*

Shaw's Corner, Ayot St Lawrence, was Bernard Shaw's home from 1906 until his death. In 1916 Ellen Terry, who was a great friend of the Shaws, visited the village of Ayot without calling on them, and G.B.S. sent after her a collection of photographs of the village to each of which he wrote a rhyme. This was the verse beneath a picture of his home:

> Here, standing sideways to the dawn,
> And looking northwards up the lawn,
> You see the house that Bernard weeps in,
> Because his Ellen never peeps in.

It was in this collection of photographs and rhymes that Bernard Shaw's last book *A Rhyming Guide to Ayot St Lawrence* had its beginning.

56. SHAW'S CORNER, AYOT ST LAWRENCE

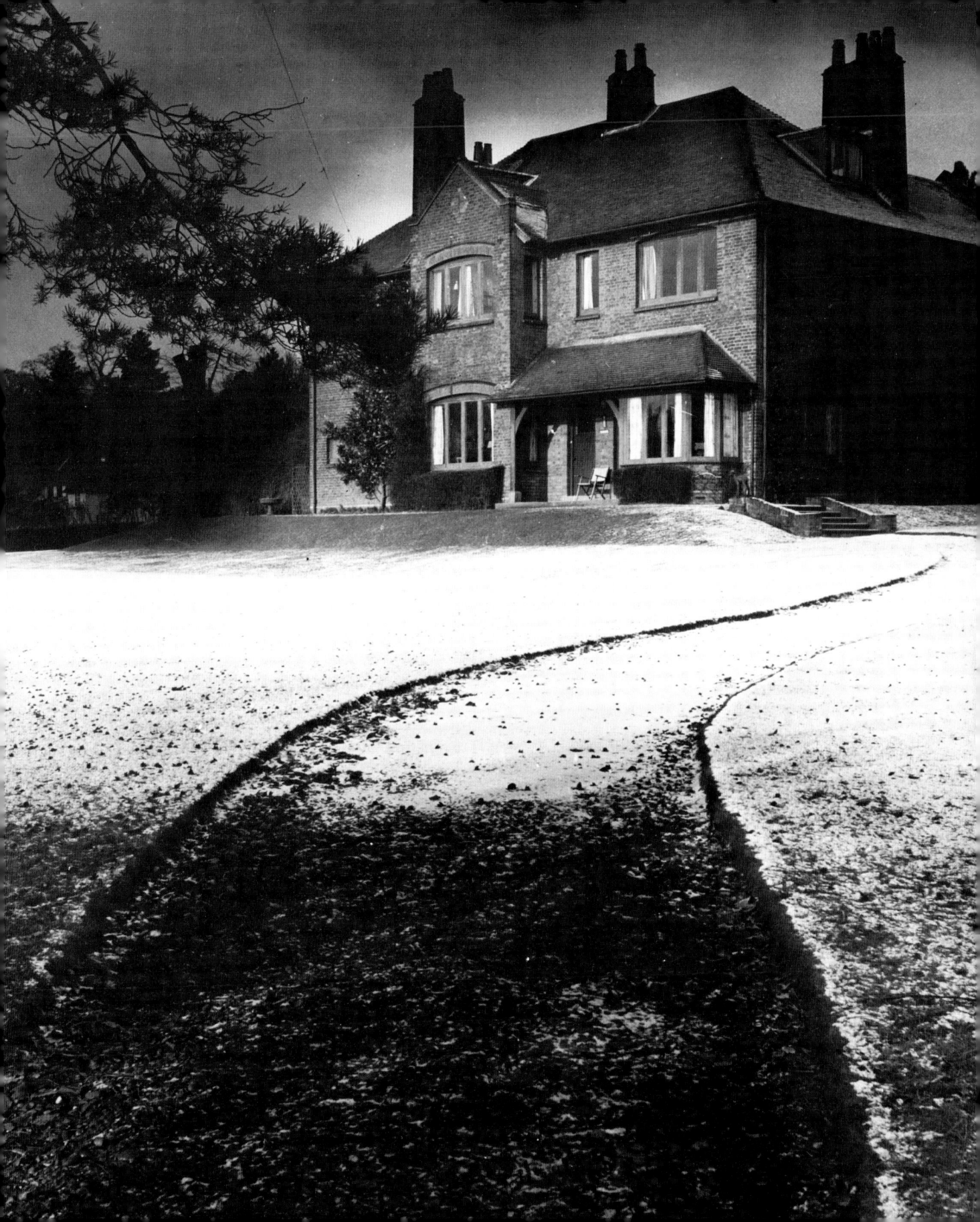

SIR PHILIP SIDNEY

Born: *Penshurst, 30 November, 1554*
Died: *Arnhem, Holland, 17 October, 1586*

The mansion of Penshurst was built in the early fourteenth century. It passed through the ownership of the Dukes of Bedford and Buckingham until, in the mid-sixteenth century, Edward VI granted it to Sir William Sidney, whose son Sir Henry built the fine façade and the gateway tower. Henry's eldest son, Philip, 'the great glory of his family, the great hope of mankind' as Camden terms him, was born at Penshurst but never lived there as its master, for he survived his father but a few months. In the park is an avenue called Sacharissa's Walk in memory of Lady Dorothy Sidney (1617–84) upon whom the poet Waller 'fixed his heart perhaps half fondly, perhaps half-ambitiously' as Dr Johnson says.

Ben Jonson wrote:

> Thou art not, Penshurst, built to envious show
> Of touch or marble; nor canst boast a row
> Of polished pillars or a roof of gold:
> Thou hast no lantern, whereof tales are told;
> Or stair, or courts; but stand'st an ancient pile,
> And these grudged at, art reverenced the while.
> Thou joy'st in better marks, of soil, of air,
> Of wood, of water; therein thou art fair.
> Thou hast thy walks for health, as well as sport:
> Thy mount, to which th' Dryads do resort,
> Where Pan and Bacchus their high feasts have made
> Beneath the broad beech and the chestnut shade . . .

57. PENSHURST PLACE

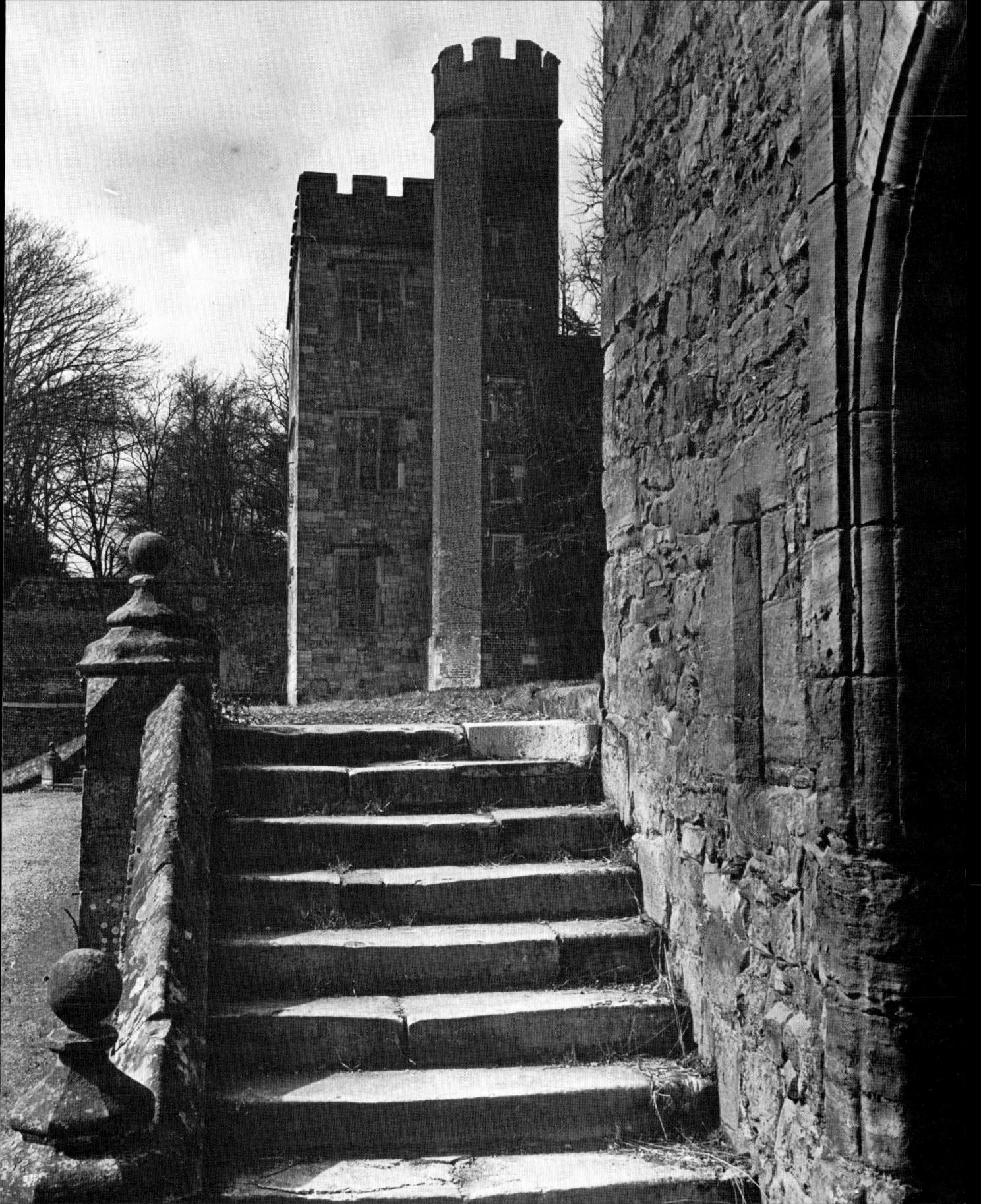

ROBERT LOUIS STEVENSON

Born: *Edinburgh*, 13 *November*, 1850
Died: *Vailima*, *Samoa*, 3 *December*, 1894

'The mist rose and dies away, and showed us that country lying as waste as the sea; only the moorfowl and the peewees crying upon it, and far over to the east a herd of deer, moving like dots. Much of it was red with heather; much of the rest broken up with bogs and hags and peaty pools; some had been burnt black in a heath fire; and in another place there are quite a forest of dead firs, standing like skeletons. A wearier-looking desert man never saw . . .'

Kidnapped

58. RANNOCH MOOR, PERTH

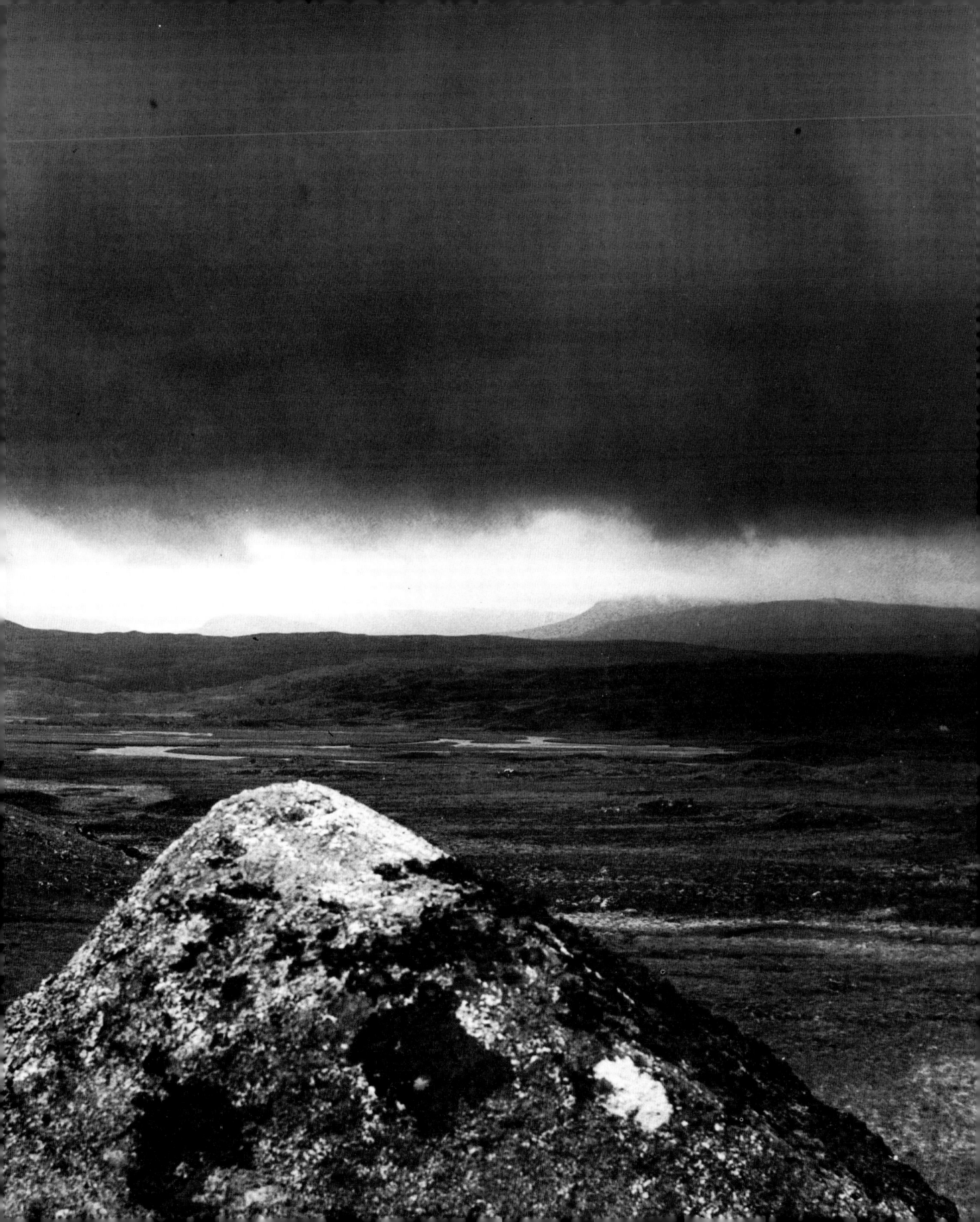

ALFRED, LORD TENNYSON

Born: *Somersby*, 6 *August*, 1809
Died: *Aldworth*, 6 *October*, 1892

We go, but ere we go from home,
As down the garden-walks I move,
Two spirits of a diverse love
Contend for loving masterdom.

One whispers, 'Here thy boyhood sung
Long since its matin song, and heard
The low love-language of the bird
In native hazels tassel-hung.'

The other answers, 'Yea, but here
Thy feet have strayed in after hours
With thy lost friend among the bowers,
And this hath made them trebly dear.'

These two have striven half the day,
And each prefers his separate claim,
Poor rivals in a losing game,
That will not yield each other way.

I turn to go: my feet are set
To leave the pleasant fields and farms;
They mix in one another's arms
To one pure image of regret.

In Memoriam: CII

59. THE OLD RECTORY, SOMERSBY

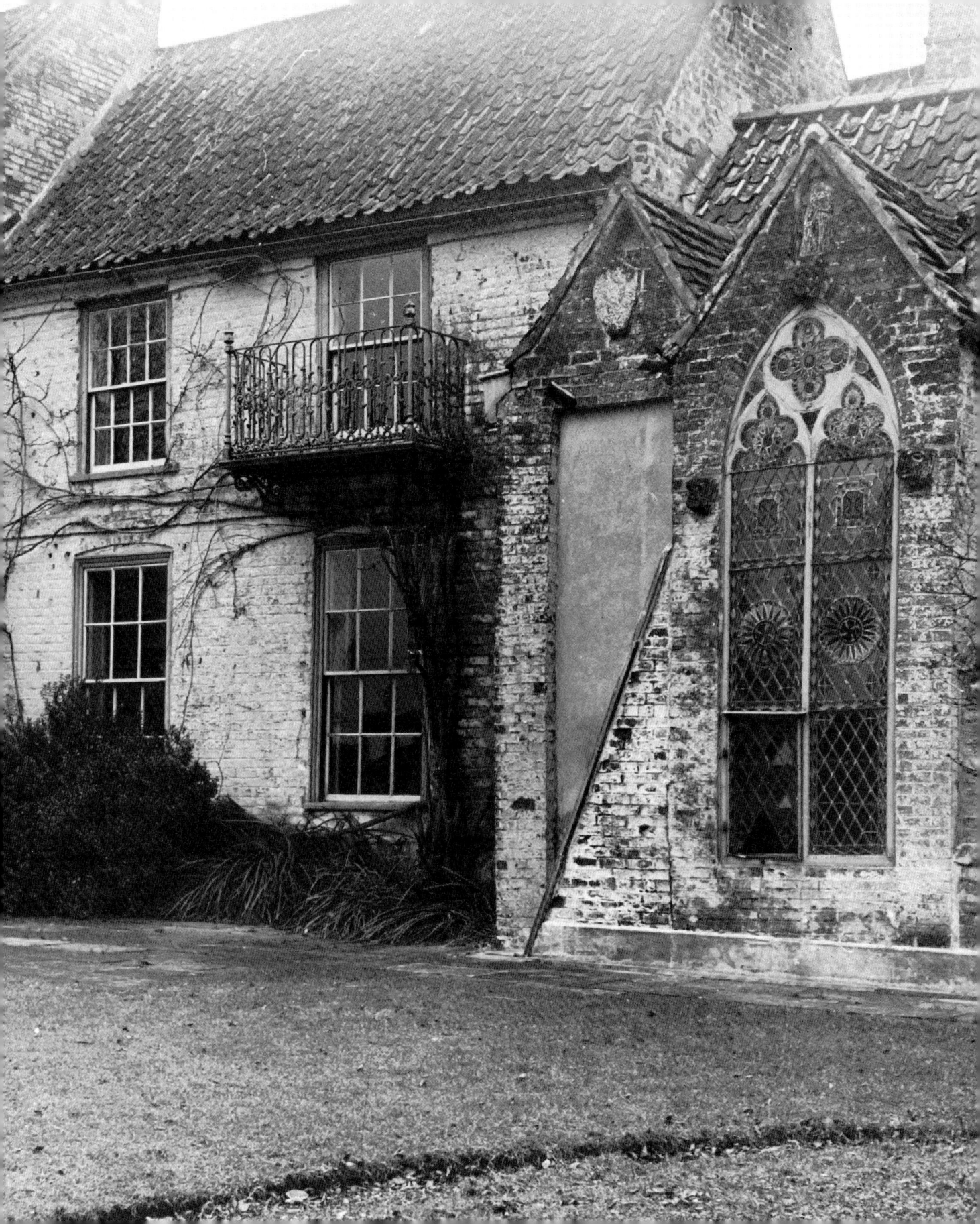

ANTHONY TROLLOPE

Born: *London, 24 April,* 1815
Died: *Harting, Hampshire, 6 December,* 1882

'Hiram's Hospital, as the retreat is called, is a picturesque building enough, and shows the correct taste with which the ecclesiastical architects of those days were imbued. It stands on the banks of the little river, which flows nearly round the cathedral close, being on the side furthest from the town.'

The Warden

60. St Nicholas Hospital, Salisbury

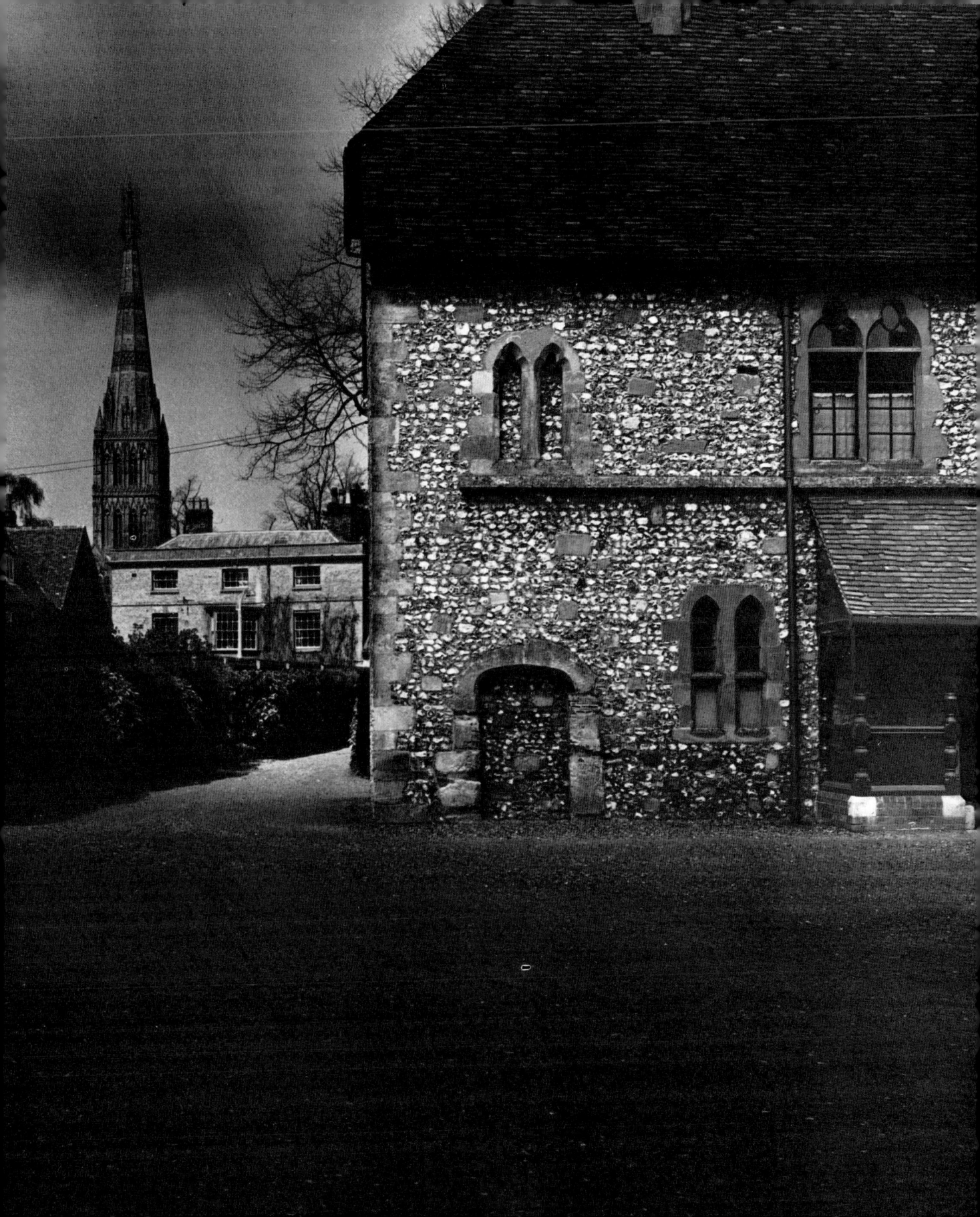

ANTHONY TROLLOPE

'. . . the new bishop took his seat for the first time in the throne alloted to him. New scarlet cushions and drapery had been prepared, with new gilt binding and new fringe. The old carved oak-wood of the throne with its numerous grotesque pinnacles half-way up to the roof of the choir, had been washed, and dusted, and rubbed, and it all looked very smart. Ah! how often sitting there, in the happy early days, on those lowly benches in front of the altar, have I whiled away the tedium of a sermon in considering how best I might thread my way up amidst those wooden towers, and climb safely to the topmost pinnacle!'

Barchester Towers

61. SALISBURY CATHEDRAL

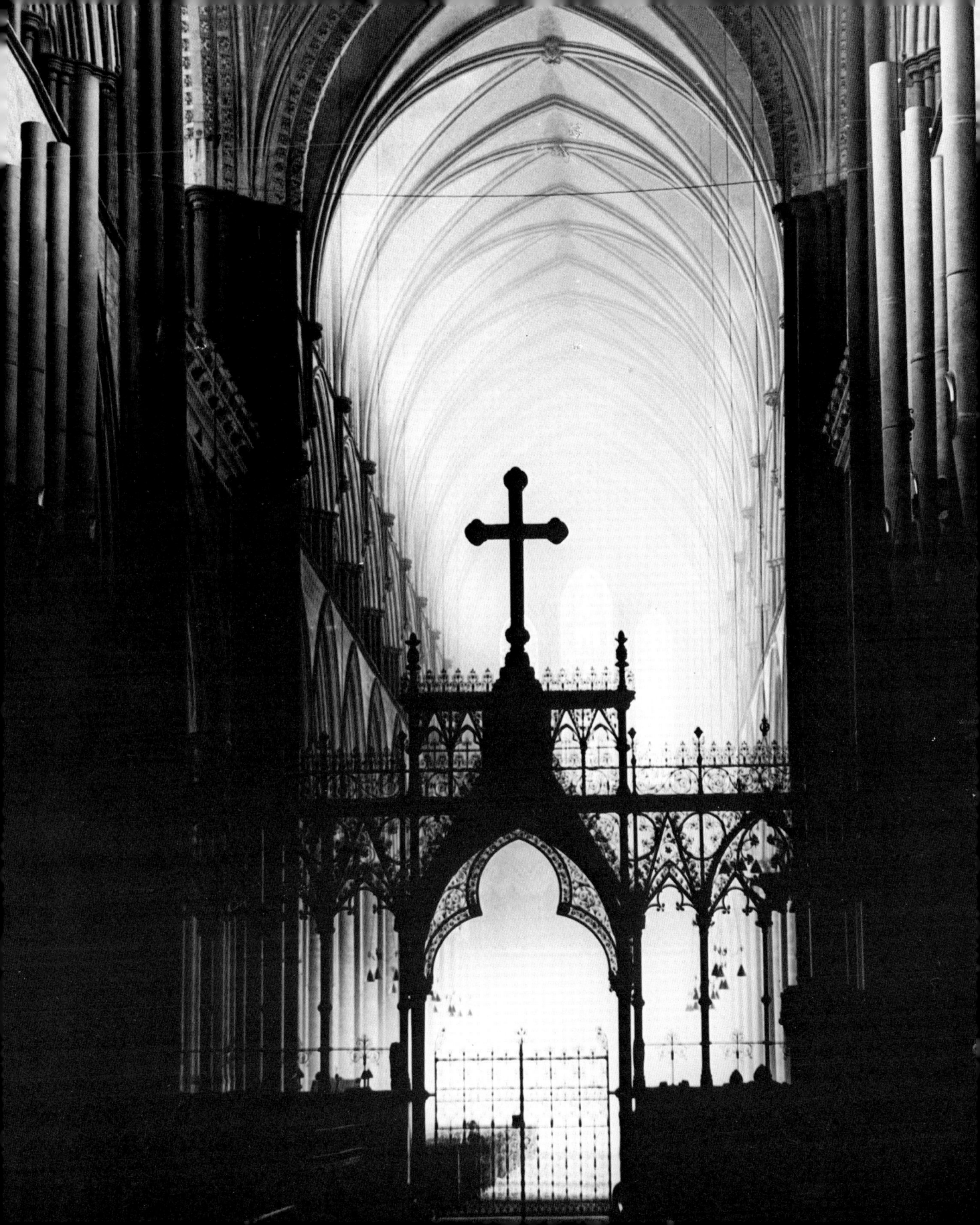

HORACE WALPOLE

Born: *London*, 24 *September*, 1717
Died: *London*, 2 *March*, 1797

'This view of the castle is what I have just finished, and is the only side that will be at all regular. Directly before it is an open grove through which you see a field, which is bounded by a serpentine wood of all kinds of trees, and flowering shrubs and flowers. The lawn before the house is situated on the top of a small hill, from whence to the left you see the town and church of Twickenham encircling a turn of the river, that looks exactly like a seaport in miniature. The opposite shore is a most delicious meadow, bounded by Richmond Hill, which loses itself in the noble woods of the park to the end of the prospect on the right, where is another turn of the river, and the suburbs of Kingston as luckily placed as Twickenham is on the left: and a natural terrace on the brow of the hill, with meadows of my own down to the river, commands both extremities. Is not this a tolerable prospect?'

Letters

62. STRAWBERRY HILL

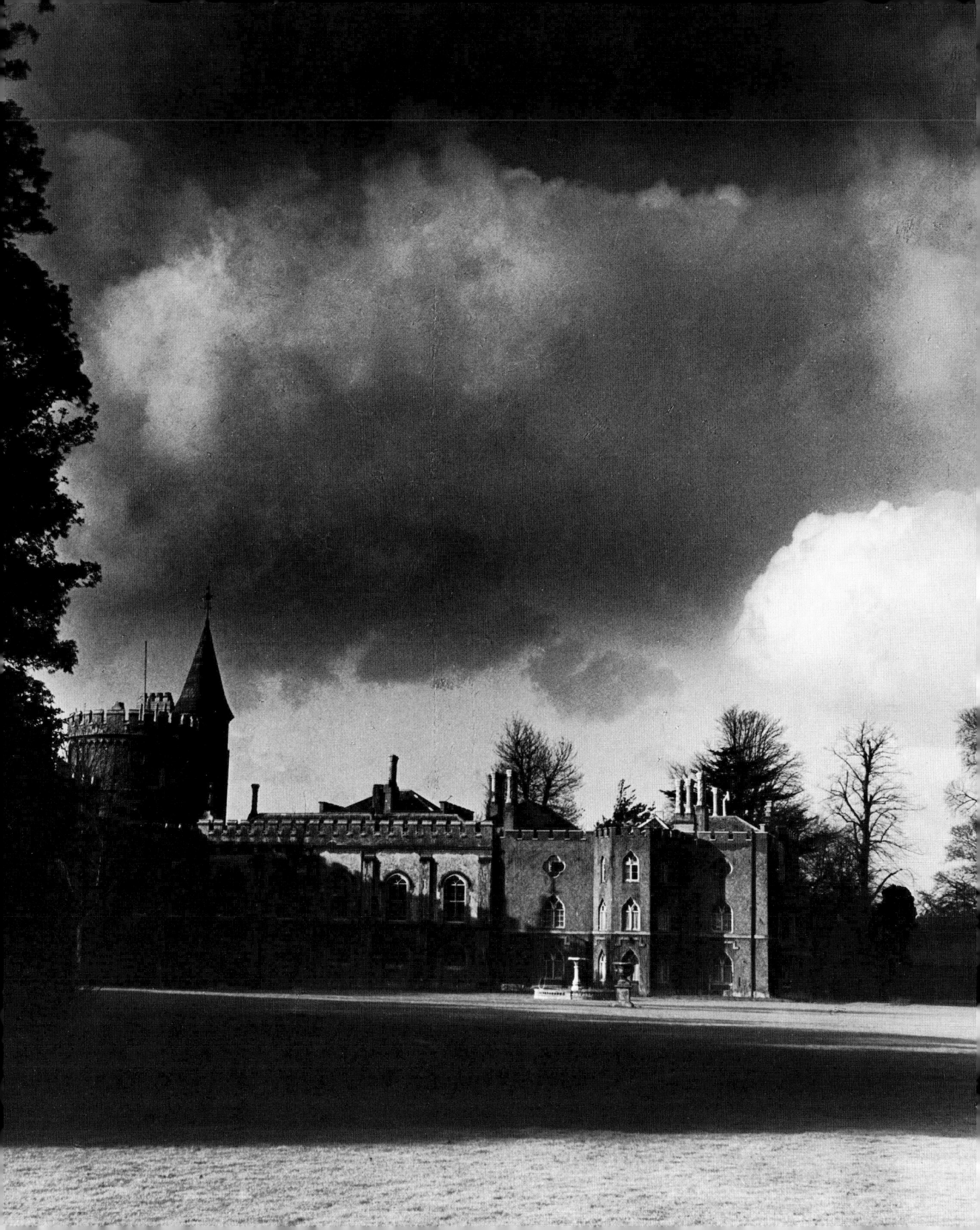

OSCAR WILDE

Born: *Dublin, 15 October, 1856*
Died: *Paris, 30 November, 1900*

I know not whether Laws be right,
　　Or whether Laws be wrong;
All that we know who lie in gaol
　　Is that the wall is strong;
And that each day is like a year,
　　A year whose days are long.

This too I know — and wise it were
　　If each could know the same —
That every prison that men build
　　Is built with bricks of shame,
And bound with bars lest Christ should see
　　How men their brothers maim.

The Ballad of Reading Gaol

63. READING GAOL

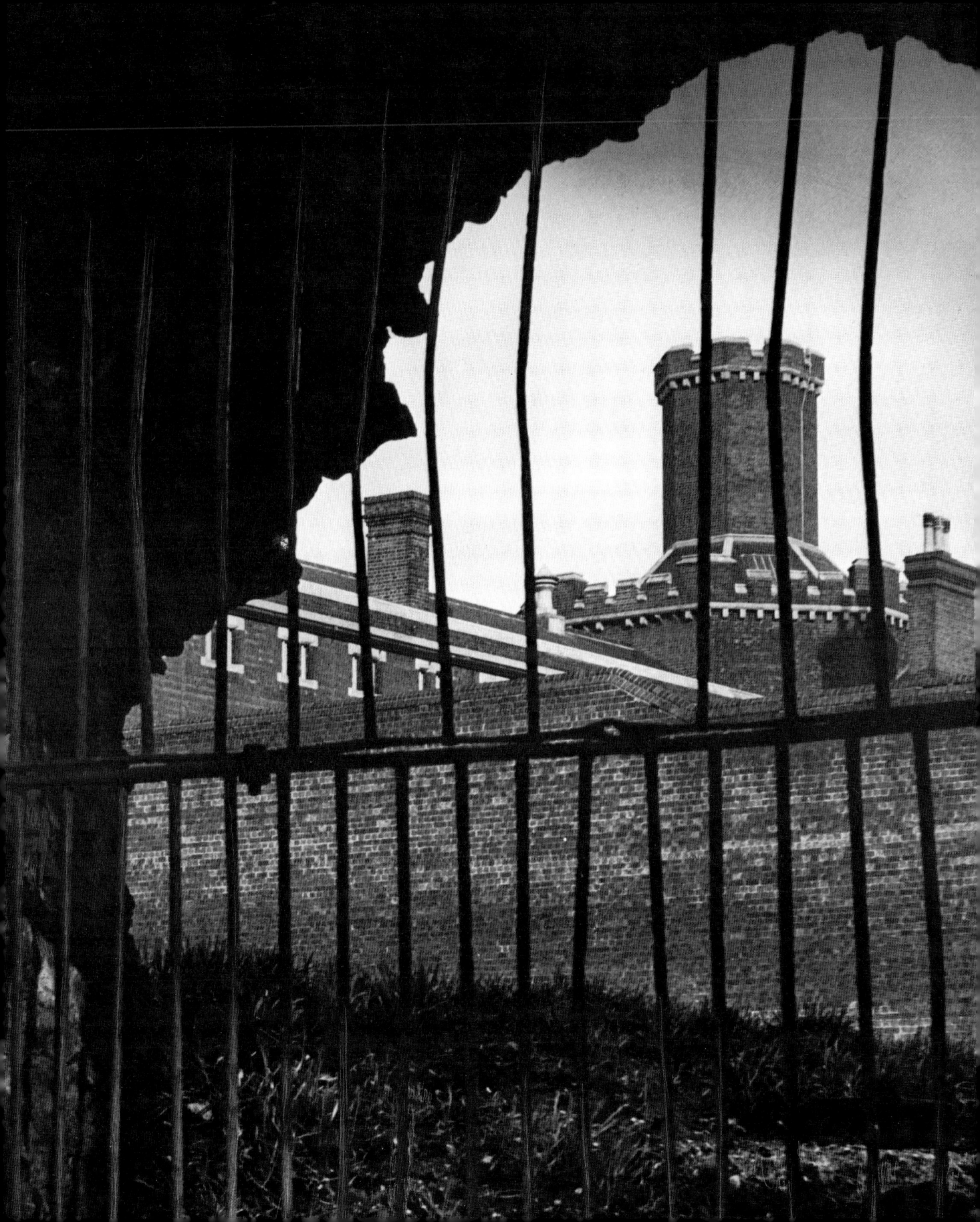

WILLIAM WORDSWORTH

Born: *Cockermouth*, 7 *April*, 1770
Died: *Grasmere*, 23 *April*, 1850

'I was ushered up a little flight of stairs, fourteen in all, to a little drawing-room, or whatever the reader chooses to call it. Wordsworth, himself, has described the fireplace of this room as his

"Half-kitchen and half-parlour fire."

It was not fully seven feet six inches high, and in other respects pretty nearly of the same dimensions as the rustic hall below. There was, however, in a small recess, a library of perhaps 300 volumes, which seemed to consecrate the room as the poet's study and composing room, and such occasionally it was. But far oftener he both studied, as I found, and composed on the highroad.'

De Quincey, *Recollections of the Lakes*

64. WORDSWORTH'S ROOM IN DOVE COTTAGE

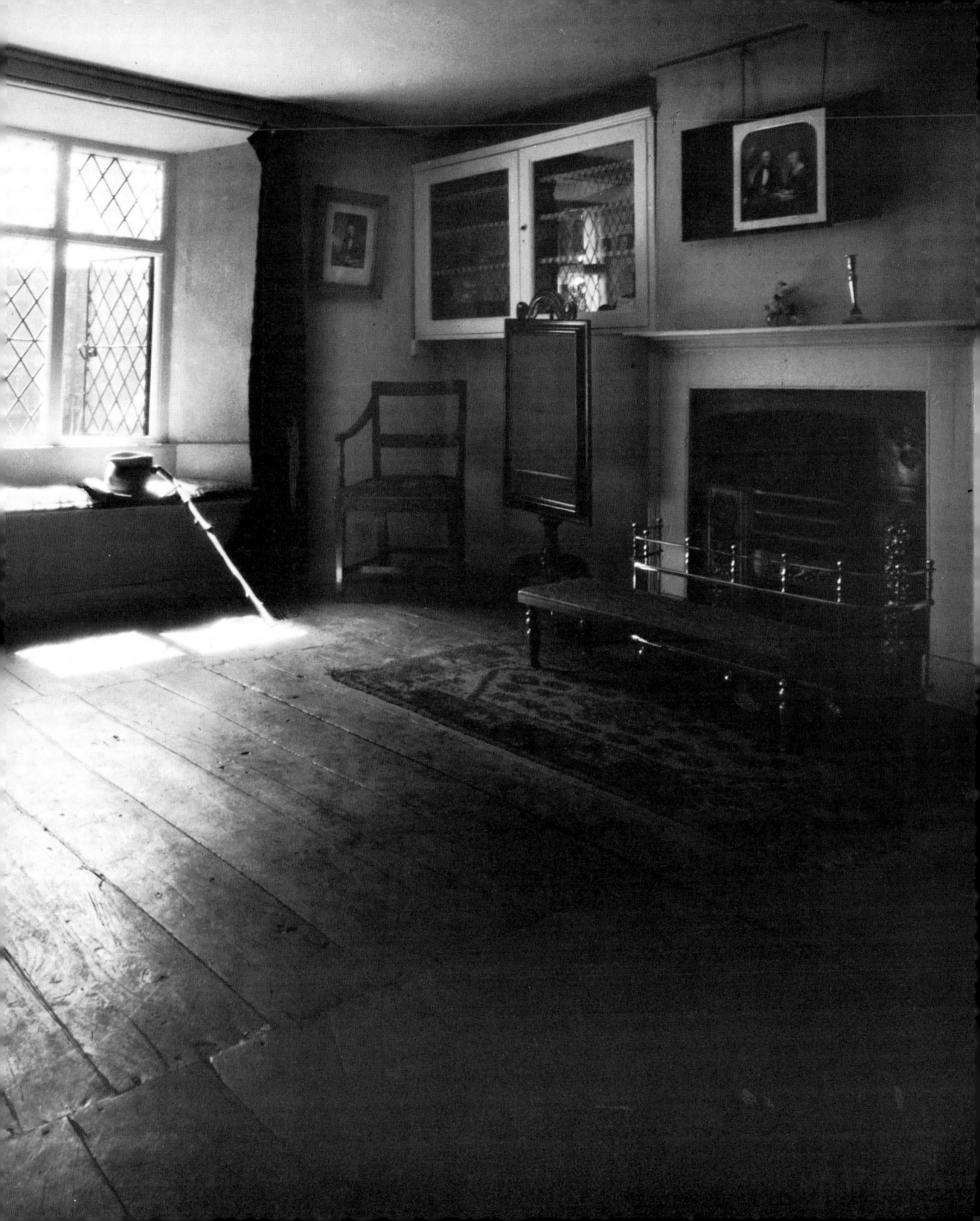

WILLIAM WORDSWORTH

the little fields, made green
By husbandry of many thrifty years,
Paid cheerful tribute to the moorland house.
— There crows the cock, single in his domain:
The small birds find in spring no thicket there
To shroud them; only from the neighbouring vales
The cuckoo, straggling up to the hill tops,
Shouteth faint tidings of some gladder place . . .
Ah! what a sweet Recess, thought I, is here!
Instantly throwing down my limbs at ease
Upon a bed of heath; — full many a spot
Of hidden beauty have I chanced to espy
Among the mountains; never one like this;
So lonesome, and so perfectly secure;
Not melancholy — no, for it is green,
And bright, and fertile, furnished in itself
With the few needful things that life requires . . .
It could not be more quiet: peace is here
Or nowhere; days unruffled by the gale
Of public news or private; years that pass
Forgetfully; uncalled upon to pay
The common penalties of mortal life,
Sickness, or accident, or grief, or pain.

The Excursion

65. BETWEEN ULLSWATER AND THIRLMERE IN EARLY SPRING

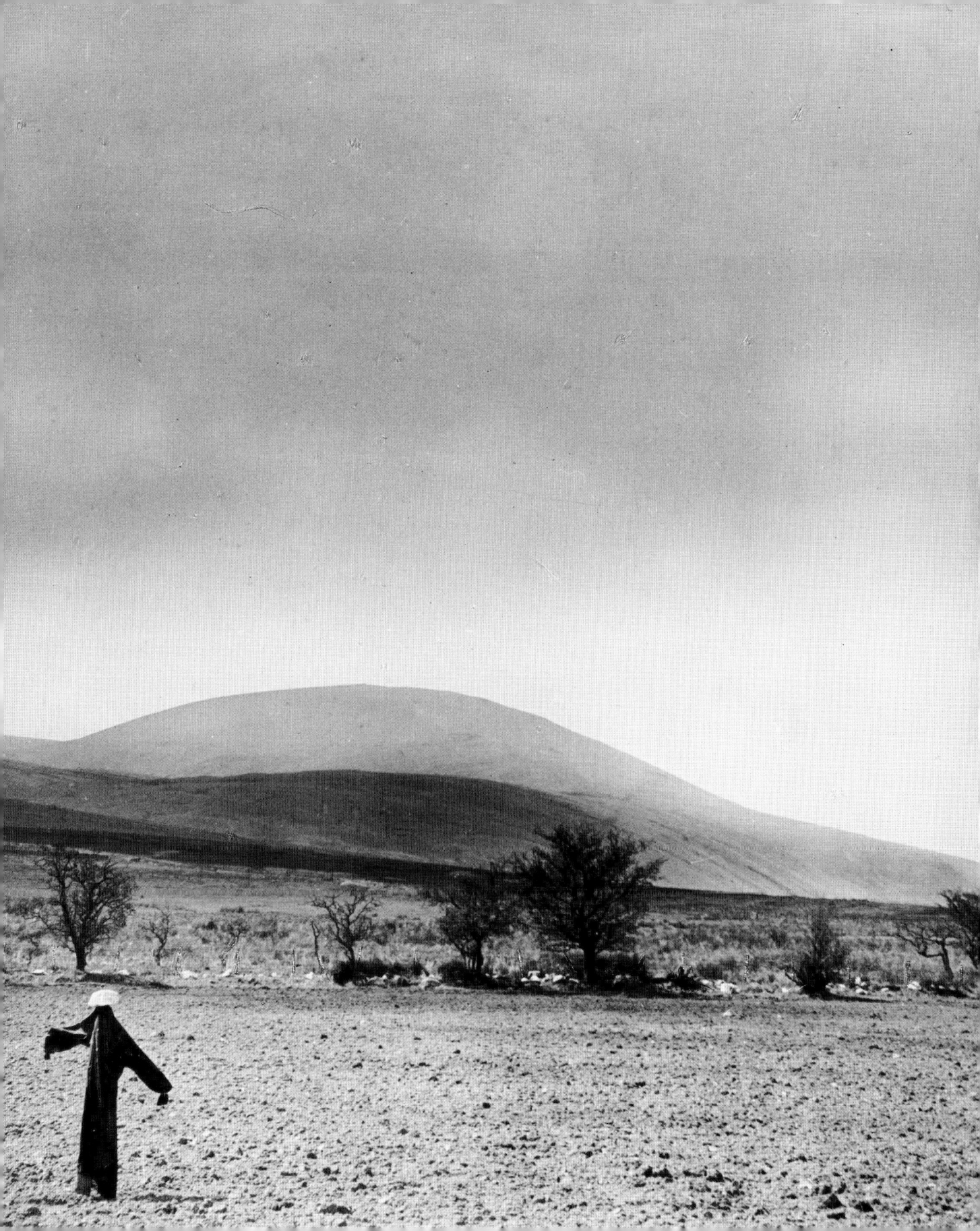

ADDITIONAL PLATES

66. ALDEBURGH

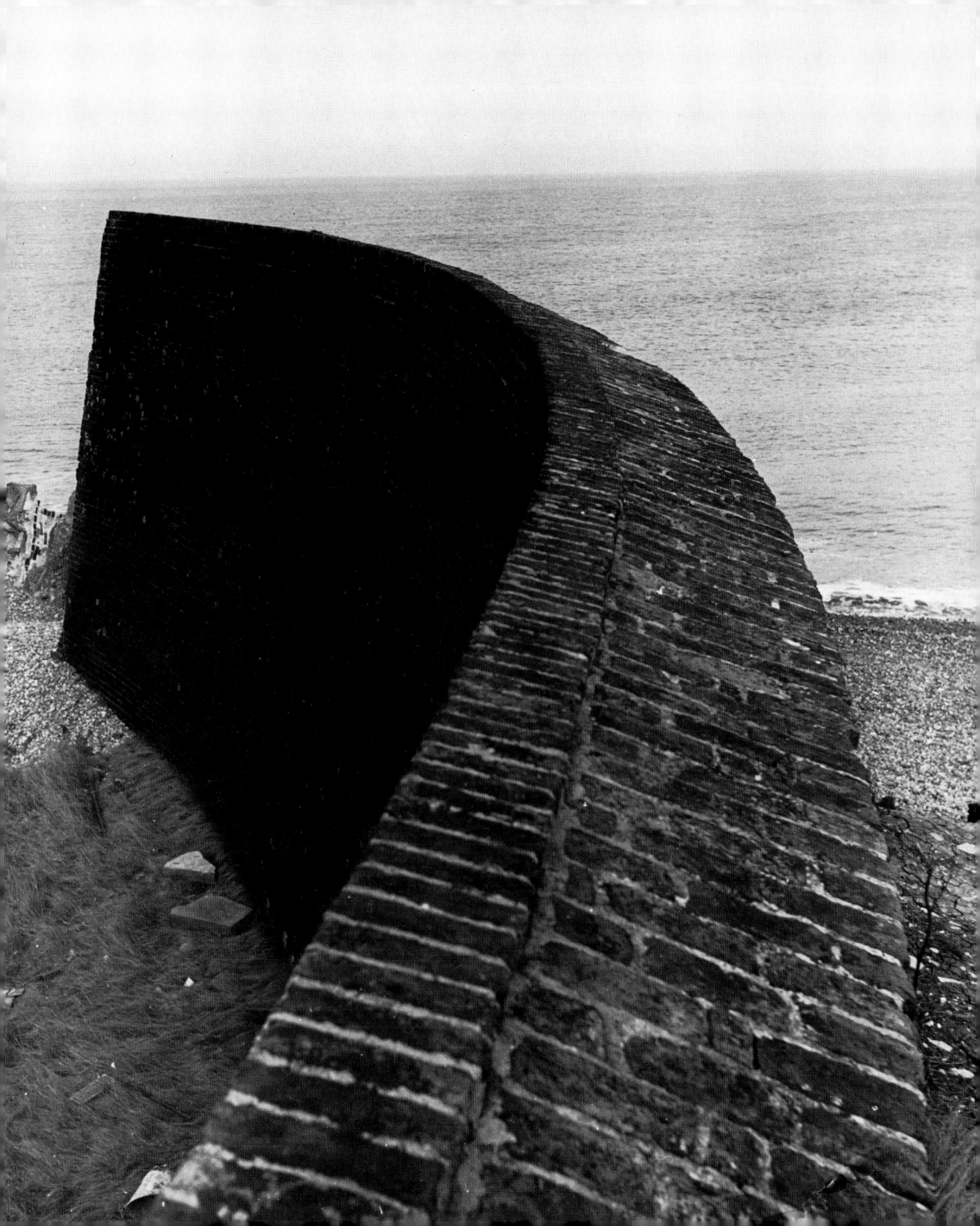

67. GORDALE SCAR

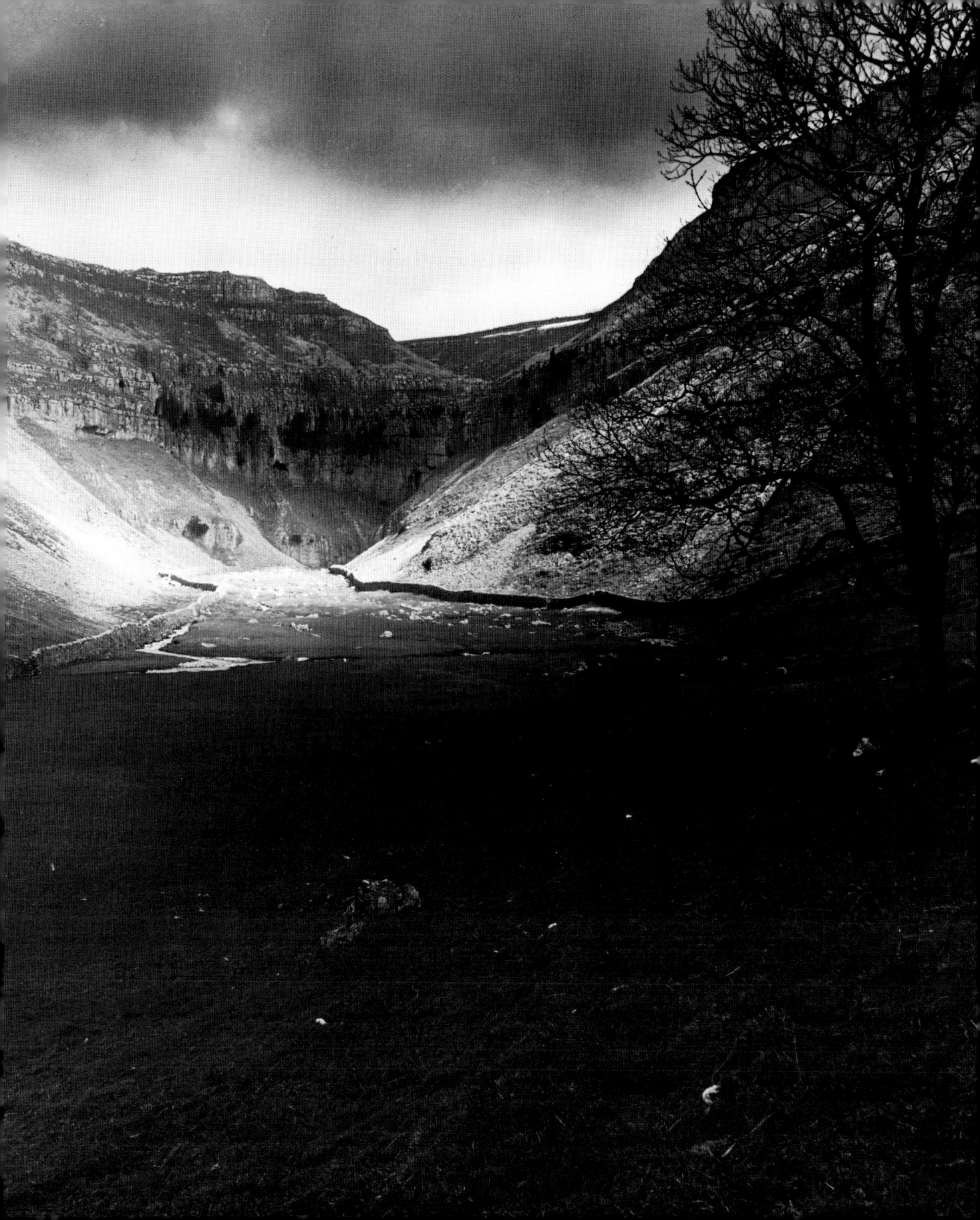

68. GORDALE SCAR

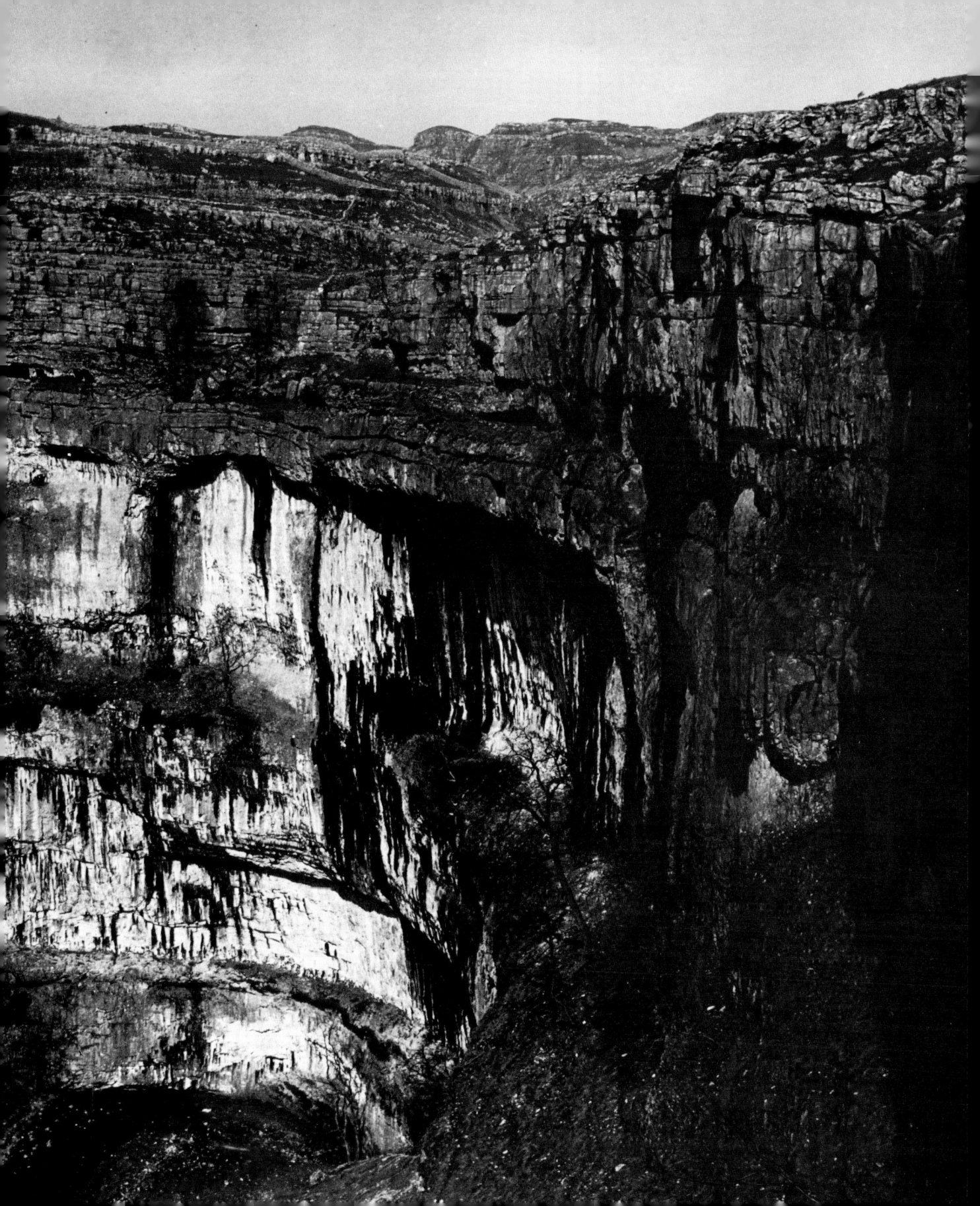

69. GIANT'S CAUSEWAY

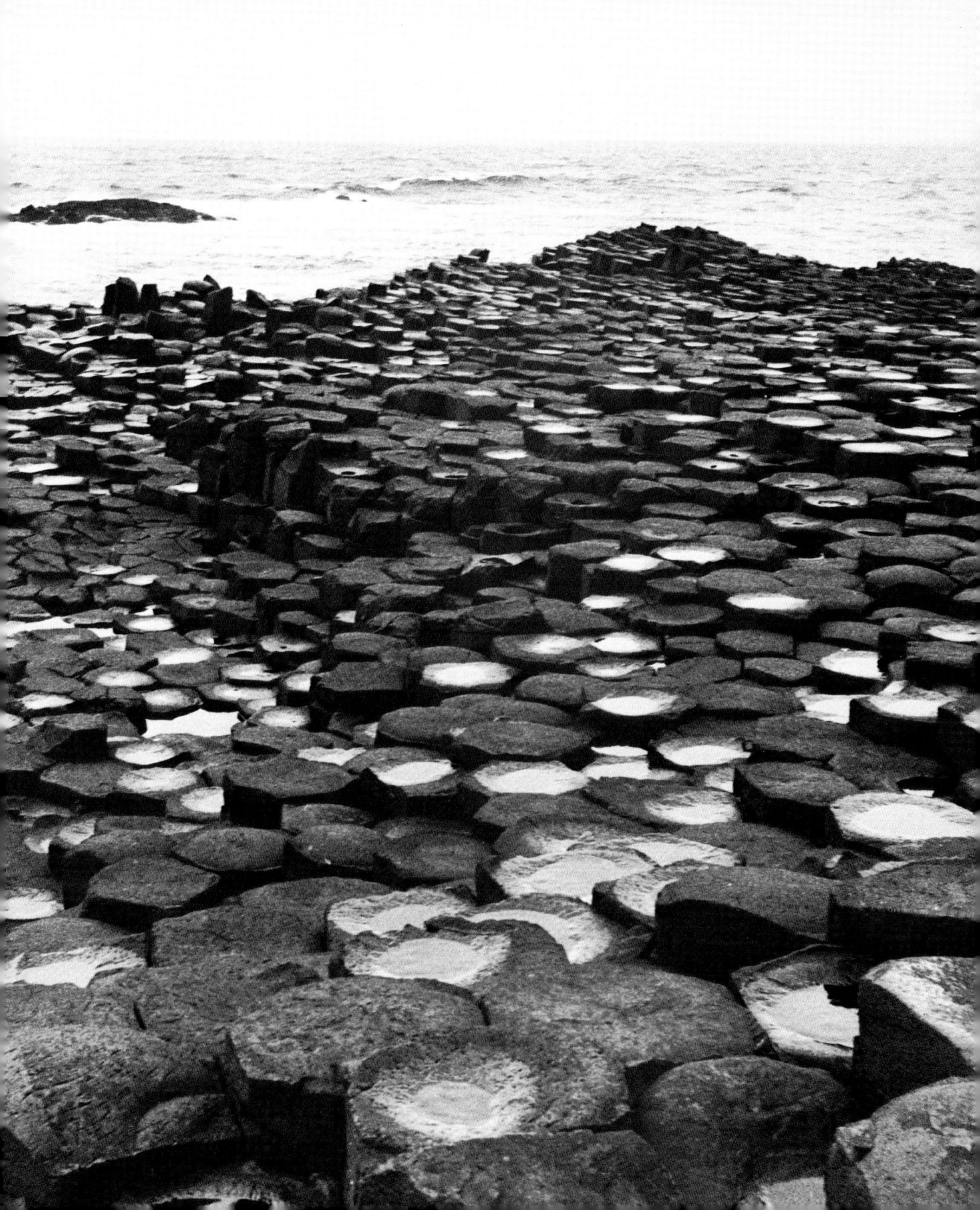

70. GIANT'S CAUSEWAY

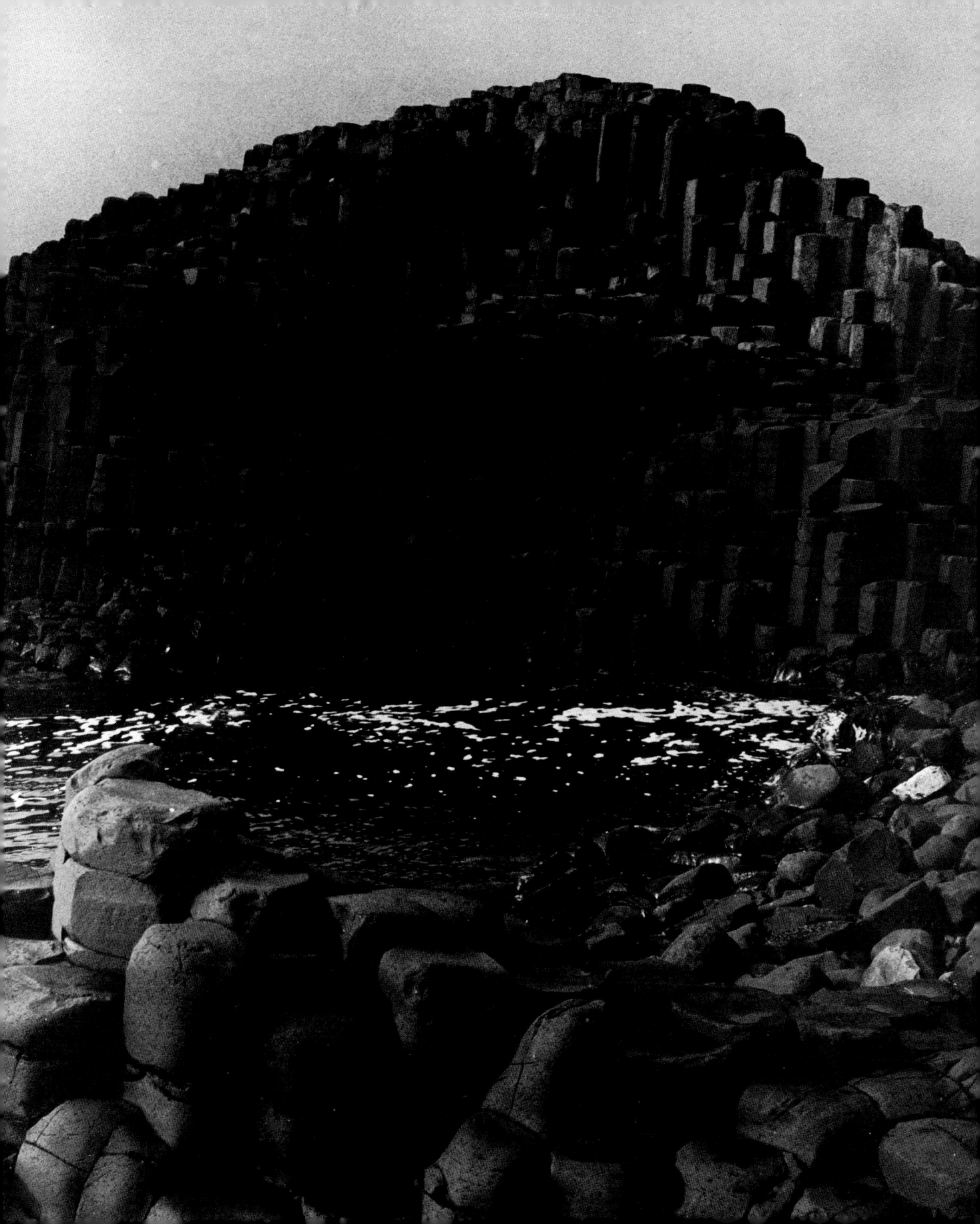

71. TOM PAINE'S HOUSE, DUBLIN

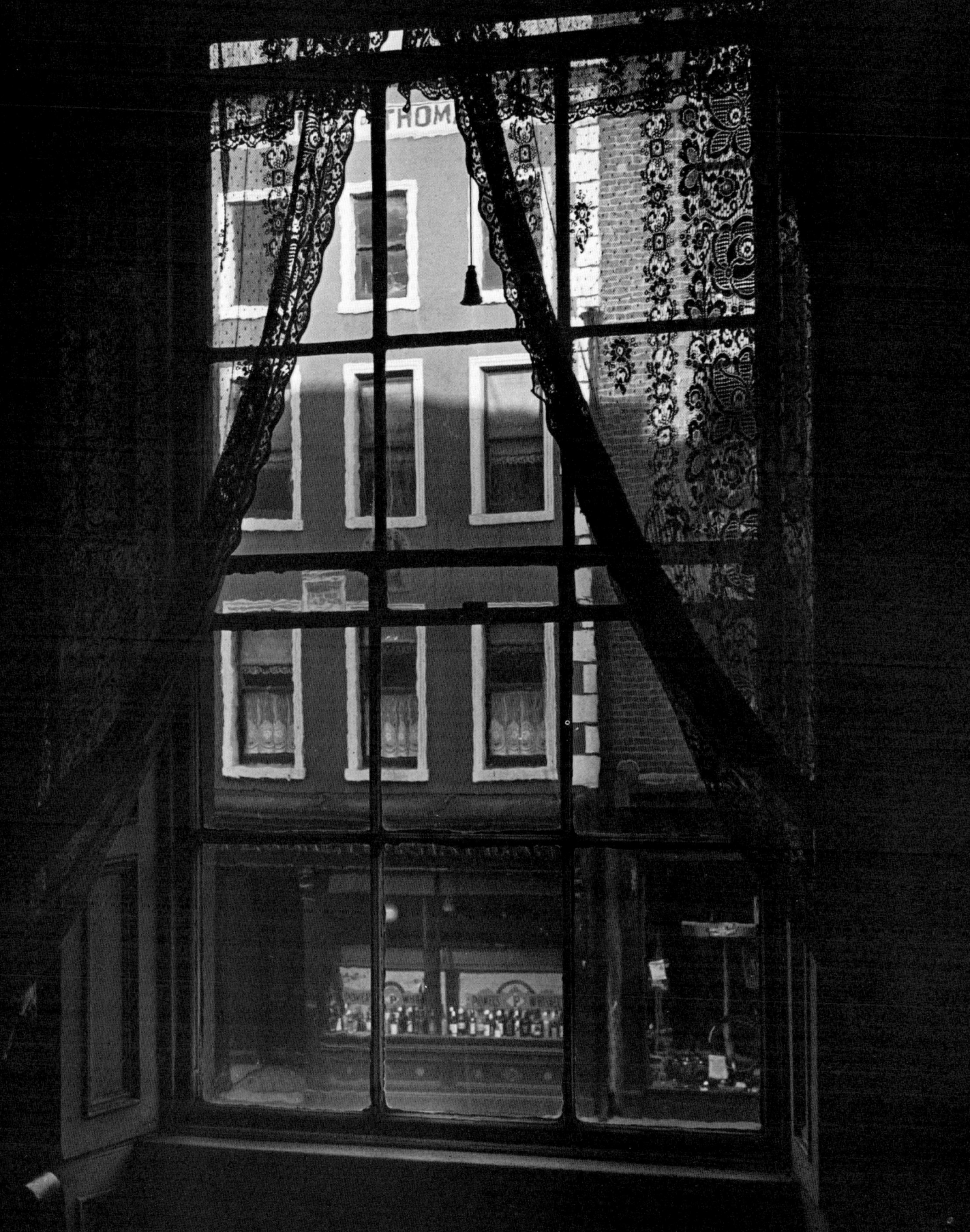

72. CHRISTMAS EVE, CAMPDEN HILL

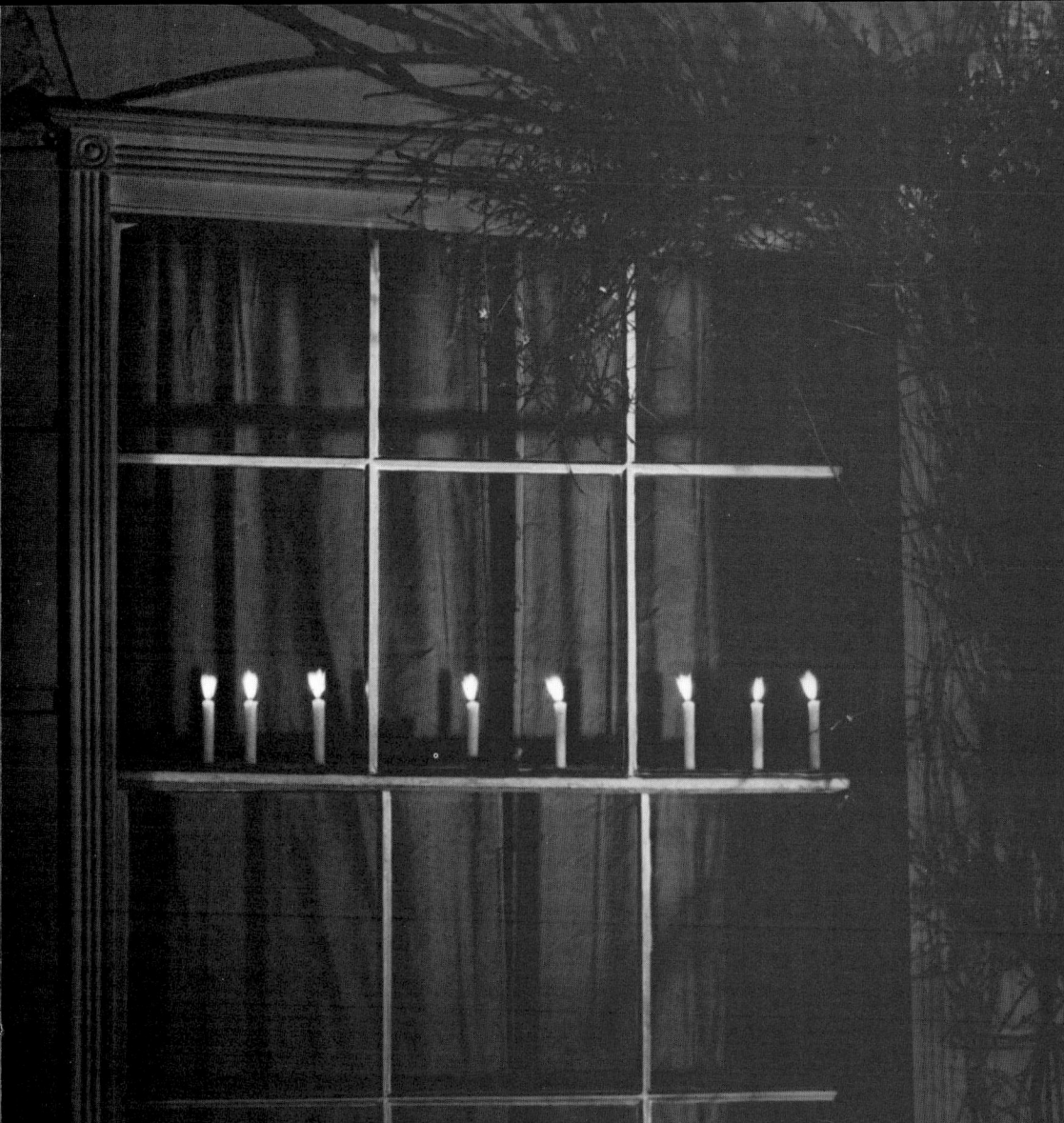

73. FOUNTAINS ABBEY

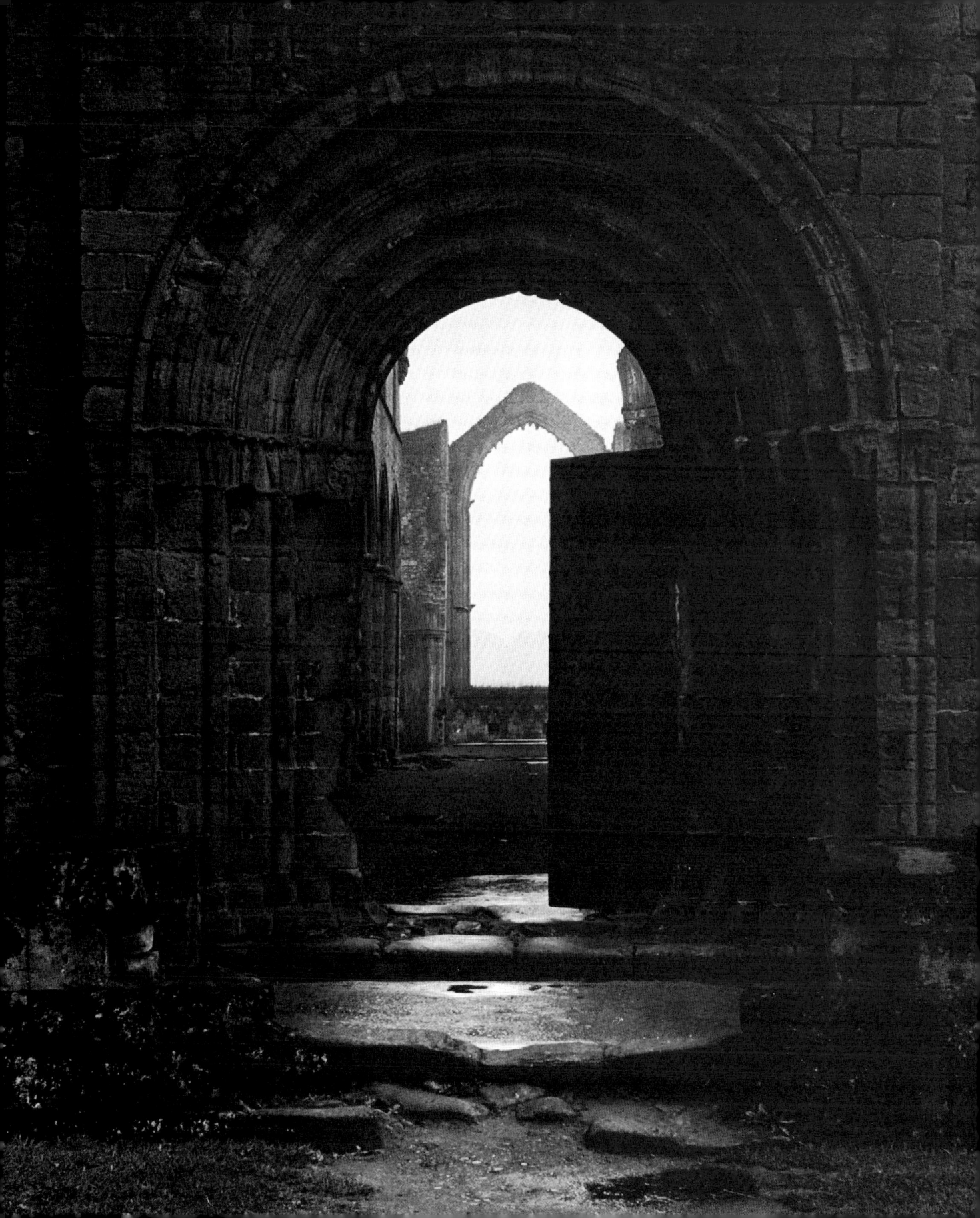

74. FOUNTAINS ABBEY

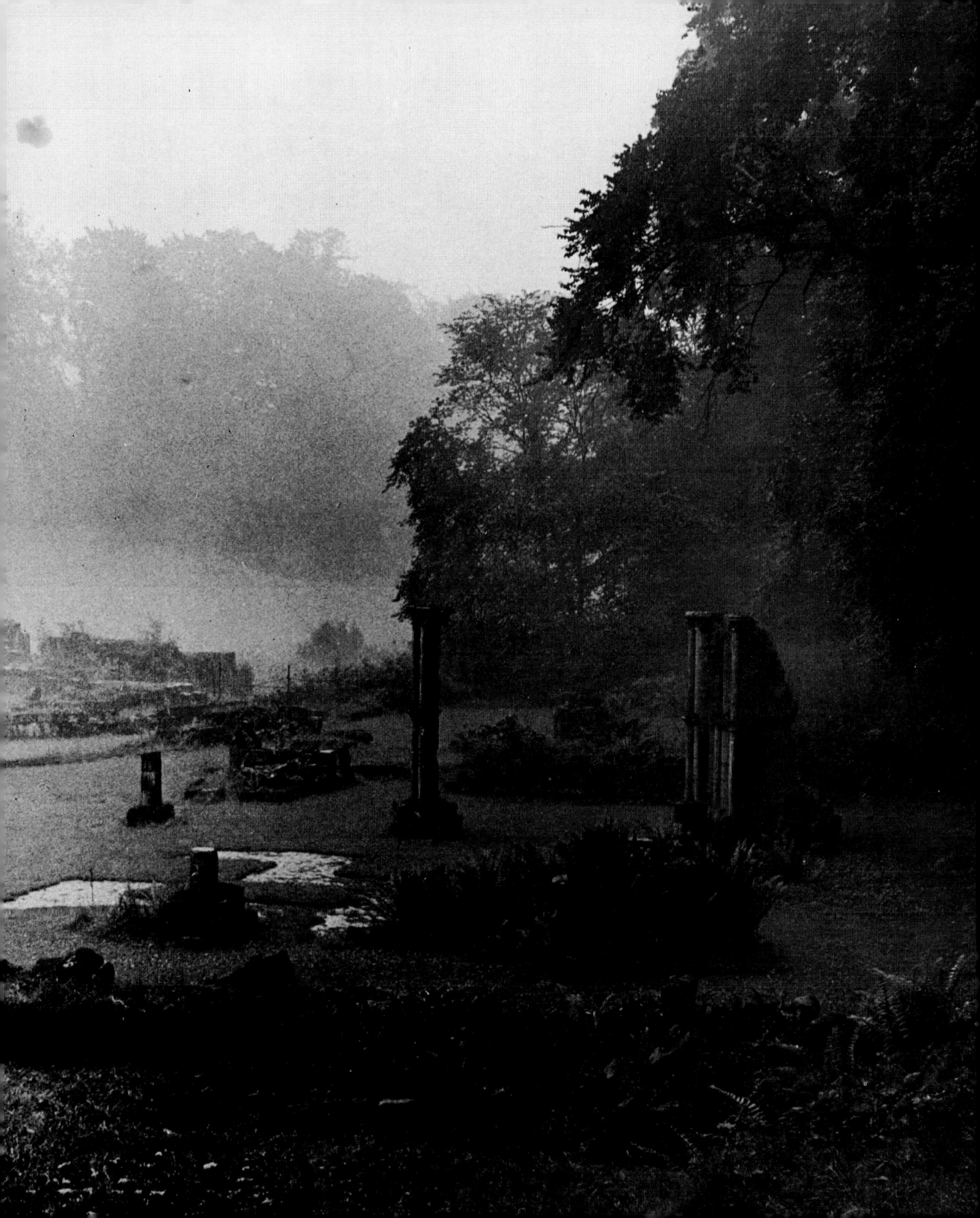

75. WEST WYCOMBE PARK

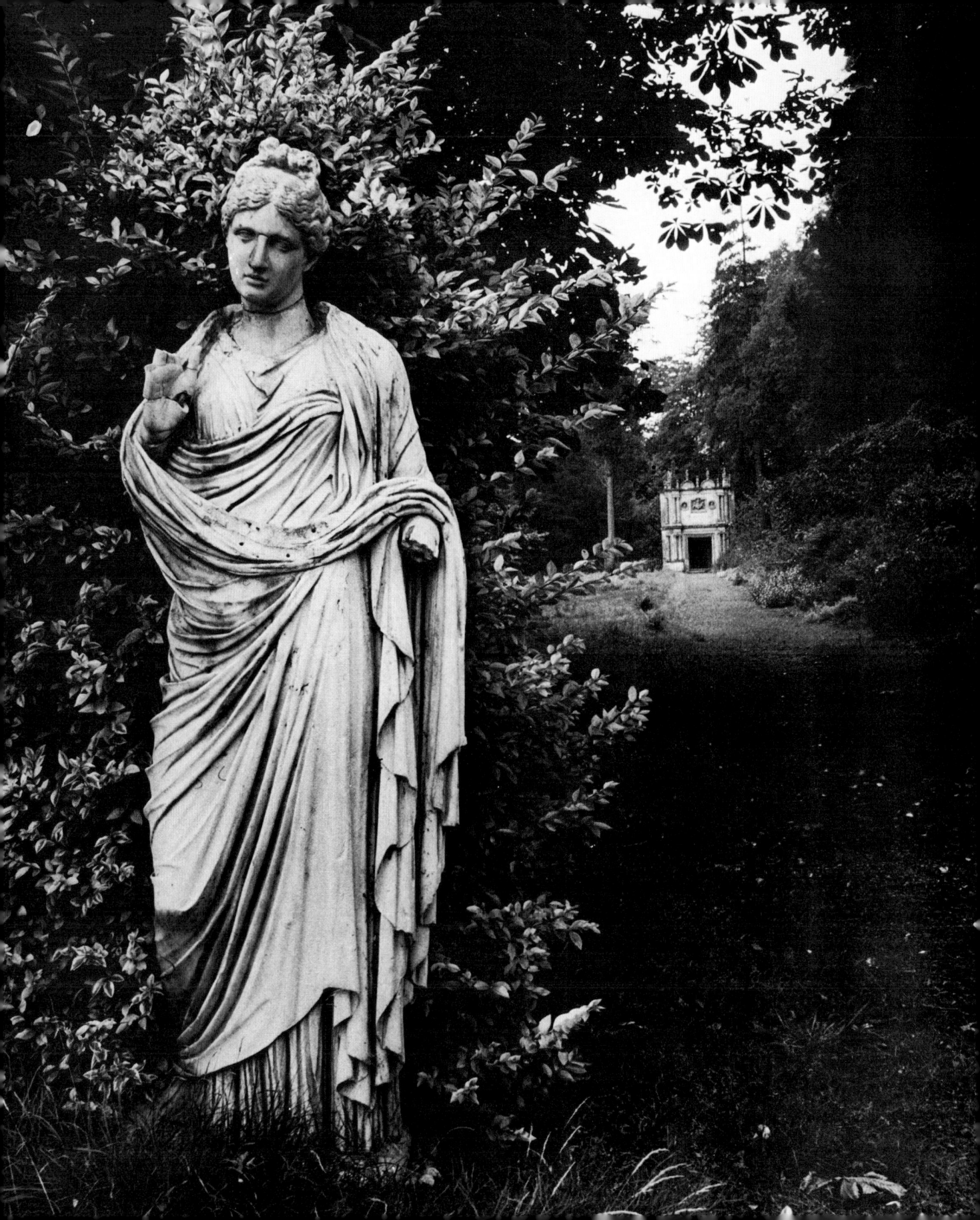

P O E T R Y: Bill Brandt – Photographer, by Tom Hopkinson

Some time in the spring of 1936 a young man came into the office where I was working. He was tall and slim, sunburned, with golden hair brushed back. He had a rather narrow mouth with thin lips, long forehead and chin, and very clear blue eyes. He wore a grey flannel suit, had a voice as loud as a moth, and the gentlest manner to be found outside a nunnery.

Altogether, he did not seem a very likely person to be given a job on a weekly picture paper. However, he carried under his arm a book, and in the book were photographs taken by himself. They were remarkable photographs, and they showed more sharply than I had ever seen before how a human eye and a piece of mechanism can combine, not so much to record the world as to impose a particular vision of the world upon it.

The photographs in the book were pictures of the London scene to which Brandt had lately come quite fresh – the elegant glitter of an evening restaurant, a gipsy on Derby Day asleep under a fence, white-capped maids at a Campden Hill lunch-party, a basement grating gazed through by three small and shrivelled faces, lovers embracing in an attic with a candle alight beside their bed.

The slim young man could take photographs – but so can a number of people who come into editorial offices. He had an eye for social contrasts and he felt them in his heart. So do many of us. On top of all this he had an acceptance of the world for what it is, and took pleasure in the apparition of its surfaces, and the warm contacts of human beings.

From my childhood I remember the phrase used, I believe, by St Paul, of a disappointing collaborator: *Demas hath forsaken me, having loved this present world*. Demas had always seemed to be one of the few Biblical characters whom I should have liked to know better at first hand. There might well be something of Demas about Bill Brandt.

Brandt worked for some weeks on the paper where I then was, and I learned rather more about him. He had been born in Hamburg of English parents.* Education at a German school during the last war had given him Vansittart views about the German people. After five years of serious ill-health in Switzerland – two of them spent entirely in bed – he had moved on to Paris, and had been strongly influenced by the photographers Atget and Man Ray; by the artists Picasso, Braque, and others; by Bunuel and other directors of the new surrealist films.

It was under these Paris influences, perhaps, that Brandt developed what is, for me, the outstanding quality of his work – its sense of mystery. In all the best of Brandt's pictures, which I feel I would choose at once from the work of all other photographers, there is a sense of immanence, of something eery just about to happen.

In the dark shadows of his background there is danger. His highlights are too brilliant to be healthy. This is not the comfortable world we know.

Certain photographs of Brandt's – such as the one of Deborah Kerr on a film set, stepping down hooded in the darkness on to a railway track – seem to belong, a century later, to the works of Edgar Allan Poe.

A sense of justice and social contrast, a keen edge for beauty, an entire absence of cynicism or contempt toward one's fellow human beings, a presentiment of the phantom in the doorway – these are rare gifts with which to start any kind of work, from founding a University to making photographs. Brandt has another, a delicate sense of irony and humour. As he went out of the door, having been commissioned by *Lilliput* to photograph 'London in the Moonlight', Kaye Webb, the assistant editor, remarked: 'And remember, we don't want a lot of whacking great moons floating about all the pictures'.

Brandt gave one of his vague, courteous smiles, and vanished. In six years I have never seen him walk out of a room. He simply smiles – and vanishes. His answer to the advice given him is in these pictures. There is not a single moon, not so much as a silver finger-nail clipping, to be seen in any of them.

From *Lilliput*, August 1942, pp.130,141

---

*Bill Brandt's family lived in Denmark Hill, South London and owned the merchant bank William Brandt and Sons of Fenchurch Street. The photographer's father, L. W.

Brandt, did not join the firm but, as the youngest son, was obliged to make his own way in business. He established himself as a merchant in Hamburg. Bill Brandt and his brother R. A. Brandt – always his closest friend and later his most valued critic – were born there in 1904 and 1906 respectively. As they grew up they heard much from their father, who lived abroad more from necessity than choice, of London, England and English ways. From their mother they gained an appreciation of the arts. She took in art periodicals such as *Das Plakat*, an up to date magazine of graphic, notably poster, art which featured such innovators as Lucian Bernhard, Julius Klinger and Ludwig Hohlwein. As children they also attended drawing lessons at the Kunstgewerbeschule given by K. E. Ort, a Czech artist they much admired. As a British subject L. W. Brandt was interned for part of the first year of the 1914–18 war. Bill Brandt's 'Vansittart', or severely anti-German views, noted by Sir Tom Hopkinson resulted from his intense unhappiness at school, an experience which may also have contributed to his contraction of tuberculosis. He underwent treatment in a sanitorium in Davos for five years, producing some paintings. In 1927 he travelled to Vienna where a psychoanalyst was said to be able to cure T. B. However, Bill Brandt was taken up by a friend of his brother's, Dr Eugenie Schwarzwald. She placed him with a lung specialist. After examination the young man was pronounced fully cured. Dr Schwarzwald then suggested a number of suitable careers for her protegé. When he immediately chose photography she found him a position in a portrait studio in the city. At her house Bill Brandt was introduced to the American poet Ezra Pound. The poet was pleased with the portrait Bill Brandt made of him in 1928 and as a result provided an introduction to Man Ray in Paris. Bill Brandt worked as assistant in Man Ray's studio for some months in 1929. He encountered at first hand the manifestations of Surrealism in cinema and the other arts. He came to London in 1931 already settled on the career of photojournalist.   M H-B

A Retrospect by Tom Hopkinson

During a lifetime of almost eighty years, Bill Brandt did more to establish photography as an art form in its own right than anyone else has ever done. But he did it in his own indirect way, without assertion, almost as if unintentionally, while he got on with his far-ranging programme of work. Few artists in any medium can have achieved more and talked about it less. Though he could enjoy a well-directed tribute, Brandt detested discussion of his own work. He made every excuse to avoid interviews; consented only when pressurised; and then, as in his last year's television interview, smilingly avoided saying anything at all.

It was, I believe, this careful conservation of resources, the preservation of his inner life through a long-sustained refusal to decline into a public figure, which allowed him the energy for a prodigious output, ranging over half-a-dozen photographic continents. He was social commentator; portraitist; photographer of landscape; he explored the nude as no one else has ever done, creating on a flat surface sculptural forms which he subtly related to cliffs, to seashore, to domestic interiors and to a variety of curious accessories.

All this he achieved with a physical apparatus of extreme frailty. His whispering voice; his slender physique which looked scarcely adequate to support his clothes; his gestures of withdrawal, all seemed necessary protection from a world of solid objects to which he did not naturally belong.

Talking to him, I have thought at times that if there should indeed appear among us a visitor from another planet, he would not be some metallic manikin, packed with clanking technological destruction. Outwardly one of ourselves, he would experience difficulty in adapting to our conditions and would therefore suffer much ill-health, which he would endure with patience and good temper. Avoiding open criticism, he would record impressions in pictorial language to alert further visitants from Mercury or Saturn . . .

In each of Brandt's creative periods the sense of mystery, of forces at work beneath the surface of life, pervades. Frightening at times, as in certain portraits, it manifests elsewhere as an added dimension, apparent in the Wuthering Heights farm; the gull's nest in the Isle of Skye; or in that moth with huge eyes on its wings gazing mournfully through the twigs in which it is entangled.

Profoundly impressed by the film 'Citizen Kane', which he saw first in 1943 and many times after that, Brandt quoted with approval Orson Welles' comment: 'The camera is much more than a recording apparatus. It is a medium through which messages reach us from another world'.

A perceptive mind, however, even when coupled with a strong artistic sense, does not produce photographs. Brandt developed and sustained these qualities by remorseless application and a surgical attention to detail. Studying his portrait of Francis Bacon on Primrose Hill it is evident that every aspect of pose, atmosphere and lighting has been organised and contrived.

Memories of Brandt's meticulous method of operating are summed up for me in a small wartime assignment carried out for *Lilliput*. Travel at that time was a fatiguing lottery; one could not be certain of arriving; all one could be sure of was of not getting a seat, or anything to eat and drink. And *Lilliput's* fees to contributors were minimal.

Bill had been asked to go up to Liverpool and photograph a certain Captain Knight, possessor of a tame eagle.

On his return Bill showed me a picture, taken seemingly in twilight in a suburban garden. The owner sat in one chair and opposite him the eagle gripped the back of another in its talons. On a table between them, lighting this cosy but sinister domestic scene, stood an elaborate Victorian oil lamp. Wilkie Collins, Poe or Sheridan Le Fanu might have visualised the setting.

'You were lucky to find that lamp there,' I remarked. 'It makes the picture'.

'I didn't find it there', Bill answered softly. 'I carried it up with me'.

Bill Brandt's indebtedness to happy chance must be the smallest of any great photographer. The tired coal-miner pushing his bicycle uphill with the day's pickings from the tip-heap was, he once said, 'given' him without planning or persuasion. The seagull in early morning mist on the Embankment had been waited for, but could not be contrived. In general though, every picture was planned in the mind before being captured on the negative; often too it was reorganised and reshaped in the darkroom to conform more closely to original intention.

No artist, I believe, has ever gone so far as Bill Brandt did towards imposing on us through a mechanical contrivance his inner vision of our world.

Afterword by Mark Haworth-Booth

The past has become identified with what in Ireland we call 'the better days'.
Imagination finds it a golden terrain.   ELIZABETH BOWEN (1951)

Literary Britain, photographed by Bill Brandt, with an introduction by John Hayward, was published by Cassell and Company Ltd in July 1951. It is a book of one hundred plates, each faced by details about or more usually an extract from a British writer and arranged alphabetically from Matthew Arnold to William Wordsworth. Although the printing is less subtle than the photogravure productions of Bill Brandt's *The English at home* (1936) and *A Night in London* (1938) considerable pains were taken with its making. The plates are full-page, bled to the margins, and measure $9\frac{3}{4} \times 8\frac{1}{4}$ inches (24.7 × 21.1 cms). The text is set in 14 point Bembo. The typography was the work of the Literary Director of Cassell's, Desmond Flower, who (in a sense) commissioned the book. The stately clarity of the design belongs to the school of British typography associated with Stanley Morison, Francis Meynell and Oliver Simon and embodies a care for tradition and materials. On starting at Cassell's in 1930 Flower found that he was sent page proofs of new titles to be passed for press on his signature:

'The proofs laid before me were so ghastly that I refused to sign them, and began by redesigning the title pages before I would allow the books to go forward. This was obviously a waste of time and money, so I decided to design the whole book before the typescript was sent to the printer in the first place ... within days of it becoming known that someone at Cassell's was interested in typography I received my first visitor: Oliver Simon.'

Simon's contributions to typography through his Curwen Press, magazine *Signature* and his books are well known; they include the founding of the Double Crown Club (1924). John Lewis, a member of this genial élite of printing from 1950, was art director at W. S. Cowell Ltd of Ipswich and supervised the production there of *Literary Britain*. The book owes to Lewis two characteristic touches. The letterpress half-tones appear to be printed on a flat tint of very pale grey which provides a platform on which the second, black, working sits to advantage.

Secondly, the text pages are printed on a flat, parchment coloured tint which recalls good-quality Basingwerk papers of the 'Thirties. This contrast achieves two results: reduces the weight of the text and adds life to the black and white illustrations. It also contributes to the traditional air of the volume – and to the price, a steep 45 shillings.

The book came out in late July 1951 and was intended as one of two 'Festival' titles issued by Cassells as part of the celebrations surrounding the Festival of Britain. The other was *Splendid Occasions in English History 1520–1947*, by Ifan Kyrle Fletcher. The character of Cassell's list at this time is shown by the full-page advertisement of new titles which appeared in a remarkable number of *The Times Literary Supplement* on 24 August 1951. The *TLS*, following the general mood of re-assessment occasioned by the Festival of Britain, produced a special series of articles on 'The Mind of 1951'. Cassell's advertisement offered Winston Churchill's Speeches, *A King's Story: The Memoirs of H.R.H. The Duke of Windsor*, *The Gilbert and Sullivan Book* by Leslie Bailey, *The Cruel Sea* by Nicholas Monserrat and the books by Fletcher and Brandt. *Literary Britain* was puffed by John Hadfield in *The Sunday Times* – 'Many [of the photographs] have a breathtaking originality of aspect ... this lovely work of interpretive art' – and *The Irish Times*: 'This sumptuous and beautiful book will delight anybody who is not blind ... an album of beautifully produced photographs'. The *TLS* for 17 August had already noted in 'Books Received' that 'Masses of shadow haunt the reproductions, and sometimes the weather seems to harass the artist: Kelmscott and Clare's birthplace [plate 16] are swathed in greyness. Altogether the subfusc spreads over the picture of homes and haunts'. The advertisement also quoted Tom Hopkinson writing (probably the first published review of the book) in *The Spectator*, for 27 July. Under the title 'A Photographer as Critic' Hopkinson described *Literary Britain* as 'the most distinguished book of photographs that has appeared in this country for some years'. He saw

Brandt as a commentator on the literature with which his photographs are associated:

'But beyond all qualities of literary enjoyment, humour, technical ability, the outstanding impression the book makes is one of beauty. Brandt's gift as a photographer is that he goes straight for the essential, discarding everything not directly connected with his vision. His pictures are almost always simple, sometimes startlingly so, though the means by which he achieves them include a complete understanding of what his cameras will do and a quite unusual mastery of printing technique . . . The negative, however, has been only the beginning. Holding back one part of the picture, stressing another, forcing the sky to lower, folding in darkness some detail that would have made the picture fussy, Brandt must have spent as much as a whole day making a single print – the work of minutes. The result is a severe and moving commentary, exactly adapted to the book form. The book is not a collection of loosely-associated artistic products. It is the work of art itself, and out of it, long after, rise images to haunt the memory.'

Some weeks later Geoffrey Grigson reviewed the book for *The New Statesman and Nation* (1 September) under the title 'The Nail File of Henry James'. 'Literary associations', he suggested, 'are something of a faint, enfeebled substitute for venerated relics. Religious magic in a jewelled reliquary around St Patrick's shin or St Piran's head, art magic in Jane Austen's reticule, Wordsworth's walking stick or the nail file of Henry James'. Was the enterprise not reminiscent, Grigson wondered, of some mid-Victorian book of haunts and homes of English poets? This echo, also discerned or half-discerned by the *TLS*, emanates from William Howitt's *Homes and Haunts of the most eminent British Poets* published in two volumes in 1847 and reprinted in 1847, 1857, 1862 and 1893. Grigson noted a similarity between Howitt's popular and prolix work (illustrated by W. and G. Measom) and *Literary Britain* but also a substantial contrast:

'Mr Brandt, an able photographer, has done it again, with fewer words, wider selection, better illustration and a brisker cunning. The photographs which are best *ad hoc* demand that you know the writings and the character of the writer. The content of association is critical and expandible. It is a compact image.'

Grigson referred to the pairing of Henry James and the Reform Club [plate 35] as an example of this compactness of image.

'For sheer photography Mr Brandt scores about 35 winners out of a hundred. The best of them are the ones least affined to the stock ways of composing a landscape from Turner or Constable down to Munnings or Lamorna Birch. But such stock composition is what pictorial editors demand.'

John Betjeman reviewed the book in *Time and Tide* for 13 October 1951 under the heading 'Only an Idea'.

'. . . Bill Brandt is an impressive photographer. He sees things as an artist, not as some dud aspirer to the Royal Academy of 1908 which is the standard of most photographers of Britain Beautiful. He knows how to compose a picture on a page. He does not use the dreary camera-club technique – tree in the right foreground, sky two-thirds of the background, long shadows and a title like "It Ringeth to Eventide". He owes much to those serious documentary and abstract photographers of the 'thirties like Man Ray and Moholy-Nagy. But he has his own vision.'

However, despite the excellence of most of the photographs, the book looked to Betjeman 'only an idea and probably a publisher's idea, born of a wise wish to publish Bill Brandt's photographs and at the same time to catch the tourist. It is the idea that spoils the book for it should not have been so literary. Not even Mr Brandt can make a beautiful photograph of so dull a house as Shaw's Corner [plate 56]; Bemerton Rectory looks more neo-Georgian than George Herbert'. Betjeman recognised the publication as 'a festival book' and thought the price put it 'out of the reach of most British people'. In *The Observer* (12 August 1951) Naomi Lewis wondered at the exclusion of certain authors – 'Herrick, Marvell, Gissing might have tempted him, you would think. And favouring as he does a moroseness as well as a richness in the landscape, why has Mr Brandt passed so slightly over Tennyson [plate 59], most topographical of poets? But what is good is magnificent.'

Recollections by those involved in publishing and printing *Literary Britain* are not unanimous on the question of the print-run, varying between 1500 and 3000 copies but a traveller for Cassell's recalls that the trade responded well with window displays, especially in areas strongly represented in the photographs. There was no separate U.S. edition.

None of the reviews refers to John Hayward, who introduced the book and (for the most part at least) wrote or assembled the texts which face each plate. The book was recognised as the work of Bill Brandt. However, John Hayward's contribution was not negligible. Parts of his introductory essay are reprinted earlier in the present volume and he showed the range and depth of his reading in choosing appropriate quotations. John Hayward (1904–65), awarded the CBE in the Coronation Honours of 1953 for his services to English literature, was described in an obituary in *The Times* (18 September 1965) as 'an anthologist, critic and editor whose enthusiasm, judgement and scholarship made him outstanding in his generation among connoisseurs of good writing and good book production'. For about ten years he shared with T. S. Eliot a flat overlooking the Thames in Cheyne Walk and 'a visit to 19 Carlyle Mansions was a required *acte de presence* for any bibliophile visitor in London'. His most notable publications are his Nonesuch Press editions of Donne and Swift, the *Penguin Book of English Verse* (1956), the *Oxford Book of Nineteenth-Century Verse*, and – in the opinion of his friend Nicolas Barker – 'the famous catalogue of the National Book League poetry Exhibition in 1947, which will remain the most individual and permanent single monument of his work'. The poet Kathleen Raine wrote of him:

'He liked to describe himself as a 'man of letters', regretting that the phrase could no longer be used (as the French say *homme de lettres*) without its seeming affected; but it is (so with his death we sadly realise) not the word but the thing itself which has almost ceased (between academic professionalism and the illiteracy, real or affected, of a new generation of writers) to exist. "I have read the whole of English poetry, *twice*", John claimed with justifiable pride; adding that his anthologies contained most that was worth reading at all. . . . The style he set for himself and others is perhaps best described in a line of [T. S. Eliot's] *Little Gidding*, whose authorship he claimed:

The formal word, precise but not pedantic'

Hayward was a general provider of material for all manner of celebrations of 'Literary Britain' including an exhibition held at the V & A for the Festival of Britain and details and quotations for a pictorial map on 'Literary Britain' designed for '51 by Kerry Lee. Among typical good works of the period was Hayward's letter to the Archbishop of Canterbury (5 October 1949) giving a character reference in favour of Sonia Brownell in support of the application for a special licence for her marriage to George Orwell.

Desmond Flower went to Hayward for the text of *Literary Britain* because, a long-standing friendship apart, he was an obvious choice. However, it appears from the researches of David Mellor that Bill Brandt had thought of bringing his photographs of the subject together in book form some time before and had hoped to work with Geoffrey Grigson. Brandt and Grigson were both regular contributors to the magazine *Lilliput* in the 1940s and Grigson supplied captions for a Brandt picture set on 'The Poet's Crib' (birth places of writers from John Clare and Elizabeth Barrett Browning to D. H. Lawrence) in *Lilliput* for March 1948 and for the set 'Six Artists', opening with Henry Moore, for the same magazine in June 1948. Among enthusiasms shared by photographer and critic were the poetry of John Clare and the sculpture of Henry Moore. Brandt's appreciation of Clare – he knew some of the poems by heart – may have developed because of Grigson's brief but eloquent account of the poet in *Lilliput* for September 1945. It seems unlikely that Brandt could have missed Grigson's essay on Henry Moore in the *Penguin Modern Artist* series (1943) which is concluded as follows:

'There is a statement which fits the work of Henry Moore:

"Nature is played out as a Beauty, but not as a Mystery . . . I don't want to see the original realities – as optical effects, that is. I want to see the deeper realities underlying the scenic, the expression of what are sometimes called abstract imaginings"

And it was made by Thomas Hardy many years ago.'
Brandt was especially attached to Hardy's novels. Desmond Flower confesses to a memory like a sieve but thought that he might have been drawn to Brandt's work by the series on Hardy's 'Wessex'. These he would have seen first in *Lilliput* (May 1946). Flower visited Hardy at Max Gate as a boy – his father was a friend of the novelist.

Thinking back in 1984, Flower thought that Brandt probably worked on *Literary Britain* for about three months – 'with enormous excitement'. Flower suggested the site of the illustration to Chaucer, the 'Pilgrims' Way' in the Kentish Weald, and took Brandt for a picnic there, presumably in the summer or autumn of 1950. He recalls that Brandt himself suggested photographing Berkeley Castle (as illustration to Marlowe, via *Edward II*: plate 46). It is likely that subjects were nominated also by Hayward. However, *Literary Britain* chiefly assembles the results of a whole series of assignments Brandt undertook during the middle 1940s for the magazines *Lilliput*, *Picture Post* and *Harper's Bazaar*. Final touches were added late in 1950, the last picture probably being that of Shaw's Corner (Shaw died on 2 November 1950; no living authors were included in the book). A couple of postcards from Lawrence Durrell to John Hayward, written soon after publication of the book, show that the idea of such a book existed earlier in 1950 but that no publisher had yet been found. Asking Hayward to 'filch' a copy from Cassell's if possible, Durrell added 'I think the original idea was mine – at least I proposed it very forcefully to Faber twice last year. Perhaps T S E [T. S. Eliot] passed the idea on?' On receipt of the book Durrell's hopes were fulfilled: 'The marvellous book arrived and I am in heaven. What a genius Brandt is . . .' In a card to the present writer he noted that 'I first realised his stature when I saw the Haworth spread in *Lilliput*.' He thought Faber might have been put off by the production expenses. He never met Brandt.

The production of the photographs which make up *Literary Britain* owes most to Bill Brandt's happy and fruitful working relationship with Tom Hopkinson and Kaye Webb at *Lilliput*. 'I hardly ever take photographs except on an assignment', Brandt wrote in his introduction to *Camera in London* (1948). 'It is not that I do not get pleasure from the actual taking of photographs, but rather that the necessity of fulfilling a contract – the sheer *having* to do a job – supplies an incentive, without which the taking of photographs just for fun seems to leave the fun rather flat'. *Lilliput* provided a constant stream of assignments during the 'Forties, the decade in which demand for Brandt's work was at its peak. Tom Hopkinson has told the story of the foundation of the magazine in the first instalment of his autobiography *Of This Our Time: A Journalist's Story, 1905–50* (1982). This cheerful, sometimes serious and generally civilised pocket magazine, now classified with the rare books collections in the British Library, was thought up and first edited by Stefan Lorant, already the founder-editor of *Weekly Illustrated* (in whose office Hopkinson and Brandt first met) and to become founder-editor of *Picture Post* in 1938. *Lilliput*, 'the pocket magazine for everyone', began its monthly appearance in July 1937. Less than a year later Lorant sold the magazine to Hulton Press and began to devise *Picture Post*. *Lilliput* offered ten articles, ten short stories, ten cartoons and colour plates and 40 photographs. Photography was fundamental to all of Lorant's schemes and *Lilliput* treated the medium with understanding and respect from the first. An abstract street view by Moholy-Nagy appeared in the first issue together with photographs from the early documentary series *Street Life in London* by John Thomson (1877–78). The first photograph by Brandt appeared in September 1937. His photographs from Spain appeared in November 1937, from Hungary in February and March 1938. In 1938 Brandt's second book, *A Night in London*, appeared and the magazine ran eight photographs from it (June). This was the first occasion on which a photo-series on one theme by one photographer appeared in the magazine. The format was used many times over the next ten years and these picture sets – sometimes ten, sometimes even 12 – later provided the backbone of *Literary Britain*. Relatively poor printing in the early issues was replaced from August 1938, thanks to Hulton funding, with high quality rotogravure. The process was ideal for Brandt's dense blacks and twilit mid-tones. From early on the magazine introduced 'camera artists' – such as Erwin Blumenfeld (July 1938) and Cecil Beaton (January 1939) – with special spreads of six or eight pictures but it is noticeable that for special assignments *Lilliput* almost invariably went to Brandt. 'Unchanging London' (May 1939) offered latter-day photographic illustrations taken by Brandt as companion pieces to the wood engravings of Gustave Doré (*London*, 1870). In December 1939 'We asked Bill Brandt, one of the most brilliant of English camera-artists, to capture the spirit of the blackout in one set of pictures'. This series of photographs of London lit only by the moon seems to inaugurate the twilight characteristic of war-time painting. At the present writer's request the historian Martin Harrison recently asked John Piper whether he could detect the influence of his work on Brandt's landscape photography: 'Quite possibly it was the other way round' was the characteristically

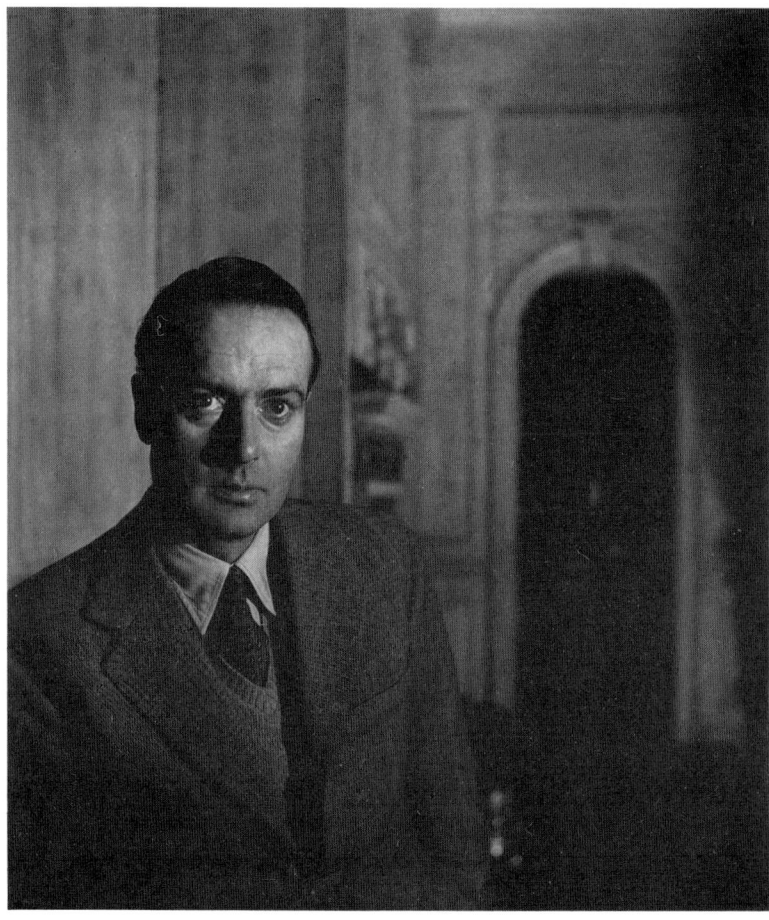

Tom Hopkinson, 1950. Photograph by Bill Brandt.

modest reply. The moonlit landscapes of Samuel Palmer received new resonance in the etchings of Graham Sutherland during the 'Thirties and became a notable influence on wartime painting, but perhaps Brandt was the innovator in transferring Romantic moonlight to the actuality of Blackout. As Tom Hopkinson recalls elsewhere in this catalogue, a further set of photographs of London by moonlight was commissioned in 1942. Twilight was to become a feature of the British landscape at large in Brandt's photographs.

One landscape, 'November in the Country', appeared in Brandt's first book *The English at Home* (1936) – an ordinary scene of field and copse tinged with mist; a well placed marker of climate and spirit of place. Landscape made its appearance in *Lilliput* in May 1940 with views by Dixon-Scott, prolific but unremarkable provider of post-cards of the sort Betjeman describes as 'Britain Beautiful'. In August 1941 a photograph by Brandt presented swans of heraldic whiteness at 'Runneymede – where ghosts walk'. In September followed a Brandt photograph – man in panama hat at the sea margin – with lines an editor (perhaps Kaye Webb) could not resist: 'I grow old . . . I grow old . . . I shall wear the bottom of my trousers rolled' (etc.). This is probably the first time one of his photographs was presented as an illustration of literature. In December *Lilliput* published Brandt's portraits of 'Young Poets of Democracy': Stephen Spender, C. Day Lewis, Dylan Thomas, Louis MacNeice, Alun Lewis, Anne Ridler,

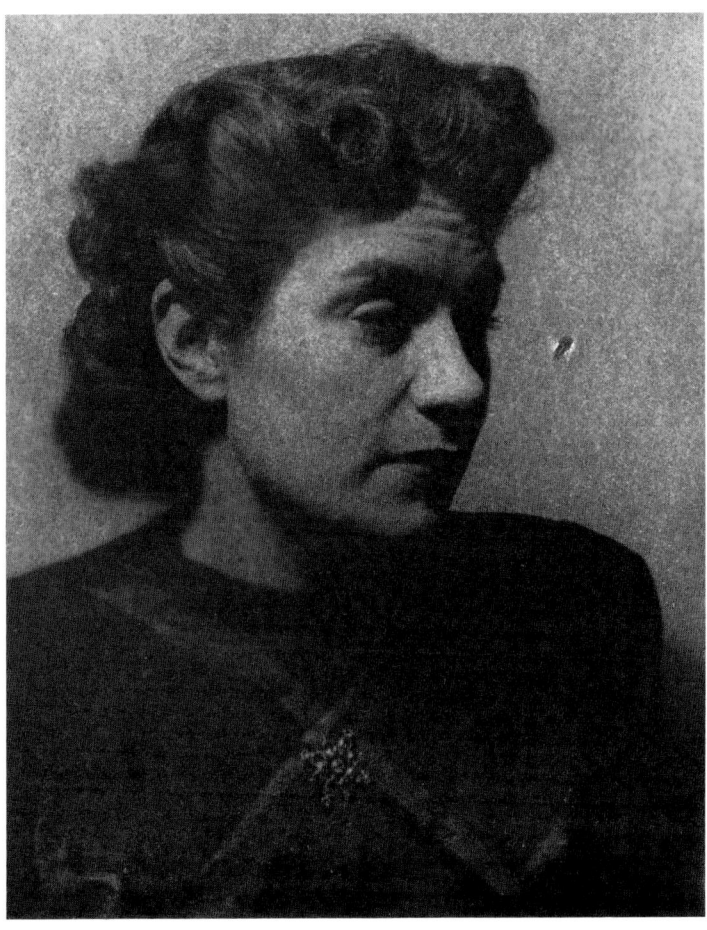

Kaye Webb, 1942. Photograph by Bill Brandt.

Laurie Lee, William Empson, – representatives of the Auden Generation but also the poets in reaction to them, outstandingly Thomas, whom Cyril Connolly named the 'new romantics'. Brandt read John Lehmann's *Penguin New Writing* regularly and Tom Hopkinson kept him abreast of interesting new writing elsewhere, such as Connolly's *Horizon* where Hopkinson's short stories were published – and in turn, in February 1942, Brandt's views of London by moonlight.

Reading through *Lilliput* it becomes clear that although landscape and portraits of writers, also of painters and composers, form an impressive, probably the most impressive, concentration of Brandt's efforts in the 'Forties, he was asked to tackle a variety of themes. Or, of course, suggested them himself. 'A simple story about a girl' which tells in eight pictures of the meeting and courtship of Mary and a sergeant called Jack (ending with two deserted chairs in a park – naturally in twilight and with 'a whacking great moon') was Kaye Webb's idea: 'something cheerful for the forces'. It appeared in September 1941. Brandt's first published nude, shot through muslin, appeared in February 1942; 'Soho in wartime – eights bits of a quarter' in April 1942; 'The explorer' (a ferret improbably caught creeping over a fence) in June 1942; a cartoon-like picture called 'The Measure of Man' (Hermann Goering – 'fifty seven inches of brawn' – being tape measured in the demonology of Madame Tussaud's) in October 1941; 'The Sleeper' – Brandt's first wife Eva asleep while searchlights pattern the night sky – in July 1941; 'Dangling' – a gnome angling – a backlit sow, a tired filly, etc., and substantial series on flowers (text by Stephen Spender, September 1942) and 'Back stage at the Windmill' in October 1942. The variety of pictorial journalism offered by *Lilliput* earned it a print order of 300,000 by January 1940.

Kaye Webb, assistant editor from 1938 to 1947, recalls that Brandt would appear regularly at the office and ask if a theme he had in mind would be acceptable; they always were. 'He thought lyrically and in series that hung together well'. He would return with eight (occasionally ten) photographs for a lay-out of eight, the pictures already sequenced by himself and with almost nothing spare for editing or cropping. Kaye Webb, who described herself recently as rather ebullient as a young woman, cropped a photograph of his *once* – to be told 'If you don't like anything, *ask* me'. The admonition was very gentle and both unforgettable and unchallengeable.

Despite the range of Brandt's wartime and post-war photography the most resonant spreads are of landscape, architecture and literary association. A photograph by Brandt prefaced 'A Dream of Winter', with a text commissioned from Dylan Thomas, in January 1942. Brandt's portrait of Edinburgh, with text by Sacheverell Sitwell, followed as 'The Northern Capital in Winter' in February 1942. September 1943 brought 'The Gardens of England' from which the picture of Garsington [plate 45] later provided an illustration to Lawrence in *Literary Britain*. In May 1945 'Bill Brandt visits the Brontë Country' – eight photographs [see plates 6–12] with quotations. (The opening shot of 'Wuthering Heights' faces an article titled 'Confessions of a Sewage Farmer' – facetiousness mixed easily with high fiction in these pages). 'Hampstead under Snow' in February 1946 featured streets and houses associated with writers but yielded nothing for the book. 'Thomas Hardy's Wessex' [see plates 28–33] was published in May 1946, following the pattern of eight photographs with quotations from the novels. Four of the Wessex photographs from this set are illustrated in this catalogue. 'The Beauty and Sadness of Connemara' in March 1947 ran to twelve pages with – for the first time – a prose commentary by Brandt himself but yielded nothing for the book (which was defined precisely as Literary *Britain*). 'Connemara peasants', wrote Brandt, 'have to pay in poverty for the beauty of their country'. 'Over the Sea to Skye' appeared in November 1947, again with Brandt's commentary. The eight published pictures included Lord Macdonald's Forest, Graveyard at Strath and the Sea-Gull's Nest, all illustrated in this volume [plates 38, 39, 5] and Skye Mountains, the photograph later used to publicise the exhibition *The Land*. The series included a photograph of a Highland Cow observing the photographer attentively from a bog. Speaking of his patience, Bill Brandt's friend Frances Rice recently remarked that 'Bill was prepared to stand in a bog longer than any highland cow'.

'The Poet's Crib' already referred to appeared in March 1948. From this series the photographs associated with Elizabeth Barrett Browning, Sir Philip Sidney and John Clare were published in *Literary Britain* [plates 13, 57 and, a variant view, 16]. A photograph of D. H. Lawrence's birth-place in Nottingham appeared; it was taken at ground level. The view preferred for *Literary Britain* [plate 44] was apparently taken from a window across the street, or some other relatively high vantage point. The downward view emphasises the shut-in, constricted nature of the street. This in turn makes more sense of the contrasting Lawrence photograph of Garsington Manor [plate 45].

'Peter Grimes Country' in June 1948 [see plates 19–21] is the last in Brandt's series of portraits of places of literary association. The *Lilliput* commission was prompted by the inauguration in June that year of the Aldeburgh Festival, founded by Benjamin Britten, Eric Crozier and Peter Pears. Brandt had photographed Britten in 1946 and his portrait of John Piper appeared in this same issue of the magazine. Piper was much associated with the Aldeburgh Festival and designer of the sets and costumes of *Albert Herring*, the centre-piece of the first Festival. It was probably through Piper that the Festival programme book – one of the earliest and most pleasing efforts of John Lewis as designer – carried eight new photographs of Aldeburgh by Bill Brandt. At Aldeburgh Romantic art was represented by an exhibition of paintings by Constable, and the new Romantic art of the 1940s by an exhibition of contemporary painting by an impressive gathering of East Anglian artists. Introducing the exhibition, John Piper wrote of the vision of the old masters of eastern England – Crome, Constable, Cotman and Stark – as 'still alive in painters working in their home counties' and noted the influence on even the most abstract painters of 'the colour of earth and the materials of buildings – the weather boarding, plaster and pantile'. Brandt's photographs at Aldeburgh, and throughout *Literary Britain*, show a similar regard for traditional materials. In *Lilliput* the photographs were presented alongside a short history of the Borough by George Goldsmith Carter and quotations from George Crabbe's descriptive poem *The Borough* (1810) from which Montagu Slater devised the opera libretto of *Peter Grimes* (composed by Britten at Snape during 1944 and early 1945).

Brandt's landscape photographs are as indelibly part of their period as the operas of Britten and the contemporary works of Piper. They are part of the dream of the decade. Perhaps Brandt's photographs informed the works of writers. His *Seagull's Nest* from Skye may have flickered at the edge of Louis MacNeice's imagination when the poet wrote *Day of Renewal* (between March 1950 and April 1951):

> . . . a wild nest
> Further, more truly west, on a bare height
> Where nothing need be useful and the breakers
> Came and came but never made any progress
> And children were reborn each night.

The same photograph seems to have struck a contemporary nerve in America too, where it was published full-page by *Harper's Bazaar* with an unlikely 'excuse' of context – an article on 'The British Export Drive' (July 1948 – the caption brings in Harris Tweed as a local industry). Hollywood paid 'literary Britain' one of its more princely tributes with the 1939 *Wuthering Heights* (with Laurence Olivier and Merle Oberon) finely photographed by Gregg Toland, whose wide-angle camera work on *Citizen Kane* was to impress Brandt so decisively. Brandt's Brontë Country made its way into the American edition of *Harper's Bazaar* in October and December 1946; 'The Hardy Country' had been featured in the previous March. Edward Steichen exhibited Bill Brandt's photographs at the Museum of Modern Art, New York in 1948 with work by three other photographers – Lisette Model, Harry Callahan and Ted Croner – and wrote in the press release:

'Bill Brandt's photographs record his experience and highly sensitized reactions to the subject material. He translates into the modern idiom of the camera the atmosphere and mood of person, moment and place, often with nostalgic suggestions of other periods and influences. He creates an emotional atmosphere within the photograph, and this is heightened by extension of that atmosphere beyond the boundaries of the photograph.'

Edward Steichen's successor as Director of Photography at The Museum of Modern Art, John Szarkowski, gave landscapes due prominence in his Bill Brandt retrospective exhibition twenty years later and quite recently wrote Brandt what he calls 'simply a fan letter': 'The winds of chance have led me to look closely at *Literary Britain* for the first time in years, and it was wonderful to discover again how very good it is. Perhaps it is even better than I knew when I was merely middle-aged' (4 March 1982).

Edward Steichen's horribly vague word 'atmosphere' was probably provided for him ready-made by Brandt himself. In the most interesting introduction Brandt wrote for his *Camera in London* (1948), he described how he found a subject that awakened his strongest interests:

'I always had an interest in architecture, so that early in my career I photographed buildings. But my pictures did not satisfy me. I looked upon the work then as the recording of buildings and as records my pictures were adequate. Yet they lacked something, some quality which I could not name and only vaguely felt would have given me pleasure. So I turned to landscapes. I am not sure why I did this, because although I appreciate the beauties of the countryside I have never thought of myself as a lover of nature. And yet here was a seeming paradox. Something in these pictures of landscapes pleased me, although I had no great interest in the subject matter. Slowly a new development took place. Almost without my realising it stone-work began to encroach upon my landscapes. Little by little – a milestone, the tombs in a churchyard, a distant house in a park – until there was a fusion, not consciously sought by myself, of the subject that interested me and that indefinable something which gave me pleasure – aesthetic or emotional, or call it what you will. I began to feel that I might produce good pictures.

The trouble had been, as I have since realised, that I came to architecture in the first place with preconceived ideas; while with landscapes I had an unprejudiced eye.

Thus it was I found *atmosphere* to be the spell that charged the commonplace with beauty. And still I am not sure what atmosphere is. I should be hard put to define it. I only know it is a combination of elements, perhaps most simply and yet most inadequately described in technical terms of lighting and viewpoint, which reveals the subject as familiar and yet strange. I doubt whether atmosphere, in the meaning it has for me, can be conveyed by a picture of something which is quite unfamiliar to the beholder. The photograph of the unknown – such photographs as those taken with a microscopic attachment of lowly forms of life or such as a close-up of the heart of a cabbage – seldom arouses in the spectator any emotion beyond bewilderment or curiosity or perhaps a logical attraction or repulsion. While if it does not show the subject in a new light, the photograph is dead, a record on the flat print and nothing more.

Everyone has at some time or another felt the atmosphere of a room. If one comes with a heightened awareness, prepared to lay oneself open to their influence, other places too can exert the same power of association. It may be of association with a person, with simple human emotions, with the past or some building looked at long ago, or even with a scene only imagined or dreamed of. This sense of association can be so sharp that it arouses an emotion almost like nostalgia. And it is this that gives drama or atmosphere to a picture . . .

When I have seen or sensed – I do not know which it is – the atmosphere of my subject, I try to convey that atmosphere by intensifying the elements that compose it. I lay emphasis on one aspect of my subject and I find that I can thus most effectively arrest the spectator's attention and induce in him an emotional response to the atmosphere I have tried to convey . . .

I am not very interested in extraordinary angles. They can be effective on certain occasions, but I do not feel the necessity for them in my own work. Indeed, I feel the simplest approach can often be most effective. A subject placed squarely at the centre of the frame, if attention is not distracted from it by fussy surroundings, has a simple dignity which makes it all the more impressive.'

The quotation may seem excessively long but it gives a good idea of the characteristic movement of Bill Brandt's mind, his simplicity, clarity (lack of pomposity) and intensely Romantic sensibility. The word 'atmosphere' was also good enough for one of the most practiced writers on art among Brandt's contemporaries. John Piper wrote in *British Romantic Artists* (1942) of the suppression by 'Thirties modernism of a native need for 'literary interest and atmosphere'. In both Brandt and Piper there is a transfer from bombed ruins to a prior, ordered sense of piously observed picturesque decay and forcefully Gothick imaginings. One of the lithographic illustrations by Piper for *English Scottish and Welsh Landscape*, poetry from 1700 to *c.* 1860 chosen by John Betjeman and Geoffrey Taylor (published 1944), provides a conspectus of motifs which occur repeatedly in Brandt's photographs. *Tomen-y-Mur and Roman Amphitheatre* shows an ancient earthwork, a dry-stone wall, exposed cottages and barns, a sombre sheet of water, darkened hills and bad weather – all arranged in stacked bands. Brandt was knowledgeable about English and Continental paintings and sculpture. The deserted, war-emptied square occupied by Burslem Town Hall seems to owe less to the 'Five Towns' of Arnold Bennett than to Brandt's well-attested interest in De Chirico and his shadowed piazzas, while the beech copses on the Wiltshire skyline seen from Barbary Castle echo the 'Wittenham Clumps' in Oxfordshire which fill so many canvases by Paul Nash in the years 1943–44. The convergence of Picturesque and Surrealist is well established in Nash's images of the prehistoric megaliths at Avebury (1934–37) which the painter describes as 'personages . . . the stones have a character influenced by the conditions of Dream' (Tate Gallery catalogue, *Paul Nash: paintings and watercolours*, 1975, page 84). Bill Brandt photographed the same megaliths from much the same convergence of interests.

Brandt's photograph of the effect of snow on the silhouettes of the darkened forms of Stonehenge was recognised by Tom Hopkinson as a graphic symbol adequate to the grim realities of Spring 1947. The photograph appeared on the cover of *Picture Post* for 19 April 1947. An article in this Crisis Issue of the magazine asked 'How Long must Austerity Last?' and described the legacy of the war:

'Great Britain may be compared to a man whose house (uninsured) has been seriously damaged by fire, who has lost a large part of his invested savings and run heavily into debt, yet is shocked to find that he is a good deal poorer than before these disasters befell him. To complete the picture, he is short of the materials needed

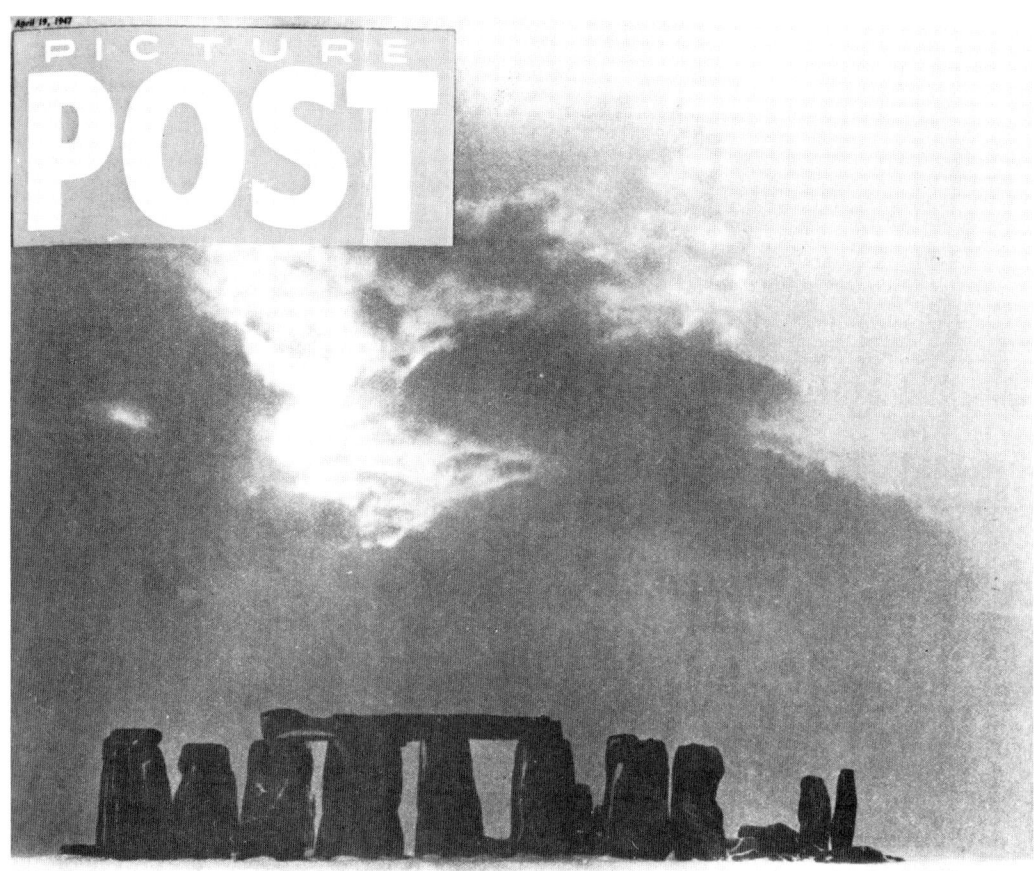

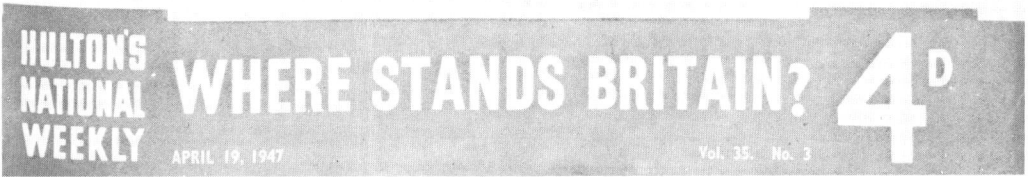

Picture Post, 19 April 1947. Cover photograph by Bill Brandt.

for rebuilding, his morale has deteriorated and with it his ability to make the best use of his resources.

Besides loss of life, the war cost this country something like one-quarter of our accumulated national wealth.' Another article, 'How did we get into this Mess?', summarised the position: 'The crisis is deep-rooted. Only its intensity is new. Only a great united effort can pull us out of it'. Brandt's Tyneside (1937) photograph of a miner pushing his bicycle wearily home faces the article full-page: 'The Wasted Years: The Man who might have been hewing coal in tons, scratches for ounces on the slag heaps'. Under Hopkinson's editorship Brandt became not only an illustrator of English literature but, so it appears now, an interpreter of national consciousness. The bleak and depleted landscape of austerity owed its most striking emblem to Stonehenge, Bill Brandt and the fall of snow for which he had waited some years. 'I'd always planned to photograph Stonehenge under snow', Brandt told Hopkinson. 'The cold would mean there were no visitors, and the snow would obliterate so much that's distracting and unnecessary'. The photograph was taken in the bitter January of 1947.

The graphic simplification of Stonehenge and its appearance as cover of a large format popular magazine is, of course, a form of posterisation. One of Bill Brandt's enthusiasms during the 'Thirties was the poster art of E. McKnight Kauffer – a man who, like Brandt, combined a singular privateness with a commanding public style intended to reach a large audience. Characterstic Kauffer subjects during the 'Thirties were shadowed, geometrical renderings of ancient buildings like the Tower of London and a starlit Stonehenge. It may be mentioned here that Kauffer was named a Royal Designer for Industry in the first awards made by the Royal Society of Arts in 1936. This honour, originally intended to be equivalent to that of Royal Academician, was conferred on Bill Brandt in 1978.

As with Lilliput, Brandt carried out a wide range of stories for Picture Post other than those concerning landscape or monuments. The BBC Hulton Picture Library preserves the negatives of many assignments and a series of folders of the contact sheets. Wartime stories included 'Spring in the Park' (10 May 1941) showing Hyde Park covered with rubble. Portrait shots (Glynis Johns), the Army Suitability Test, the Stirling Bomber, Fire Guards

on the House of Commons, A Town that Takes Care of its Troops and Saving Britain's Plum Crop, these suggest something of the range of Brandt's assignments for the magazine. Assignments which may have furthered Brandt's collection of photographs more or less associated with 'Literary Britain' are 'The Threat to the Roman Wall' (23 October 1943), the National Trust (22 January 1944), Fountains Abbey (28 September 1946), 'The Horizon of Richard Jefferies' (6 November 1948) and 'The Vanished Ports of England' (24 September 1949).

The English edition of Harper's Bazaar often published Brandt's photographs of country houses and gardens. 'The Forsaken Garden' appeared in June 1944. 'Our war-neglected gardens, with their overgrown paths, their lawns now pastures, their unclipped bushes and shrubberies, have a sad poetic beauty which would have delighted the original landscape gardeners of the Eighteenth Century'. Brandt photographed the strangeness of unkempt topiary ('In those times') and Bowood, Wiltshire, the lake at Stowe, Highcliffe Castle and Prior Park, Bath. The Prior Park photograph, taken after a day photographing bomb damage at Bath, originally appeared in Lilliput in April the previous year. Brandt constantly reused his photographs where appropriate and there seems to have been small concern among the magazines over repetition. For example, Brandt's portraits of 'Young Poets of Democracy' reappeared in Harper's (June 1945) to illustrate Stephen Spender's article 'The Common Reader and the Modern Poet' although Brandt used a variant study of Dylan Thomas and added a portrait of T. S. Eliot. After looking at Picture Post and Harper's Bazaar it is clear that Lilliput took the key role in forming the 'Literary Britain' collection.

Three and possibly four photographers have a bearing on Brandt's photographs of 'Literary Britain'. Atget he knew about from his days in Man Ray's Paris studio and the passage of time, momentarily suspended by certain conditions of lens, light and geometry, became one of Brandt's persistent interests. As a working photo-journalist of the 'Thirties and after Brandt is most closely linked with Brassai. His emphatic style of printing favoured the chiaroscuro effects characteristic of Brassai. The so-called 'Vitalist' landscapes of Edward Weston, with extravagantly orchestrated shadows, may play a substantial part in Brandt's print-making in the photographs of 'Literary

Britain'. The photographic press apart, Weston's work was introduced to the English public by John Davenport. Whereas Hopkinson profiled Brandt in *Lilliput* under the heading 'Poetry', Weston was thought to qualify as 'Genius'. Davenport's article and a set of photographs appeared in *Lilliput* in November 1942. The West Coast art dealer Howard Putzel introduced Davenport to Weston in 1936 when the English writer immediately bought two prints. He gave Weston a copy of William Empson's *Seven Types of Ambiguity* and received in return Weston's first book of photographs (published 1932, now in the collection of the painter R. B. Kitaj, London). *Lilliput* published one of Weston's decisively shadowed Oceano dune-scapes in April 1943. Brandt always spoke enthusiastically of these photographers. An unlikely fourth was suggested by Lawrence Durrell on first looking into Brandt's *Literary Britain*: 'only one other photographer in the world has nearly as much sensibility as him – Herbert List . . .' Such photographs as Brandt's 'Gull's Nest, Skye' almost preclude stylistic analysis by their perfection but if there is any substantial photographic anticipation of the composition of Brandt's masterpiece it is List's 'Goldfischglas, Santorin' (1937). This photograph was handsomely reproduced in *Photographie 1940*, the annual brought out by Brandt's Paris publishers Arts et Métiers Graphiques (1939) which also included pictures by Brandt. The subject is a close-up still life – a goldfish swimming in a bowl placed on a sea-wall – a stretch of sea, and the dark outline of a distant island. List used the same equipment as Brandt, a Rolleiflex, and very probably a Proxar close-up lens. The comparison may be far-fetched but it is not intended to suggest that Brandt did other than note the possibility of the kind of photograph List had produced. Equally, he could have noted Paul Nash's use of the same elements of composition during the mid 'Forties.

Technically, Brandt seems to have owed much to the approach of Man Ray. This was described by Lee Miller in an article called 'I worked with Man Ray' in *Lilliput* in October 1941. Noting Man Ray's allegiance to Dada and Surrealism she wrote: 'his lack of respect for his material and his irreverence of reality is in this tradition . . . whether he just presses the button and lets someone else do the rest, or manipulates the prints and negatives in the lab himself, fiddling with formulae and control – he is interested in the end, not the means'. I have seen only one

solarised photograph by Brandt – that side of Man Ray's work he did not pursue – but he was a tireless experimenter in the darkroom. 'I consider it essential that the photographer should do his own printing and enlarging', he wrote in *Camera in London*. 'The final effect of the finished print depends so much on these operations. And only the photographer himself knows the effects he wants. He should know by instinct, grounded in experience, what subjects are enhanced by hard or soft, light or dark treatment'. The 6×6cm negative of the Rolleiflex, which he always used stopped down to the smallest aperture possible under existing lighting conditions and usually therefore on a tripod, provided Brandt ample scope for darkroom manipulation. An example of his methods is the illustration to Kipling's *Puck of Pook's Hill* in this catalogue [plate 42]. His printing from the negative has made of the Roman Wall a vertiginous causeway. A negative taken from an almost identical position – and perhaps taken during the same visit – is held by the BBC Hulton Picture Library. It is illustrated overleaf. Comparison of Brandt's published photograph and the full-frame Hulton negative shows that, a change in natural lighting apart (the sun falls on the distant view in the Kipling illustration) Brandt chose to use only the centre of the negative and to create an abyss at the right. He regarded his negatives as (sometimes very) raw material and his prints as the (often much retouched) starting point for rotogravure printing. The relief on the black forms of the *Picture Post* cover was clearly applied by hand. An article on Brandt's landscapes by Tom Hopkinson (*Photography* April 1954) gives some technical details: that a Proxar close-up lens was used for the Gull's Nest, f.22 a favourite focal length and that an afternoon picture of the Yorkshire Moors could become an evening scene during the printing stage. The same issue of *Photography* contains an appreciation of the Rolleiflex camera by a close friend of Brandt's – and a steady supporter of his controversial experiments in nude photography at the time – Norman Hall:

'Like the first Leica, it came [in 1929] as a completely new design and opened up a fresh era of photography. It gave the photographer big camera quality, without the weight and bulk; its quick, easy action was a revelation and it had the precise workmanship of the famous Leitz miniature . . . Perhaps it is closer to being a universal camera than any other type or make.'

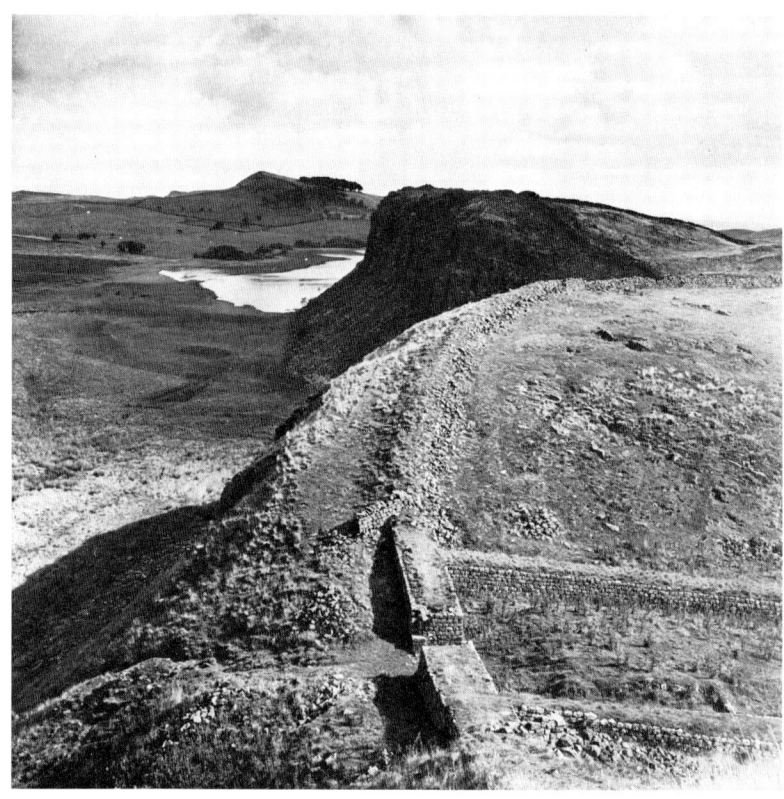

Hadrian's Wall. Variant view, full frame.

The camera continued in production until 1981. Brandt's technical notes to *Camera in London* state that 'he never uses filters', 'does not usually snap pictures in a hurry, but works slowly and deliberately' and that his equipment included enough flex to stretch the length of Winchester Cathedral. His only technical essay, on night photography, appeared in L. A. Mannheim's *The Rollei Way* (1951).

Kaye Webb remembers Bill Brandt as an 'intensely literate' person. In the 'Forties he was especially interested in the idea of illustration. Reading habits were much affected by the war, of course, and the classics found an expanded reading public in the years of long, slow train journeys and suspended social life. As paper supplies became more generous after the war the classics were again reprinted – *Wuthering Heights* was issued in three editions in 1946 and three more the following year. The photographer's brother R. A. Brandt shared an interest in illustration. R. A. Brandt (born 1906) studied at Ozenfant's academy of painting in London and with Paul Colin in Paris at the end of the 'Thirties. For the publisher John Westhouse R. A. Brandt illustrated *The Devil's Heir: Nine Tales from Les Contes Drolatiques* of Balzac (1945) and made illustrations also to Poe, Rabelais and Dickens. His best-known illustrations today are for *The Earth-Owl and Other Moon-People* by Ted Hughes (1963).

In the 'Forties Bill Brandt became so attracted to a story by Elizabeth Bowen that he set out to illustrate it photographically but the material proved intractable and he had to give up the idea. The story, 'Ivy Gripped the Steps', first appeared in *Horizon* in September 1945. It is set in 'Southstone'; Brandt travelled to Folkestone to try to photograph his illustrations. The town had been declared 'in the front line' in summer 1940. The ban on access was lifted when the tide of the war turned. The story evokes the strange, suspended life of the place in September 1944. A deserted house, singled out for a 'gothic fate' by an unchecked growth of ivy, is at the centre of the story. It is easy to see why Brandt was so entranced. The notations of light would probably have had a special appeal – 'from the awnings the rooms inside took a tense bright dusk' (as in Brandt's portraits of the period). 'The sky being clouded, but not dark, a timeless flat light fell on to everything' [see plate 26]. The story's contrast of adjacent family lives, one closed the other open, was of the kind that inspired *The English at Home* but for Brandt, perhaps, the crucial ingredient may have been the sense of a war-time actuality suffused by distinct voices from a remote past apprehended with the sharpness of memories of childhood. His sympathetic portrait of Elizabeth Bowen appeared beside her short story 'Mysterious Kôr' in American *Harper's Bazaar* in April 1946.

Literary Britain appeared at a time which provoked reassessment; the turning of the half century, with its Festival, provided an occasion for consideration. The real Britain of 1951 suffered the wettest first three months for 70 years, the threat of defeat in Korea and war with China, a grave trade deficit, the demoralising *deja vu* of rearmament, and by the autumn the end of the Labour Government and the return of the Conservatives. 'The theme of the time at best is inevitably *reculer pour mieux sauter*. Meanwhile, each western country is thrown back upon itself, simply by practical difficulties' – such was the conclusion of a writer in the *TLS* in its issue on 'The Mind of 1951'. Another anonymous writer in the issue found that English fiction might attend with judgement and affection on 'our unimportant but finely woven existences' but had produced nothing of the order of *The Naked and the Dead*, *La Peste* and *The Sheltering Sky*. The

TLS commended the subtlety and honesty of a recent article by Elizabeth Bowen. 'The Bend Back' appeared in *The Cornhill Magazine* for Summer 1951:

'after a second world war, with its excoriations, grinding impersonality, obliteration of so many tracks and land-marks, heart and imagination once more demand to be satisfied – to be fed, stabilised, reassured, taught. The demand is, that writers should reinstate the idea of life as liveable, loveable. Can this demand be met only by recourse to life in the past? It at present seems so'.

She deplored this entrapment of writers, and not writers only, by this past. Yet, 'Atmosphere has been conditioned out of the air, and impermanence attached even to the 'oppressiveness of brick and concrete' – 'all this in a second could become nothing':

'As creatures of feeling we register this dismay. Is it not, all the same, something to *be* a creature of feeling? Our power to idealise, to desire, spells life in us. We perceive the past in terms of vital glittering moments; but, if we had not ourselves experienced such moments, how should we recognise them? ... All those sublime moments, great or little, were victories – one must remember that'.

Such victories were abundantly remembered in Bill Brandt's book. His absorption with the subject followed a decade of documentary, a genre whose prestige fell away sharply in the realities of wartime, and landscape was to be followed in turn by a decade in which his subject became the portrayal of creative men and women, and, much more seriously for him, images which mix idealisation and desire: *Perspective of Nudes*. From about 1943 to about 1948 and for some months in 1950 literary Britain was for Bill Brandt 'a golden terrain'.

Acknowledgements

I am grateful to his friends for sharing their knowledge of Bill Brandt with me and to those who have generously made available records or collections in their care, in particular: Mrs Noya Brandt, R. A. Brandt, Martha Chahroudi (Philadelphia Museum of Art), Brian Coe (Kodak Museum), Stephen Croad (National Buildings Record), Mrs Valerie Eliot, Dr Desmond Flower, Dr Michael Halls (King's College, Cambridge), Martin Harrison (Olympus Gallery), Sir Tom Hopkinson, Peter Kernot (Executor of the Estate of Bill Brandt), David Lee (BBC Hulton Picture Library), John Lewis, Barbara Lloyd (Marlborough Fine Art), L. A. Mannheim, Mechtild Nawiaski, Alex Noble (V&A), Colin Osman and his colleagues at *Creative Camera*, Terence Pepper (National Portrait Gallery), Mrs Eva Rakos, Simon Rendall, Mrs Frances Rice, John Szarkowski (Museum of Modern Art, New York), John Ward (Science Museum), Kaye Webb, and Curtis Brown Ltd, on behalf of Lawrence Durrell, for permission to quote from him in the text.

Many appreciations of Bill Brandt are in print and a substantial exhibition and catalogue *Bill Brandt: Behind the Camera* (1985) recently appeared at the Philadelphia Museum of Art in association with Aperture Foundation Inc. Bill Brandt did not particularly welcome the stylistic analysis of his work and the credit for writing the first strictly art historical assessment belongs to David Mellor of the University of Sussex who contributed an essay to the catalogue *Bill Brandt: A Retrospective Exhibition*, edited by Valerie Lloyd, held at the Royal Photographic Society, Bath in 1981. Note that a misprint in that catalogue places the date of Bill Brandt's birth in 1905, an error that has travelled widely and should not be repeated; 1904 is the correct date. I am indebted to Robert Hewison's *Under Siege: Literary Life in London 1939–45* (Weidenfeld and Nicolson, London 1977). Desmond Flower's reminiscences of his earlier days as a bibliophile are published in *The Private Library*, Third Series, vol 1 no 1, Spring 1978. John Hayward was remembered by friends in *The Book Collector*, vol 14 no 4, Winter 1965. His papers, including the Durrell postcards, are preserved at King's College, Cambridge. 'The Book Illustrations of R. A. Brandt' by John Keir Cross was published in *Graphis*, vol 2, 1946, pp 374–79; see also *Publimondial*, no 11, 1948, pp 53–55. The (marvellous) TV film on Bill Brandt, referred to by Sir Tom Hopkinson, was produced by Peter Adam for the BBC in the series *Master Photographers* in 1983. Bill Brandt professed himself pleased with a profile of him by the present writer (*Vogue*, September 1982) but he was always kind, courteous and encouraging; 'Kitaj/Brandt/Screenplay' has some relevance to *Literary Britain* and appeared in *Creative Camera* in June 1982. The portraits of Kaye Webb and Sir Tom Hopkinson have been kindly lent for use as illustrations by the sitters and are copyright of the Estate of Bill Brandt. The photograph of Hadrian's Wall illustrated in the essay is copyright BBC Hulton Picture Library.

M H-B

Notes

Literary Britain is based on such vintage prints of the relevant photographs as Bill Brandt had retained. He and his wife kindly allowed the Victoria and Albert Museum to borrow a group of about 160 prints for the original exhibition in 1984. Studying them closely it seemed that the best possible exhibition would concentrate on the finest of the prints – those in best condition and most satisfyingly executed. This select group covered only about half of the original plates of *Literary Britain* as it appeared in book form in 1951. However, the subject was a fertile one for Bill Brandt and he made a number of variant photographs of subjects in the original plates. Also, when the major series of photographs appeared in *Lilliput* during the 1940s – 'The Hardy Country', 'The Brontë Country', 'Over the sea to Skye', 'The Poet's Crib' and 'Peter Grimes Country' – each set comprised eight photographs. In the interests of balance the original *Literary Britain* reduced these quantities; also in the interests of literary balance some weaker photographs, never subsequently published by Bill Brandt, were shown as representing scenes or more usually houses associated with well-known writers. It seemed no impiety to omit the lesser photographs in favour of stronger representation of the places and writers which particularly inspired the photographer. Unfortunately some fine plates in the book were not available in the form of original prints; possibly in due time fine prints, faithful in tone to the plates published in 1951, could be made. However, such time was not at our disposal and it seemed desirable to keep to our original plans for the date of the show. In order to include extra plates without breaking the original lay-out of the book, this publication includes texts not chosen by John Hayward. Usually, these could be provided from *Lilliput*, where quotations from writers usually captioned the illustrations. In other cases quotations were, with some reluctance but I hope justifiably, chosen by the editor of this volume. Those from Thomas Hardy are copyright Macmillan London Ltd. The changes from the 1951 book are tabulated below to save confusion.

The following plates are not illustrated in this edition: 1, 11, 13, 14, 15, 16, 19, 20, 21, 22, 23 (a variant appears here), 26, 27, 28, 29, 30, 33, 36, 37, 38, 39, 40, 41, 43, 44, 45, 48, 50, 51, 52, 54 (a variant view appears here), 55, 61, 68, 69, 70, 75, 76, 77, 79 (a variant view appears here), 81, 82, 84, 85 (a variant view appears here), 86, 88, 89, 91, 92, 96, 98.

Plates newly added: 9 (used on dust-wrapper of 1951 book), 11, 12, 19, 21, 28, 31, 32, 33, 39, 40, plus all additional plates section.   M H-B